MW00807135

Mr. Awana

Mr. Awana

Years ago God implanted a vision in the heart of Art Rorheim which has resulted in hundreds of thousands of boys and girls around the world coming to Christ through Awana. Never have I met a person with a greater passion for the gospel and the souls of boys and girls and every person he meets. He was my hero sixty-four years ago when, as a boy of seven, I felt his unconditional love and acceptance which brought me face to face with Jesus the Christ. This humble servant continues to be my hero in the faith today. I love this man.

John Dobbert
Businessman and Awana board member

Art Rorheim is called Mr. Awana, but I think he also should be called Mr. Gospel! Few people are as committed to the purity and spread of the gospel as Art is—always ready to share it, ready to explain it, and, yes, ready to live it.

This book will give you insight into Art's life, but more importantly, insight into the development and success of the great ministry of Awana that has been used by God in many countries of the world.

Dr. Erwin W. Lutzer
Senior Pastor
The Moody Church

In the summer of 1969, I was a nine-year-old, caught up in the wonder of Camp Awana. It was there I first met Art Rorheim. It was there I first saw a grown man cry, pondering the eternity of a lost soul. Even at that age, I knew there was something extraordinarily right about a heart like that.

Over the decades, I have watched and wondered at the heart that is yours, Art. Watched as you have traveled the globe and simply tried to be obedient to the Lord in your singular passion and calling: the other boy and girl for Christ.

I remember seeing you come back from those early international trips, heavy with emotion. And when at last I traveled to Kenya and Zambia this past fall, watching kids round an Awana game circle scrawled out in the African dust, I could not hold back the emotion.

Elisha of old asked for a double portion of Elijah's spirit. I seek no such thing.

Me? I want a heart like yours, Art. If I had that, the sun would never set on a day not lived for the other boy and girl for Christ.

Jon Gauger
Christian radio producer and former Awana clubber

I just read Art's book. Wow, it is incredible! I would recommend everyone buy two copies: one to keep and one to give away. You will see firsthand in this book his passion for the clear presentation of the gospel, his love for people, and his deep love for the Lord Jesus Christ. I don't know of a more exciting person than Dr. Art Rorheim.

Dr. James Scudder
Senior Pastor, Quentin Road Bible Baptist Church
Weekly TV program, Victory in Grace
Chancellor, Dayspring Bible College and Seminary

A long time ago, Art Rorheim had the idea that if a child participated in a systematic way of memorizing Scripture, combined with the joy of games, the Word of Life would be indelibly written on the tablets of that child's heart. His small beginnings are now a global phenomenon. Praise God: Art Rorheim continues to remind us that His Word will always be a "a lamp unto our feet and a light unto our path."

Janet Parshall
Nationally syndicated talk-show host

Art Rorheim has probably done more for children in America than any other human being regarding their morality and their growing up to be productive citizens. His book tells a story of an incredible man whom God has used to do incredible things for the most important thing in our future, our kids.

Burl Cain
Warden, Louisiana State Penitentiary

The Lord never blessed Art Rorheim as a world-impacting visionary. He did something far better! God gave Art a passion for the gospel of the Lord Jesus Christ, coupled with a strong desire to reach out to boys and girls. The sum total of the Awana vision was captured long ago in Art's original motto: "The other boy for Christ." Art has succeeded over the years in holding on tenaciously to that priceless statement. Because of him, Awana remains to this day deeply committed above all else to getting the gospel to boys, girls, youth, and adults all over the world. The stories in this book will inspire you to do the same.

Jack Eggar
President/CEO Awana International

There are few people who bring such fond memories and challenge to me as Art Rorheim. Art is a man of tremendous passion for our Lord and children. I have seldom talked with him where his voice does not begin to quiver and eyes swell with tears as he talks of God's goodness, grace, and mercy and the various ways he was thinking about to get this message to the multitudes.

I have never been challenged by any man as powerfully as I have by Art. He is ordinary and knows it, yet his love of and availability to God have made him extraordinary. He knows God and has memorized much of God's word. He has led by example and continues to set the pace well into his nineties.

I am certain that you will find the stories he shares in this book entertaining, exciting, and educational; more importantly, I am sure that when you are finished you will be encouraged to love, give, and memorize. Art was never about Art, but he has been about our Father's business and millions of us have benefited from his efforts and examples to move Christianity from concept to reality.

Dave Wager
President, Silver Birch Ranch
Founder, Omega Force

No other Christian youth organization has done more to reach the youth of our world than Awana. And no other person is better qualified, spiritually and academically, than Dr. Arthur Rorheim to review the organization's history and ministry. He has had a vital part in Awana's beginning and continuing ministries. Awana Clubs exist all over the world, advancing the cause of Christ, the grace of God, and Scripture memorization. This very readable account of Awana's history and present ministry will thrill your heart and challenge your life.

Dr. Robert P. Lightner
Dallas Theological Seminary, Retired

Awana is the strongest program I know to get young people into the Word of God that will transform their lives. Far more than just Bible memorization, Awana teaches

Christian character and responsibility, and produces young men and women who will live for Jesus Christ. Everywhere I minister, I recommend that churches begin an Awana program to transform the lives of their young people.

Elmer L. Towns
Co-founder, Liberty University, Dean School of Religion

It is my privilege to strongly suggest and support not only the writing, but also your reading of this great book from one of God's good men—Art Rorheim. We know well "the steps of a good man are ordered by the Lord." And there has been no man or ministry whose steps seem more directed by God than [the] ministry founder of Awana. Read its pages and cherish the miracles of a man who "suffered little children" and brought them unto Him.

Steve Curington
Founder, Reformers Unanimous

Our family will be forever grateful for the faithful, caring outreach of the Awana leaders. As a ten-year-old boy, my late husband, Jack, was invited to Awana by a missionary kid attending the same school, whose family was on an extended furlough due to World War II. By God's grace, that set the course of Jack's life, and later he became an Awana and camp leader. I was a ten-year-old girl when our family first attended the Awana Clubs and Camp Awana. Jack and I met at Camp Awana, were married, and later served with New Tribes Mission as missionaries to the Tagbanwa tribe in the Philippines.

Awana is a creative and innovative approach to making the gospel of the grace of God relevant and alive today! This timely book tells only a fraction of what God has done in the lives of so many individuals, and how Awana is continuing to reach way beyond our borders, for the glory of God!

Dottie Connor Bingham
Founder, Gracestoration

Art Rorheim is a man of God, a soul winner, and a children's ministry pioneer. As the founder of Awana, he is a man with a message that we need today. His testimony will inspire others to share the clear gospel message of salvation in Jesus Christ. Art would tell you that he is just an ordinary man who had the privilege of doing extraordinary works for his Savior. Millions of people will be in heaven because of his life work.

David Gibbs III
Christian Law Association

I want to thank God for the ministry of Awana for sixty years. I thank God how Awana has impacted our family and our church. For many years, millions of boys and girls and parents worldwide have been reached with the message of the Gospel because of Awana.

I encourage you to read this book and I know it will bless you as you read of God's miracle since Awana's inception sixty years ago.

Tony Evans
Pastor, Oak Cliff Bible Fellowship

Mr. Awana

Sixty-Plus Years of Changing the World for Christ

ART RORHEIM

GRACE ACRES PRESS

CULTIVATING JOY

LARKSPUR, COLORADO

Grace Acres Press
P.O. Box 22
Larkspur, CO 80018
888-700-GRACE (4722)
(303) 681-9995
(303) 681-9996 (fax)
www.GraceAcresPress.com

Copyright © 2011 by Grace Acres Press.
All rights reserved.

No part of this publication may be reproduced, stored in a
retrieval system, or transmitted in any form or by any means,
electronic, mechanical, photocopying, recording, scanning,
or otherwise, except as permitted by law, without the prior
written permission of the Publisher.

Grace Acres Press also publishes books in a variety of
electronic formats. Some content that appears in print may
not be available in electronic books.

Scripture taken from King James version.

Photos used by permission of Awana Clubs International and Art Rorheim.

Library of Congress Cataloging-in-Publication Data:
Rorheim, Art, 1918–
   Mr. Awana : sixty-plus years of changing the world for Christ / by Art
Rorheim.
     p. cm.
   ISBN 978-1-60265-028-2 — ISBN 978-1-60265-027-5 (pbk.)
1. Rorheim, Art, 1918– 2. Church work with children. 3. Awana Clubs
International—Biography. I. Title. II. Title: Art Rorheim, Mister Awana.
   BV4447.R663 2010
   289.9'5092—dc22
   [B]   2010017685

Printed in Canada
13 12 11 10   01 02 03 04 05 06 07 08 09 10

Dedication

Writing this book has been an exciting challenge and blessing to me, as I have relived God's blessings and miracles of yesteryears. It has taken several years of worldwide research to assemble the many stories and articles contained in this book.

I wish to dedicate this book to Lynn Jorgensen, who has been my executive assistant for many years. With all of her research, typing, and editing, she has poured her heart into making this historical book a reality. She is a special friend and an encouragement to me.

I trust that this book, written and compiled by two ordinary people, will be an encouragement to God's many ordinary people, whom God wants to use in His extraordinary, miraculous way to bring glory to His name.

About Art

Art Rorheim is co-founder of Awana. Art built Awana from the ground up from its early days as a weekly club program at the North Side Gospel Center in Chicago.

Art was introduced to youth and children's ministry in 1935 at age 17 when Lance Latham, his church's pastor, asked him to serve as a club leader at the North Side Gospel Center.

In 1941, Art became the Gospel Center's youth director and oversaw the church's weekly programs for kids and teens. As the weekly clubs grew, Art and Lance named the program Awana, and Art put in place many of the signature features that characterize Awana today.

Art guided Awana as executive director when he co-founded Awana as a resource and training provider to churches with Lance Latham in 1950. He served in this capacity for 42 years before becoming Awana president from 1992 to 1999.

Contents

Foreword

Art Rorheim has changed the lives of more young people than anyone I know, including my own. I remember the first time I experienced an Awana meeting. The excitement among the boys was intense. Soon, Awana became the highlight of the week for me, featuring games, competitions of all kinds, and, of course, Scripture memorization. I had the privilege of attending Camp Awana, where I remember Art and Doc entertaining and ministering to us for hours, but also teaching us God's Word. Many of the verses I know today from memory are the result of my times with Awana. Just as Art influenced my life, he has continued to reach people around the globe on 6 continents, ministering now to more than 20,000 churches in 100 countries each week, extending Awana's reach far beyond what Art ever imagined. This is in addition to the numerous ministry leaders, pastors, teachers, missionaries, and church workers, who, like me, extend his impact to countless others.

When Art first told me of his plans to write a book based on his experiences in starting Awana, I knew it would be a story many would need to hear. Seeing it in print only confirms my first thought. This is a book of encouragement from a Christian layman who cared about kids and was willing to sacrificially follow God's lead to do something about it. His story will encourage and instruct a new generation of lay people who will apply the message of these pages.

When you get to know Art, the first thing you become aware of is his focus on the love and grace of God as demonstrated in the salvation purchased by

Christ on the cross. As a result, he has always centered his work on presenting the gospel and teaching the Word of God to boys and girls. There is a reason Awana has focused on Scripture memorization: Art is a man who knows and applies the Word. One time I had the opportunity to visit the Awana headquarters for an event. To begin their meeting, the staff recited verse after verse from the Bible that they had been memorizing as a team. Why? Art knew God's Word was what changed lives. He did it, he expected his staff members to do it, and he has helped countless young people build their lives on the solid foundation of the Bible.

For those longing for a deeper walk with God, a clear presentation of the true gospel message, and a powerful example of one who has been doing it for a lifetime, this is the book for you. I look forward to how Art's stories will affect the lives of many in the days ahead, helping the next generation to know and follow the Word of God, as Awana's key verse declares, "Study to shew thyself approved unto God, a workman that needeth not to be ashamed, rightly dividing the word of truth" (2 TIMOTHY 2:15).

Dr. John Ankerberg
Founder and President
The John Ankerberg Show

Acknowledgments

Life to me has been a thrilling adventure, to have been chosen by God to share the exciting news of the gospel to a world that has no eternal hope. I will forever thank God for my salvation; for my loving wife, Winnie; and for my children, grandchildren, and great-grandchildren, all of whom know and love our wonderful Lord.

I thank God for choosing me to have a part in the amazing worldwide ministry of Awana, which He started and has blessed these many years. We know that the heartbeat of Awana is the Good News of the gospel and memorization of His precious Word. I thank God for our present Awana headquarters leadership and our faithful missionaries around the world. I greatly appreciate our Awana friends, the Robert Vaughan family, especially for their assistance on this book.

My greatest desire is that Awana will continue to fulfill its calling given in Colossians 4:17 (paraphrased): "Take heed the ministry that *Awana* has received of the Lord and that *Awana* fulfills it." And then, the heartbeat that the apostle Paul displays as he is to turn to give his mantle to his son in the Lord, Timothy, with the pleading in his voice you can hear in 1 Timothy 6:20 (paraphrased): "O, *Awana,* keep that which is committed to thy trust." I thank God that I know this is also the heartbeat of our present Awana leadership. May God help all of you to keep on serving our wonderful Lord until He takes you home.

Art Rorheim

Preface

1,440

Each day God gives us 1,440 minutes. These minutes, along with the days, weeks, and even years of one's life, seem to pass so quickly. As we grow older, they seem to pass even more quickly.

The average human life span is approximately seventy years. During that period, most people spend approximately three years in school, eight years in recreation, six years eating, five years in transportation, four years talking, fourteen years working, three years reading, twenty-four years sleeping, and three years convalescing.

As each day slips by in my life, I have become aware of something: time is irretrievable. Merrill E. Dunlap once said, "There is no way on earth to save time; all you can do is spend it." I can't change one iota of the past. It is sealed in God's record book forever. Whether the past week or year has been one of blessing or regrets, I cannot change it.

But I can do something about today, tomorrow, and the weeks that lie ahead. And that is to allow the Lord to direct my thoughts and my activities for His glory.

The cry from all of us seems to be, "There are not enough hours in the day." But God allows us enough time to do the work He has given us. When we say we don't have enough time, we are really announcing to everyone that we are poor managers of our time. E. J. Grit said, "Our days are identical suitcases, all the same size, but some people can pack more into them than others." ECCLESIASTES 3:1 says, "To every thing there is a season, and a time for every purpose under the heaven."

As Awana leaders, it is imperative that we plan our time wisely each week, month, and year. If we only respond to the needs in our clubs, rather than a planned personal objective, we will be wasting the precious commodity of time. The Awana Clubs that have the most success always have an overall club year plan. However, as a leader, you also need a personal plan. If God called you as an Awana leader, remember, He has trusted you with the precious lives of those kids.

One of the most challenging verses to me personally is 2 TIMOTHY 4:5: "But you be watchful in all things, endure afflictions, do the work of an evangelist, fulfill your ministry." These are the Apostle Paul's last words to his spiritual son, Timothy. That's not a suggestion or an exhortation, but a commandment to all believers who love and want to serve our wonderful Lord.

I will always remember the wise counsel I received from my good friend, the late Clarence Jones. He was the founder of the worldwide ministry of HCJB in Quito, Ecuador, and also the author of the Awana theme song. He said, "One of the most effective lessons I've learned is to regularly, each year, take time to get alone and take personal inventory as to how wisely I am spending my time, and if you are honest with yourself you will see where you have wasted time and can rearrange it with goals to be a more effective leader for the Lord."

Personal discipline is another major factor in using your time wisely. You cannot say, "Yes!" to everyone who needs assistance. Learn how to say no rather than having your life drained by so many sources that you're not really effective in anything. People will respect you for it. If you're an Awana Commander or Director, be a good delegator. Persuade people to share responsibility with you.

Yes, time is a very precious commodity. Some day, when we stand before Him, God will allow us to look back over our lives. Let's trust that we will not have too many regrets on how we spent our time. Looking back over this past year, we can benefit from an evaluation of how we spent our time. Let us press on into the new year to serve our wonderful Lord—it could be our last.

Introduction

I praise God for all of the people who will read this book and learn of God's precious teachings to me. He has led me step-by-step all of the way and I trust that you will allow Him to lead you, too.

This book is a collection of memories from many parts of my life. As such, there has been no attempt to try and present these as a complete chronology of my life. Rather, these stories have been organized into topical areas. Each story is complete in and of itself, but you will, I hope, find great joy in reading as many as you can. While you are reading, you may find some overlaps from story to story that were necessary to make each memory complete. This is intentional and should not detract from your enjoyment of watching God's leading in my life.

I encourage you to be intentional about seeing God's work in your life, perhaps even keeping a journal or a diary yourself.

CHAPTER 1

Personal Stories

FAMILY

I have traveled to more than fifty countries, and God has always reminded me, as I entered each new country, of one amazing truth: I could have been born into a pagan country and never have heard the name of Christ, and therefore be headed to a Christless eternity. By God's grace He allowed me to be born in Chicago to godly parents who lived, talked, and daily walked the Christian life before me each day.

I am truly blessed because I am a part of a seven-generation family of born-again Christians. My ancestors came from a remote island in Norway called Ombo. My great-grandparents, whom I never met, impacted their family for Christ. Their name was Rorheim. My grandparents had a vibrant heart for foreign missions. My grandfather's name was Ole Golv and he was the founder of China Inland Missions in the Scandinavian countries, even though it was originally pioneered in China. His mentor was Hudson Taylor, the founder of China Inland Missions. My parents, Ole and Alida Rorheim, married in Norway and then came to America.

When I was just two or three years old, my folks took me to Norway with the possibility of us living there. However, it wasn't long before my folks returned, because they felt the Lord wanted them to live in America. They decided to make their home a haven for Norwegian immigrants who didn't have any place to go when they came to America. So I lived in a home just filled with Norwegian immigrants.

Art Rorheim at four years old

After a few years of living on a farm in Iowa, our family moved to Chicago. As a boy, I was quite proficient in speaking Norwegian. It wasn't long before everyone was learning English and many of the boys were getting interested in some of the English-speaking ladies they met. In their desperation to write letters to these young ladies, from time to time I was called upon to help them express themselves properly to these American ladies whom they wanted to date. That got to be quite interesting and humorous at times.

Art (middle) and friends

We soon started attending Bethel Free Church, a church that had a heartbeat to win souls. As I grew up into my teens, I had little interest in the things of God and spent several years emulating the neighborhood kids. The Lord protected me from the life-threatening hazards that I was enslaved by. After the death of my brother and my conversion, I soon met my mentor, Lance "Doc" Latham, with whom God so wonderfully blessed me, and I had the opportunity to minister alongside him for more than forty years.

Together, Doc and I were blessed to start the worldwide Awana program. We also founded the North Side Gospel Center where the Awana roots were planted. It was there that I met my dear wife, Winnie Hofmann, whom I have been blessed to have as my wife, encourager, and co-worker in the development of the Awana program for more than seventy years.

Almost every year my father would make a trip back to his home country there in Ombo. Of course, at that time there were no planes, so he traveled by boat. The boat trip was usually eight days long. I was intrigued, as he would share with me how he had practically memorized just what was to take place each day.

On the seventh day, he would get up on the deck and look out, and far in the distance he would see just a small dot. It was a little boat that kept coming closer and closer and finally the ship's crew docked this boat alongside the huge passenger ship. They had a unique way to bring a man from this little boat on board using a rope ladder. Of course, this man was very special; he was the harbor pilot, and only he was capable of taking the boat through the fjords, which were so narrow that there was a possibility of running into the rocks that protruded from the water.

When he would board the ship and come on the bridge, it was like a beautiful ceremony. He would come up to that big captain's wheel and the captain would turn it over to him, saying, "It is all yours now." It was a magnificent procedure and from then on, the ship was his responsibility. What a pleasure it was to see how he maneuvered in and through the fjords until the ship got to its destination.

Even more beautiful is the thought of how Christ is like that harbor pilot. When we allow Him to take the helm of our lives, He takes us through all the problems of life. We know that we can completely trust Him; He is not only our harbor pilot, but He is also our heavenly pilot, and He will continue to do that until He takes us home. I know this is the message that all of us can apply to our lives.

CONVERSION

My mother and father were immigrants from Norway. They came from a little island nestled way up in the fjords. When my dad came to this country, he worked on a farm in Iowa, and shortly after that he married my mother, Alida. I had an older brother named Roy who was four years my senior. Our home had an open door to immigrants coming from Norway. None of them knew English or even had jobs when they arrived. My mother had a big heart and was willing to board them until they were able to get work.

My dad directed a team of elevator operators in one of the large office buildings in the city of Chicago. It took him an hour and a half each day to get to work and he worked there for forty years. He was late to work only twice during that entire time, so you could see the discipline that my dad had for doing things right.

My father became an officer in the Salvation Army, where we attended for several years. Then he felt God leading him to a Norwegian church in Chicago called the Salem Evangelical Free Church. For several years, I sat through many Norwegian sermons where I understood very little, but my folks instilled in me that church was the place we go every Sunday whether we feel like it or not. Of course, quite often I did not feel like it, because I didn't enjoy listening to these sermons in Norwegian all the time. Occasionally, I would hear a missionary speak who had a real burden to reach the lost, but I was not yet ready to respond to God's direction in my life.

When my brother was thirteen years of age, he was invited to a boys' club at the Chicago Gospel Tabernacle in Chicago. He would often come home just raving about the tremendous time he had had and the good friends he was meeting. Then one day he came home and announced that he had trusted Christ as his Savior and wanted to give his life to serve the Lord. These, of course, were the most beautiful words my folks could ever hear. The club program there was called Tabernacle Scouts and it was under the direction of Clarence Jones, who later became the founder of the radio station HCJB in Quito, Ecuador.

One day my brother came home from the club very sick. They rushed him to the county hospital, where they found that he had spinal meningitis. It was a very rare disease at that time, so there was very little medicine available to counteract it. There were only two cases in the entire city of Chicago then, so most of the medics were very interested in watching his case. While my parents were visiting my brother that night at his bedside, my brother became aware that his life was heading out, and in a trembling voice he said, "Dad, you are a Christian. Mom, you are a Christian, but Art is not a Christian and we have got to win him to the Lord."

By then I was attending the Bethel Community Church in Chicago, which had a very evangelistic pastor. I heard the way of salvation and it reached my heart. I knew that Christ had died and paid the price for my sin, but it was only a head knowledge that had not truly affected my life. But those last words from my brother—"We must win Art for the Lord"—kept flooding my mind and my heart. I knew that I would never see him again if I did not trust Christ as my Savior. I remember going out into our family car where I told God that I was a sinner for whom He died and right then and there I wanted to trust Him to be my personal Savior. At that moment, after personally talking to God, I became a Christian because I put my trust in the finished work of Christ at Calvary. I left the car with joy in my heart and I knew for sure that I would see my brother again in heaven.

We lived on the outskirts of town where each little neighborhood seemed to have its own gang of kids. They did not do violent things, but I became enamored of them and wanted to be accepted in their crowd. This led to a careless period in my life when I did not obey God's leading in my life. Still, I walked some three miles to school each day and enjoyed being on the honor roll several times. How little did I suspect then that the miracle of the Awana program would be born and that God wanted me to direct it.

Then came World War II, and I became employed as a machinist in a company that was making parts for the atom bomb. I worked nights with a friend of mine, Truman Robertson. We knew that God had something in mind for our lives but we didn't know what. At two o'clock in the morning, when we had our lunch, we would get together and pray and ask God to direct our lives.

At this time, I was married to my wife, Winnie, and we had two children, Kathlyn and Kenny. I was asked by Doc Latham if I would help him direct the camp that we were operating in Michigan, called Michawana. I was honored to have the privilege of directing the camp and felt that God was leading, but in the fall when camp was over, I was unemployed. I really wasn't certain what God had planned next. It was then that Doc Latham recommended to the North Side Gospel Center board that I be hired to be the church's youth director. Not having any previous training in this, I felt very inadequate. I was to direct the clubs in this converted furniture store that was now a church.

CAMP

Every morning of the summer when I was ten years old, my eyes would fly open and I would instantly think, *How many more days until summer camp?* First I counted the weeks, then the days, marking them all off on the calendar—and finally the hours.

I had never been to camp before, so was eagerly looking forward to Camp Chic-Go-Tab. Back in those days, merely getting to camp was an adventure. There were no parents or bus drivers to start us off safely on our grand adventure. Instead, we arrived at the Navy Pier in Chicago just in time for our midnight voyage, climbed aboard, and spent the next eight hours boating to Muskegon, Michigan. With the prospects of summer camp looming before us, there was no way any of us could sleep, so we didn't even try. Instead, we explored as much of the ship as we were allowed. Eight o'clock the next morning found us crowded around the railing, each trying to get the first glimpse of the harbor and our waiting leaders.

By today's standards, the camp would have seemed primitive, to say the least. There was one large dorm that was meant to serve as ten separate cabins. That, along with Lake Michigan, a tennis court, and a ball field, comprised Camp Chic-Go-Tab, but none of the boys seemed to mind. To them there was plenty to do, and plenty of space to do it in. Every day we spent two hours studying the Bible with Doc Latham. Most youngsters today wouldn't be able to handle that, but none of us minded because Doc had a way of unlocking Scripture that kept us interested every minute.

With plenty of sunshine, sports, food, and study, everyone had a good time—except for me. Although I had been counting the days until camp, it hadn't occurred to me that I would be away from home without my family for the first time, and now I was suffering a terrible bout of homesickness. To make matters worse, I ate one too many green apples, which led to a painful stomachache. While everyone else was enjoying themselves and having fun, I struggled through each day and solemnly vowed that I would never again go to camp at any time or any place.

The Lord has a sense of humor. I recovered from my first camping experience and went the next year for four weeks. In fact, I didn't stop going to camp for more than sixty years. You see, any camp that places an emphasis on Bible study and challenges its campers to serve the Lord is a tool that can be used for good and is effective for any youth ministry.

The Lord showed me that, and after that first camp I attended as a home-sick boy with Doc Latham at Chic-Go-Tab (which eventually changed to Michidune), we transferred to a government camp the Lord provided that was called Michawana. As the camping ministry continued to grow, the Lord put it in our hearts to buy a piece of property in Wisconsin, known today as Camp Awana.

When we first bought Camp Awana, that's all it was: just a piece of property. Within eight months, we had tents, a mess hall, and latrines, and we were ready for business. It was in those early summer days, full of archery, diving, fun, and fellowship, that God began to teach us the basic structure and principles of what is today known as Scholarship Camp. Every camp would be two to four weeks long, with heavy emphasis placed on daily Bible lessons and Scripture memorization. By having the kids for twenty-four hours a day for two to four weeks, we were able to make a long-lasting spiritual impact on their lives.

Today thousands of kids have gone to the more than forty Scholarship Camps, and the fruit is seen as those same kids grow older and begin setting off around the world as missionaries, pastors, youth workers, camp directors, and Christian workers. There are seven Bible camps today, whose staff have been leading boys and girls to Christ for more than thirty years. All seven of these camps were founded by former Awana campers. The big advantage to camp is that we have the campers for twenty-four hours each day, away from their ungodly distractions and even broken homes. Within this time frame, we can influence their hearts and minds to give their lives to serve our wonderful Lord.

It just shows, when we embed in the hearts of these kids and leaders the importance of camp, and they see how their own lives are being impacted, they realize that this is a ministry God could call them to be a part of later in life. Perhaps millions of kids have gone through the camps that were started as the result of the heartbeat of the North Side Gospel Center.

WHITE SHIRT BRIGADE

Without question, one of the great highlights in my Christian life as I grew up was singing with a boys' group called the White Shirt Brigade. Its leader was my mentor and pastor, Lance Latham. He was a tremendous musician

Art (back row, third from right) and the White Shirt Brigade

who majored in the gospel and was also a tremendous pianist and organist. His group was wanted in churches all around the country.

In those yesteryears we were able to take off from school for one to two weeks at a time, and the teachers considered it an education that we could not have gotten anywhere else, which was certainly true. I question whether it could be done today.

Our group consisted of approximately eight to ten boys. We would pack ourselves into one or two cars, which in those days had no trunks for suitcases, so everything we took with us had to be tied on the running board or roof. We could write many a story about our travels! One time we went through a downpour of rain that left most of our things soaking wet, and our clothes actually were discolored by some of the black socks that were packed together with the shirts. Can you imagine what we looked like when we arrived at the church with not enough time to get things washed again?

Traveling in the car with Doc Latham was a life-training seminar that I couldn't have gotten anywhere else. I saw a man who was not just preaching the gospel, but living it every day. What a tremendous, godly example he was to all of us. When he counseled us and talked to us, yes, we listened. We knew that God had given him some insights as to how to live as a Christian that we couldn't get anywhere else.

White Shirt Brigade reunion performance, about 40 years later

Some of our trips were twelve to fifteen hours long, which was very tiring in those crowded conditions. However, we did love the fellowship we had with one another, and especially with our leader, Doc.

The White Shirt Brigade was quite famous in those early days. We would often sing in churches to a thousand or more people. The Brigade was also God's way of teaching us the basics of leadership. I remember especially one time when we were going to sing in a church in South Bend, Michigan. It was a large high school that was going to be filled with students. About an hour before arriving, Doc turned to me and said, "Art, tonight I want you to be the leader of the program." I had never done anything like that before. I was as frightened as anyone could be, but still I didn't want to disappoint Doc by saying no.

Yes, I led the group that night. I was scared and felt that I had failed utterly, but Doc's encouragement afterward was a real blessing. I had no idea how much that experience was going to help me in the years to follow in Awana, when I was called upon unexpectedly to speak to many large groups. Doc would often tell me that we're not here to talk about ourselves or even an organization. First of all, we're here to represent the Lord and let people know that God has a wonderful plan for their lives, if they first of all trust Him as Savior and put their entire life in His hands.

Humorous things often took place on these trips. I remember so well when we were in the Calvary Church in Grand Rapids, Michigan, where the late Dr. Martin DeHaan was the pastor. The church was filled to capacity with people standing everywhere.

One of the features of the White Shirt Brigade program was Lance Latham playing *The Storm* on a large organ. He certainly could make it sound like a storm. But once during *The Storm,* in the midst of one of its loudest bursts, some of the large bellows of the organ began to fall off. This was humorous but scary. The pieces could have fallen on some people below, but the Lord once again protected us.

I could go on and on sharing the many humorous things that took place in the car as we drove, but I can assure you it was the challenging times of blessing that Doc shared with us that had the biggest impact on my life, for which I will be forever thankful. He taught me lessons that I could never have received in a seminary school.

ANGELS

I have often said, "When I get to Heaven I want to meet my guardian angel who protected me during the many foolish adventures in my life." Here are a few examples of those adventures.

Birds, Birds, and More Birds

"Here's another one," hissed Art.

"Watch it!" Bill whispered. "If the cops hear the squawking from these bags, we'll be in for it."

"Aw, we aren't doin' nothing bad," Joe said.

Art swooped down on another sparrow. "Hey, you guys, I bet we got more'n two hundred. We'd better quit, my bag is full."

It was night, and the three boys were scrambling around city rooftops catching sparrows, just for the "fun of it." Each boy carried a gunny sack, and the uncomfortable birds inside were letting the world know they didn't like their captivity. The boys held a pow-wow near a street light. Art Rorheim, a wiry, energetic boy, asked, "Now that we've caught 'em, what'll we do with 'em?"

"I know," Joe said. "There's a delicatessen down the block. The owner always gives me a rough time. I've been itching to get even with him. I say let's give him some customers that he doesn't want."

The plan met with hilarious approval, so the boys approached the store, kept to the shadows, and waited. When the owner went into the back room, the trio heaved the bags through the doorway, then hid between the buildings to watch.

Sparrows fluttered out of the bags and scattered everywhere, roosting on smoked hams, Swiss cheese, the meat grinder, and the white porcelain showcases. One floundered momentarily in a barrel of dill pickles. The screeching sparrows were everywhere.

As the chuckling boys headed for home, they were pleased at the success of their prank. But a pinpoint of guilt stirred in Art's mind. His parents were dedicated Christians, faithful in the local Evangelical Free Church. They regularly attended Sunday school, Sunday morning and evening worship services, and prayer meeting. Art and his older brother were always with them.

Art thought he was fooling his parents and many of the church members who saw him as a model son. How could they understand his desire for adventure? Though only nine, Art, enamored of the older boys in the neighborhood, emulated their standards and activities. Because neighborhood youth recognized and esteemed the most daring among them, individuals were challenged to prove their abilities.

Toccoa Falls

When I sang with Lance Latham's White Shirt Brigade, we visited Toccoa Falls College in Georgia. A small waterfall there is actually higher than Niagara Falls. While wading in the river that leads to the dropoff, we got the daring idea to see how close we could get to the edge of the falls for a photograph. My friend Chester and I walked carefully to the falls and stood on slippery rock covered with moss.

Within six feet of the edge of the falls, my buddy said, "Let's make this a daring picture. Why don't you get up on my shoulders?"

I said, "Why don't *you* get up on my shoulders?"—as if it made any difference! There we stood for the sake of a picture, only a slip away from going over the falls. A couple weeks later, we heard the tragic news that a young fellow, who had been doing exactly what we had done, went over the falls. It took them three days to find his body, which was wedged under a huge rock.

I have often thought that that could have been me. YES! I believe God's angels protected me. Had they not, there might not have been Awana as there is today.

Chester on Art's shoulders at Toccoa Falls, Georgia

Bus Skitching

When I was a teenager, peer pressure was just as challenging back then as it is today. Drugs and alcohol are more prevalent today, but back in my days, peer pressure was perhaps just as dangerous. I remember when the first trolley bus was introduced to the city of Chicago. The trolley bus had a couple of trolley cars that were connected to the electrical wires above. There were yokes that held them in place. That was so superior to the regular bus trips that we had taken; we really made progress when the trolley buses came along.

There was a little bumper on the back of the trolley cars where we could hop on and, of course, the trolley ropes came in right at that spot. We thought it was really exciting to be able to travel along on the trolley and when we got to the stop where we wanted to go, we would just reach up and pull the trolley rope down. Everything would go dead and all the lights would go out.

What we did was really not very nice, but we thought we had accomplished a great feat to be able to fool the bus drivers and everyone. Once the trolley car stopped in place, we would run as fast as we could run. This began happening quite often, and the drivers were just waiting for it to happen once more, to make sure that whoever was doing it would be taken care of. I remember one time when one of the boys pulled this prank: after the trolley suddenly stopped, this boy ran down the street but, believe it or not, the bus driver ran after him for almost a block. When the bus driver caught the erring prankster, he spanked the boy but good. Of course everyone in the bus was cheering, because that fellow certainly got what was coming to him. Today the bus driver would have been rebuked and his name would be in the papers for abusing a child.

Car Skitching

The next daring step was to be able to "skitch" automobiles. Back then cars had a small little bumper on each side and a spare tire on the back. It was quite an art to be able to sneak up in back of a car when it stopped at a light, making sure the driver could not see what we were doing. When the light changed, along we would go with that car, hanging onto the tire with our feet on those little bumpers. We would total up the number of miles we had traveled, and the more miles you had, the more macho you were; you were really somebody! This was very, very dangerous and although I seemed to be fearless back then, there were times when the cars we were skitching would hit bumps that made our feet actually come off the bumper. If I hadn't hit it again on the way back down, I would have gone right out in the streets.

One of the times when I wanted to get a whole lot of miles, I decided to see if I could take a trip to one of the suburbs to accomplish my desires. It was a warm day and when I found the car I wanted to skitch on, I was able to turn around and actually sit on the bumper. Then I saw we were coming into the town. I looked ahead and noticed that there was a railroad crossing ahead, and right over the crossing there was a policeman standing there. I was determined not to let him see me, so as I came to the railroad tracks, I jumped off—and to my surprise, I found that after sitting on the bumper my legs had gone completely to sleep. I just lay on the railroad tracks until I could get my feet working again.

Skitching Tragedy

Skitching automobiles was a risky activity. My father heard about this activity and took me aside to share his concern. He reminded me how much he and my mother loved me, and advised me that this activity was too dangerous. I pretended I was listening to him, but really, down in my heart, I felt he was just spoiling my fun.

A few weeks later my closest friend, Andy, and I prepared to go skitching again. We stood at the corner of Diversey and Central Avenue in Chicago. Along came a huge truck, pulling a trailer. This was a whole new adventure! My buddy got between the trailer and the truck cab just as I did and the truck started to pull away from the red light. Suddenly, a tragedy occurred. Andy got his foot caught in the wheel of the truck, and he actually went around with the wheel as it began to turn. In desperation, I got the truck driver to stop. There was a lot of activity and ambulances and my buddy was rushed off to the hospital. The next morning I got the sad news that Andy had had to have his leg amputated and died after the operation. That was what it took for me to realize that the warning from my dad was the real thing.

However, the greatest tragedy was that I, a born-again Christian, walked two to three miles to school with Andy every day and I never shared the gospel with him even though he was my best friend. I was a Christian and I knew the Lord as my Savior, but I was really not Andy's best friend because I did not share God's way to heaven. To think that most likely he is in eternity without Christ today because I neglected to be faithful! I will never forget how important it is to be sure you witness to everyone you come in contact with. Because I failed in telling Andy about the Lord, I trusted that from that time on I would be more aware of trying to be the witness that God wants me to be.

Unlawful Entering

Another of my peer-pressure activities was breaking into buildings under construction to play our rubber-band war game, in which we shot each other as heads came peeking out of another window. Lots of fun, but foolish fun.

There was police protection to guard against intruders on these construction sites, but that was only a challenge to us. If we saw the police car arrive, we'd make our way to the roof and jump into a sand pile from a two-story building. I'm amazed we didn't break our legs.

Tobogganing

We also went tobogganing down a huge toboggan slide about a block long. After going down the slide the conventional way, we decided to add some thrills to it. We began to go down the slide standing up or even standing backward on the toboggan. Any mishap going down would have been tragic.

One time I slipped off the back of the toboggan and traveled down this enormous slide on the seat of my pants. The big problem was that the slide was made of rough timbers, with wood slivers and splinters everywhere, and it didn't have enough snow on it to protect me on the way down. My pants became fastened to me by large slivers that required an emergency trip to the hospital for removal.

I can fully understand why teenagers today are so daring and have no thought about the possible dangers that their foolish activities may incur. However, with the collapse of our moral structure, drugs, and the breakdown of the family, the satanic hazards for teens are far greater. PROVERBS 1:7 says, "The fear of the Lord is the beginning of knowledge, but fools despise wisdom and instruction."

In some ways things were no different then than they are today. As teenagers, we wanted to do the thing that was cool to get the approval of our peers and let them know that we were part of their team, regardless of how dangerous it might be. Peer pressure is truly one of Satan's effective methods of capturing people.

PHOTOGRAPHY

I have often shared how blessed I was to have Christian folks who loved the Lord and who also made their home sort of a refuge for Norwegian immigrants. One of those immigrants was a young man whom my father brought from Norway, because his mother and father had passed away and he was all alone. He was a very creative and aggressive young man and soon decided that he wanted to start a photo business of his own.

Before long he got married, and he began developing pictures in his home and thinking about starting a mail-order business. He was very successful and wanted me to come and work alongside him. I was just a teenager, but my father took me out of school to do it, as he felt I would learn more working with this man. Well, this happened to be God's plan for me, even though as I look back, I wonder if it was the right thing to do. But as I worked for Mr. Skrudland, I became intrigued with being a photograph printer. It was back in the days before electronics controlled all the aspects of the picture business, so you had to be very skilled at doing this. Since I was just a young fellow learning, I was determined to be the very best at this. I became very accomplished and made good money while working at Skrudland's Photo Service. Of course it was named after the owner, George Skrudland.

It was in the days before air conditioning, and I sat in an almost-dark room with dim lights, printing and developing my pictures. I would get to work in the summertime at 6:00 in the morning and would work straight through until 8:00 at night because the business orders were so demanding. Mr. Skrudland would plead with me to stay there and get the work finished. Between the extreme heat and the chemicals in the room, I really had quite an odor when I left. One of the difficult things on this job was the special orders, where he would give them a thousand prints for $10. All of the prints came in different sizes and it was difficult to print all of the different sizes with different paper. Then when something would go wrong with the developer, these pictures had to be replaced. If you had a thousand negatives, you would have to find just those pictures among those thousand negatives and reprint just those pictures. This all had to be done virtually on your own time, because you were paid piecework for every batch that you finished. It was a very trying job, but I think if there was anything that it taught me, it was real patience. If you did not have patience, you could never have worked for Skrudland's.

It was while I was working there that the war broke out. I had an opportunity to get a job at the Chicago Crane Company, working to make supplies for the war, but I didn't know that I would be involved with machinery that was actually making parts for the atom bomb.

I look back at my days at Skrudland's Photo Service as a real time of testing for me, but there was also a crossroads time there, too. Because I had learned the business virtually as a teenager, I knew every aspect of the job. They felt that the business had progressed and so they were going to open another store. They were wondering if I would be the one to go ahead and be in charge of that new store.

That was really quite a challenging thing presented to me, but somehow the Lord was not in it and I did not take that attractive offer. Then along came the offer from the Chicago Crane Company for work as a machinist. That was my time in the photo-finishing business: a time of learning and a time of testing for me.

CROSSROADS

We all arrive at crossroads in life. Some are not that important, but then there are the big ones that really change one's whole ministry and life. Before the Lord called me to full-time ministry with Awana, I worked as a machinist for the Chicago Crane Company, a large manufacturing firm. I was employed by them during World War II and unknowingly helped make parts for the atom bomb.

More than 2,000 employees worked one of three shifts in the plant every day but Saturday. I enjoyed my Saturday off because it was then that I directed a Pals Club at the North Side Gospel Center. I worked the night-to-early-morning shift and felt blessed to meet another Christian man on the job. We would have lunch together, usually somewhere close to 2:00 AM.

One day, a big notice went up notifying all employees that we would be required to work on Saturdays. I was dumbfounded. What would I do? I was married, had two children, and knew it was my responsibility to support my family. Still, I knew that God had also called me to direct the Pals Club. While I was wrestling with what to do, Doc Latham shared MAT-THEW 6:33 with me: "But seek ye first the kingdom of God, and His righteousness, and all these things shall be added unto you." I had my answer.

It wasn't an easy decision to make, but I knew I had to talk to my boss and request time off. His office, a small isolated square, was in the middle of the manufacturing plant. In the wee hours of the morning during my lunch break, I knew the time had come to face him. I made countless circles around the office, all the while praying and working up my courage to go in and face him. The clock said 2:00 AM when I finally knocked at his door.

"Come in!"

I swallowed my fear at the sound of his voice and opened the door. The man seated before me had a big surly air about him. He had been smoking a giant cigar when I entered, but threw it down in disgust when he saw me.

I prayed that he wouldn't use any of the profanity he was known for. "What do you want, Rorheim?"

I wasn't sure, but I seemed to detect a measure of curious surprise in his voice. I plunged in. "Well, sir, you see, I lead a club for boys every Saturday, which, as you know, is a day I'm now supposed to work. I was wondering if I could have Saturdays off to continue working with the boys." I went on to explain more about Pals Club and what we did. As I finished, I braced for the blow that I was sure would come. Instead, I got a pleasant surprise.

He brightened. "Rorheim, I think what you're doing sounds great. I've never heard of anything like it! I'm going to make an exception for you, so you can keep right on helping those boys."

I breathed a prayer of thanks. After thanking my boss, I was soon back at work. To this day, I'm so grateful I followed the Lord's leading. If I hadn't trusted Him, I wouldn't be involved with Awana. This instance reminds me so acutely how easy it is to miss the Lord's will in our lives. Unless we're completely committed to following Him, we'll miss the greatest things He'd have us do for Him.

WINNIE

It is hard to believe that more than seventy years ago, I met this cute teen-aged girl at that original North Side Gospel Center. She came from a broken home; her father had left the family when she was just a young girl. She was the oldest of three girls and some of the time she had to be the mother of the family.

It so happened that God was in all this, because Mrs. Latham was there at the church and she led Winnie to the Lord. Winnie lived about five miles away from the church and the club, so it was difficult at times for her to attend. She was so anxious to come to club that she would walk to the club and try to scrape together five cents for the streetcar fare to take her home.

Winnie was so embarrassed to tell people that she came from a broken home. She vowed in her heart that if she ever got married, she wanted to be certain that this would be a marriage that would last a lifetime.

Club became an exciting part of her life, as this was the only true happiness she had. She would meet with leaders who would encourage her and she just enjoyed their fellowship so much. It was not long before they shared with her that there was a camp that they were planning for the girls in Muskegon, Michigan. They encouraged her to try and save her money so that she could attend that camp, which she succeeded in doing.

She was really excited to meet the boat at Navy Pier in Chicago. She went alone with nothing but a duffle bag. Her mother did not even take her down there. She got on a paddle boat and over to Lake Harbor they went. It was an all-night trip and early in the morning they would arrive over there and the cars would come and pick up the campers and take them to the camp.

Camp had a real spiritual impact on Winnie's life because she listened to the Bible-hour lessons each day, taught by Mrs. Latham. She also met many of the leaders and clubbers and she fit in with everyone because she had such a warm personality. It was not long before they asked Winnie to be the director of the Junior Guards Club. This was all prior to Awana, while it was in the learning stages with no tests, but they were reaching kids with the gospel. They had a good time of fellowship.

At this time, I was directing all of the clubs because I was the youth pastor and I was also in charge of the Pals Club for the boys, which was my main responsibility. The North Side Gospel Center was planning a big banquet and Paul Rader was coming in as the speaker. The banquet was to be held in one of the beautiful hotels in downtown Chicago. I decided to invite Winnie

Winnie and Art on a date in Terre Haute, Indiana, circa 1938

to be my date for the evening. It was during that date that someone lit the fire of romance, and from there on in we began dating on a regular basis.

The North Side Gospel Center in those early days was a very interesting church, as it had afternoon Sunday school and after Sunday school was an afternoon meeting, and then there was also an evening service. It was an all-day church time. Many of us were excited just to be together. We would come to Sunday school and would stay all the way through the evening service. We would go out and get something to eat, and all the fellowship we had was just tremendous.

It was there with all of these kids that I had the opportunity to meet Winnie Hofmann. When we were both twenty-one years of age, we decided to get married, but the North Side Gospel Center was just a hub of Christian activities every night. Even though I was the youth director and on the staff, there was not even one free night to arrange for us to get married there at the Center. So we did not make an issue of that; we found a small Norwegian church in the area that worked out very nicely for our wedding.

Of course, there was a wedding dress to purchase, as well as dresses for the bridesmaids, which was really an issue at that time because of the shortage of money. So Winnie, being as handy and capable as she was in sewing, decided to make the wedding dress and also the dresses for the bridesmaids, which turned out just beautifully. The wedding was quite interesting; Doc Latham performed the ceremony, and my friend, Jim Gunderson, was the best man. When the time came in the ceremony when Doc Latham asked the best man to present the ring, Jim had forgotten which pocket he had put them in. You can imagine the chuckle that went through the church as he frantically searched through each of his pockets! Finally he came up with the ring and everyone cheered. A year later, I acted as the best man at Jim Gunderson's wedding.

We could not have known at that time the part that the Gundersons would have in Awana's first missionary film, *Hitting the Mark*. The book of Proverbs says, "He who findeth a wife, findeth a good thing." I never looked at Winnie as a thing, but as a wonderful wife who contributed so much to the ministry of Awana in the days that followed.

By then she was the mother of two children, Kathlyn and Kenneth, so she had those added responsibilities as well. But in spite of all of the challenges, she helped me in attending to the many needs I had as we took the beginning steps in the Awana ministry.

Winnie and Art on their wedding day

One of the first challenges we had was when I found all of those beanie hats—red, blue, green, and yellow—that we converted into nice little uniform hats. I got little monograms, which became Winnie's first Awana job. She sewed the monograms on all of those hats that were a part of the uniform. Later on, as the program was progressing, we needed to make neckerchiefs. I would buy the material in bolts and we would cut them up in different sizes and then we would turn them over to my dear wife, Winnie, who would sew them up and put a nice Awana monogram on each one of those neckerchiefs. She was so very efficient in doing that. I was really happy to see the nice supply we had of neckerchiefs. It was not long, though, before Awana was growing so fast that she was unable to keep up with the supply. God wonderfully provided another way for us to get the neckerchiefs we needed, as they were being sold all around the country by that time.

First Awana Building Challenge

Then came the challenge of finding another building, since we had completely outgrown the present facility. It was then God just said, "Why don't you get into your car and go for a ride and let's see what we can find?" We did find a nice double storefront that looked just perfect for meeting our needs, but the problem was we did not have any funds that could even come close to purchasing it, at $43,000. We thank the Lord we had a church committee that had a real heart for Awana and thought that God was in it and that we should consider trying to raise money with interest-free loans, which we had done to purchase the North Side Gospel Center building.

We thought about having a fund-raising banquet and inviting all the Awana people. We were amazed by the enthusiasm! Even though we had only eight people on our staff at that time, we found ourselves with a banquet of about a thousand people attending! Then we had to find a facility that could handle a group of this size, and of course the question immediately arose: Who would handle all the food and be able to take care of that part of our banquet? Winnie said simply, "I will assume that responsibility."

She took over that responsibility wonderfully, got a crew together, and they handled all the food for that entire banquet. I was so thrilled to see the capability she showed in reaching all of these people who enthusiastically worked along with her. As a result of that banquet, all the people gladly responded with interest-free loans and we were able to purchase that first Awana building.

Winnie's Camp Leadership

Awana was growing rapidly, but I was still responsible, as the director of Camp Awana, for all the leaders and all the wives of the counselors. Winnie set up a separate camp for the wives, who became the working team at the camp. They were responsible for taking care of the camp team, doing the inspection of the cabins, and cleaning the latrines. There were many, many jobs for them to take care of. Winnie was able to help them feel that they had a vital part in making the camp successful.

Winnie and Art, Camp Awana

Depression Days

I remember we went through a time of financial depression. Everyone was put on food stamps to buy groceries and gas, and Winnie watched the use of the stamps carefully. She also invited people to come over during those times, and they gladly brought some of their stamps along so that we could buy food as a group and still have a good time of fellowship together.

Marriage-Testing Decision

Winnie had many abilities for which I thank the Lord. It was my responsibility to get up to at least one hundred volunteer workers every Saturday for about six weeks to work at the camp. This one Saturday I had about a hundred coming up to camp, and I had made all the plans for them—and all of a sudden, Winnie became sick. I had to take her to the hospital and I was deeply troubled, wondering, "What do I do with my wife in the hospital and with all of these people coming up to camp?" I was the only person who could direct the volunteers.

Winnie said, "Listen, this is what God has called you to do. You go right up there because God will take care of me." This was special to see the heart attitude she had to stand behind me and do what God laid on my heart to do. I saw this spirit in Winnie constantly, that all those years she wanted to serve the Lord. She knew that I was her husband and she was there to be my encourager and to help me in any way she could.

Another Testing Decision

In the later years we had another real test. I had a very important trip planned for Japan and Korea—a trip I really needed to make. Thirty minutes before my friend arrived to take me to the airport, Winnie fell and I had to call the ambulance to take her to the hospital. Winnie said, "Listen. God will take care of me and you go ahead to the airport and make your trip to Japan and Korea." I certainly appreciated her self-sacrifice, but my heart was just tugging at me. Do I leave my dear wife, without even knowing at this point what is wrong with her? I decided to go and the Lord took care of her in my absence.

She had such a sweet spirit and peace about me going on this trip that I will always appreciate. Later I found out that her hip was broken. But, as always, God was in control and took care of her in my absence.

During the beginning years of Awana, Winnie worked as a volunteer in any way that she could possibly help. She worked in the finance department and also learned how to operate the first card printer (the computer printer) that we had. It was so much easier than what we have today.

Winnie on Awana Staff

One of my biggest assets was having Winnie work at Awana and be able to feel the heartbeat of everything that was going on, so that together we could pray and talk and see how God was going to lead us along. There again, it was Winnie's happy, cooperative personality that made everything go so well as she worked with people who respected her. If that had not been so, it would have been very difficult; I would not have been able to handle everything at Awana without Winnie's help.

Physical Testing

The last couple of years have been challenging for both of us: Winnie had an accident and broke her ankle and then some time later she broke her hip, which was very painful. She went through a very difficult time with rehabilitation, and I soon found out that I simply was not able to take care of her at home. God would have to provide a special care person to meet her needs. It is so beautiful how God provides when we really need His help.

God's Angels

Along came a lady from our church, Lynn Erickson. She was the first angel God sent to help with caring for Winnie. Lynn was wonderful with us, especially with caring for Winnie's needs. We knew Lynn was planning to go to Korea to be a missionary, and we were not looking forward to losing her, but we knew God was calling her and her family to be missionaries. Before leaving for the mission field, she introduced and trained Mercedes to take her place in caring for Winnie.

KATHLYN AND KENNY

We were blessed with two children, Kathlyn and Kenneth. Our first child, Kathlyn, married Dennis Brock and had four God-loving daughters, who have given us ten treasured great-grandchildren. Yes, we are truly blessed to be the proud parents of both Kathlyn and Kenneth. Kathlyn and her family have been a real blessing to both Winnie and myself. Kathlyn has a true servant's heart, and a real passion for foreign missions. She is also a great encourager and persuader for people who are discouraged and hurting. She is a beautiful Christian people-person who radiates her love for the Lord wherever she goes.

Winnie's surprise ninetieth birthday party with daughter, Kathlyn, and granddaughters, Julie and Kim. Left to right: Julie, Kim, Winnie, and Kathlyn

Art's granddaughters (from left to right): Julie Bales, Amy Roedding, Kerry Gwaltney, and Kim Ahlgrim

The Brock daughters all graduated from Toccoa Bible College with teaching degrees, which they are all presently using in their ministry as they serve the Lord. Amy and Gary and their three children have been missionaries to Quito, Ecuador, for more than eighteen years. Our youngest granddaughter, Kerry, and her husband, Rich, along with their two children, are missionaries in Malaysia and are enjoying God's leading in their lives there. Our granddaughter Julie, and her husband, Joel, have three children and Joel has a real pastor's heart. Kim is an executive at the Cedarville Bible University and has a real impact on the students there, as well as on her husband, Tom, and their two children.

All parents know so well that the most challenging thing in life is raising our children. Each stage that they go through is very challenging. A big part of my son's life was attending Camp Awana. An exciting part of the activity at camp was a 40-acre archery golf course. This fascinated Kenny to no end and he strove to master the sport so he could get one of the lowest scores. He did just that.

Camp Awana is a beautiful 123 acres of ground with many lovely trees creating a gorgeous wooded area. One day, by chance, I discovered that my son and his friends had been building a tree house back in the woods. They had chosen one of the tallest trees in camp and were secretly allowing some of the campers to come up there with them. I soon realized that this could be a very dangerous activity and that the camp would be liable for any injuries. But it was such a unique idea! So, I decided to join his venture. I enlisted a couple of skilled carpenters to construct, in that same area, a beautiful tree house that was safe. It became a real feature of the camp.

It wasn't long, though, before the tree-house excitement seemed to wear thin. One day, Kenny came home and said, "Dad, I know now what I want to major in. I'd like to be a scuba diver." Kenny didn't go into things halfway. In fact, I believe Kenny could be nicknamed Mr. Adventurer—there doesn't seem to be anything dangerous and exciting that he hasn't tried.

He was determined to get all the training he needed, plus a complete set of scuba equipment, and then he traveled to some of the most exciting scuba-diving areas he could find. For quite a while this seemed to fill his life satisfactorily. Then, again one day he came home and said, "I have finally found some daring excitement like never before."

I said, "Ken, what is this?"

He said, "I am now engaged in mountain climbing. I'm going to classes and learning this challenging but scary technique." It wasn't long before I found him practicing on the side of our two-story home. It wasn't long thereafter that he got involved in some precarious mountain climbing.

Then the excitement of that passed, and Ken, with that familiar enthusiastic look on his face, said, "Dad, I would like to get involved in skydiving. It just fascinates me to see people jump out of planes and glide down with a parachute." Well, I knew he was quite determined and I did not even try to discourage him. Before long, he was involved in a regular skydiving venture each week, and was getting to be very good at it.

Then along came Uncle Sam and the challenge of the war, so he enlisted in the United States Air Force. It wasn't long before he was transferred to Germany and became a member of the U.S. Air Force skydiving team. This assignment was very attractive to him, as he got involved in putting on exhibitions for the Air Force as well as participating in skydiving tournaments. My wife and I hadn't seen him for more than four years, because he took all of his leave over in the East so that he could travel and see the world. We knew approximately when he would be coming home, but we weren't really sure.

One day, while Winnie and I were visiting my daughter, she received a phone call and the caller suggested that she should get her parents out into

Art and Kenny, Camp Awana

the back yard. We went out into the yard and looked up into the sky and down came my son, parachuting right into the yard. That's when you can say literally, "I'll be 'dropping in' on you some time."

Ken wasn't home from the Air Force very long before he got involved in flying an airplane. After learning that, he decided to start a flying school as a business venture, which he directed for some time. Since he had become so proficient in flying, he decided to get into aerial photography as well. This also became part of his business venture for some time.

Shortly after that, he married one of his college schoolmates from Western Illinois University. While they were going to school there, he also directed a skydiving school for the college. Then he became very enamored of sailboating. He had friends who were excellent sailboat navigators and he really got hooked on sailing. They were very adventurous and decided they wanted to sail across the ocean over to Europe. Ken decided that would be a tremendous challenge.

Unfortunately, during this period of Ken's life, he had really gotten out of touch with things of the Lord; all of his exciting adventures were taking first place. But the Lord had a plan to bring him back to his senses. While Ken and his friends were out in the middle of the ocean, a tremendous storm came up and that sailboat was tossed around like a cork. Ken really thought that his life was going to come to an end and they were all going to be drowned. It was there that he and the Lord had a conversation and Ken said, "Lord, if you'll bring me home safely, I'll allow you to use my life." It wasn't long after that Ken and his new wife decided to purchase a sailboat of their own, one that they could consider their home. For twenty years they lived on *Assurance* while his wife taught school and he carried out some of his navigating adventures.

He became the captain of a tour ship, another job that intrigued him. One of the most exciting vacations my wife and I ever had was sailing with him on his boat to the Aleutian Islands and visiting some of the beautiful remote areas there. Later Ken was stationed in the Bahamas and became a full-fledged navigator, conducting a ship transport service.

One day they thought it would be good for my wife, Winnie, and me to come down and spend two weeks with them on their boat traveling around all of those beautiful islands. Because he was then based in the Florida Keys and would be traveling over to the Bahamas, he told us to meet them in Nassau. "When you get into Nassau," he told us, "go to the Coast Guard and you'll be able to track us down. They will find out just where we are located on

Kenny and Art on Kenny's sailboat

the ocean. They will send out radio signals and they will get a response to you very quickly."

So, we looked forward to that great event, being reunited in Nassau. We followed his instructions and went to the Coast Guard and said that we were looking for our son and that his ship's name was "*Assurance.*" The fellow there said that he would put out the call for *Assurance* and he was sure we would be getting a reply soon. In a short time, we got the most unusual reply: "*Temptation* is towing *Assurance.*" Now, *Temptation* was the name of another boat; evidently my son's boat had broken down, and *Temptation* was actually pulling his boat. While we were still there waiting for him to arrive, another couple came in to the Coast Guard and said, "We've lost track of a boat as well." The person in charge asked what that name would be, and to our amazement, the name of that boat was *Hallelujah.* This message went out on the airwaves to all the boat people in the area and the comments were coming back from them. "*Temptation* is pulling *Assurance, Hallelujah, Hallelujah.*" Winnie and I thought what an unusual story this was going to be.

It wasn't long before we saw a boat by the name of *Temptation* pulling in, and there was *Assurance* behind it. They got some engine repairs done, and Ken was able to take care of some additional errands, and then we were off on a wonderful two-week tour all through the islands there in the Bahamas. That was a great time for all of us. You could plainly see God's handiwork in some of these islands, especially where it seemed like no one had ever been there before.

Yes, that was an exciting, exploring two weeks that Winnie and I will never forget. My wife and I have often watched our son skydiving and parachute-jumping. I can remember up at Camp Awana when he came to put on a demonstration for the campers. He went up to 15,000 feet, which is really higher than normal, and as he jumped out, it was just like a little dot in the sky coming down. It seemed like it took forever for him to open that chute. *When is he going to open that chute? When is he going to open that chute?* was our hearts' cry as he plummeted through the air. Finally, we saw the beautiful sight of the chute opening, and then he landed right there on the campground.

We would watch our son after he landed, as he took and folded his chute ever so carefully. I watched him fold it very meticulously and I asked, "Ken, why are you so careful with folding that chute?" And he said, "Dad, my life depends on how careful I am with my chute."

I think about each of us who are dealing with the lives of boys and girls: We realize that their lives depend upon how faithfully we witness to them and how we prepare ourselves to speak to them as we care for them. So yes, our lives depend upon how faithful we are in obeying what God calls us to do.

We have been very thankful to the Lord for giving us such a wonderful family that want to give their lives to serve our Lord. My dear wife Winnie and I thank the Lord constantly for the long wonderful life He has given us to minister for Him. One of the treasured verses that David gives us in the later days of his life is Psalm 71:17–18: "Oh God, you have taught me from my youth, and I have declared your wonderful works and now I am old and gray-headed; Oh God, forsake me not until I have shewed thy strength to this generation, and thy power to the generations that are to come."

It is truly our hearts' desire that all of the people to whom God has allowed us to minister will in turn minister to others and they to yet others, and so keep on sharing this wonderful message of the gospel and God's wonderful plan for everyone who will put their trust in Him and allow Him to direct their lives.

Rorheim family reunion, Psalm One Club, Starved Rock Lodge, Illinois, 2007

HOSPITALS

My wife, Winnie, and I had the privilege of hosting two trips to the Holy Land on behalf of Awana. I found that to thoroughly enjoy these walking trips over the many hills and rolling terrain, you needed two major pieces of physical equipment: a good pair of shoes and good feet. Next to that were knees that were not worn out. I found out that my shoes and feet were just fine, but that I had a knee that needed to be replaced. With the modern technology available today, I found that replacing a knee was a very practical thing to do. So, I made arrangements to have this done.

Down through the years God has blessed me with a healthy body. Yes, I have had a few minor surgeries, which were very successful. However, I found that my body could not adjust to the antibiotics that one needs during surgery. My body reacts violently to them and they have sent me to the hospital three times with severe reactions. So, as I prepared for this knee surgery, I encouraged many folks to pray that I would not have a problem reaction to the antibiotics that I would have to take to avoid infection.

I went through all of the pre-operation information sessions and training and finally was scheduled to arrive at the hospital on the morning of the operation at 6:30 AM. There was much anxiety as they prepared me for the operation; they placed the intravenous equipment into my vein and the antibiotics began to feed into my system as they wheeled me into the operating room.

After several hours I awoke in my room, just delighted that the operation was over, and learned that it had been very successful. The nurse told me there would be pain that would range anywhere from 1 to 10, but I need not be too concerned about it because they now have new self-injection equipment and you are able to regulate the pain medication yourself. Everything seemed to be just routine and going fine—but that afternoon I became very uncomfortable and began experiencing quite a lot of pain.

As the doctors examined me, they saw that I was having a violent reaction to the antibiotics. I was developing a rash over my whole body and some parts of my body were also having other reactions. To add to my frustration, I thought of all the people who had been praying for me that I would not get an allergic reaction to the antibiotics: Had God not heard their prayers? Of course, I knew that God always answers prayer; sometimes it is "yes" immediately and sometimes it is "wait" and sometimes He says "NO." Evidently

Art and Winnie at the Tomb of the Resurrection in Israel

this was a time that God said "no." This reminds me of when the Apostle Paul prayed to have his thorns removed and God said "no" to him. He said, "My grace is sufficient for you," and this was obviously God's answer for me.

In my distress, I thought about how many times I had quoted Scripture to other people. There is 1 THESSALONIANS 5:18: "In every thing give thanks: for this is the will of God in Christ Jesus concerning you." Then I thought of EPHESIANS 3:13: "Wherefore, I desire that ye faint not in my tribulations for you, which is your glory." Yes, I wrestled with the Lord at that moment and asked Him for help. I said, "I know this is all true, but give me the grace to really apply it to my own life this very moment."

Both of the doctors there were conferring about what they should do to combat this situation. They were now doing blood tests and many other tests to see really what had taken place in my body. In spite of the entire drama, and the trauma that was taking place, how wonderful it is to know that the Lord fully understands and, as He says, "He is touched by the feelings of our infirmities." It is times like this that you really have to completely rest on that truth.

I was wondering who was going to be sharing the room with me. Would this be someone I could witness to? To my dismay, I found out that my roommate was afflicted with Alzheimer's. All through the night there would come these loud bursts of despairing screaming and, yes, I continued to ask the Lord, "Why all this?!" To my further dismay, I found that this situation was going to last for two nights. I was physically in distress and completely exhausted. Then I received the good news that my partner was going to be moved and that most likely I would be alone for the next night. This was truly the best comfort I had had thus far.

For a short period of time, everything was quiet in the room, until suddenly the door opened and they brought in another patient coming out of surgery. I remember in my heart saying to the Lord, "Please, I am so exhausted I do not even want to talk to this person." This is truly the first time in my life that these thoughts had ever come to me.

In just a few moments, this new patient introduced himself and began to share his family background. He was a father of five children, and he told me that he had been raised Catholic all of his life. These past few years he had become somewhat disenchanted with the Catholic religion because it had not helped him or his family in any way. I just quietly listened and tried to be polite, adding just a short remark here and there.

Then he shared that a big change had just recently taken place in his family. He said that a couple of his girls had been invited to another church for something that was called, he thought, Awana Clubs. He wondered if I had ever heard about anything like that. For a moment I was just speechless and couldn't even respond. It was like a miracle took place in my body. All of a sudden, God gave me renewed strength so that I was able to talk with enthusiasm, and share with him a bit about Awana. At that time I did not mention my affiliation with Awana, but instead shared how God had mightily used Awana around the world to show boys, girls, and their parents how they could be sure they could go to heaven.

My new roommate then told how his twelve-year-old daughter had come home from Awana and said that she was saved and sure of going to heaven. I said to him, "That certainly must have made you real happy, didn't it?" He said, "It sure did," and it was then that the Lord prompted me by saying, "Art, this is the prime opportunity to ask him the big question." So I turned to my roommate and said, "How about you? Are you sure of going to heaven?"

Winnie and Art, 2005

In an honest reply, he said, "No, I have no assurance of going to heaven at all."

I immediately said, "Wouldn't you like to know that for sure right now, and would you allow me the privilege of showing you how you can be sure?" What a thrill it was to present to him God's beautiful plan of salvation that took place at Calvary. Then what a joy to see the receptive heart that he had, as right there in the hospital room he put his trust in Jesus Christ as his personal Savior.

I have thought of those two preceding days that to me were a complete disaster both physically and even spiritually. I had really wondered why God didn't answer the prayers of so many of my people who were praying that I would not have a reaction to the antibiotics, but God again taught me a big lesson to completely trust Him and to realize that His ways are always the best. What a joy it was from there on to fellowship with my new brother in Christ, whose name is Jim Josetti. When we left each other at the hospital, he said, "Will you please keep in contact with me? I need you to help me to grow spiritually." Every day without fail, he has called me or asked me to call him so that we could talk and pray together.

During my stay in the hospital and at the rehab center, I had opportunities to talk to at least twenty-five nurses, doctors, and workers about salvation. Two of the nurses indicated that they, too, were now trusting Christ as their Savior. Several of them shared how concerned they were for their children, who were growing up and having to face the world of sin. They were interested in getting their children into Awana Clubs in their area. Of course, I found many of them who had big burdens and were very much ready to talk to people who had a concern for them. But, as we know so well, they will never have peace in their hearts until they get that new life that only Christ can give them, when they put their trust in Him. Yes, my hospital experience was truly an adventure.

Rehab

During my stay at the rehab center there must have been twenty-five to thirty nurses, staff workers, and doctors who came to my bedside. The Lord gave me an awareness that regardless of their positions in the hospital, they all were in two classifications: They were either heaven-bound or hell-bound—and He made me realize that I may be the only one who is going to cross their path in a lifetime to challenge them about the big question as to where they are going when they die.

I found that often, in the quiet of the night when they would come in to check my vital signs, they were open to conversation. Some of the nurses had broken homes, and many of them had burdens and were searching for answers. There were several Filipino nurses with whom I could share our heart interest in the Philippines. Of course, I have personally been there several times and so that made them listen to why I cared about Filipinos. Two of them indicated that they were trusting Christ to be their Savior.

As you may know, I always have my little camera handy so that I can take pictures with all of these dear folks. This makes for a good follow-up when I write to them and send them books or other pieces of literature that I feel they might need.

At the rehab center I ate all of my meals with two other gentlemen. One was a Catholic about my age, who was as kind a man as you would ever meet, but then it would break my heart when I saw the priest come in to give him communion periodically. The other man was a devout Lutheran, who from all indications didn't have the slightest idea how or why God takes people to heaven. So, as you could imagine, we had a lot of interesting conversations. I asked them if they would mind if I prayed to ask God's blessing on the food. They seemed just delighted that I would do that.

Rehab Once Again

I was in another rehabilitation center after my new knee procedure and I found that this second rehab center was another opportunity to witness for the Lord. Yes, I had many opportunities to witness—too many—but there were some that God gave me an even greater opportunity with, especially those with whom I sat at meal times.

I remember one fellow who was new to the center who came and sat at my table. I thought, *I must witness to this man,* so I thought, *I'm going to give him one of my tracts.* "How can you be sure of going to heaven?" I asked. "Would you read this tract over? I would like to be able to talk to you about it further, maybe tomorrow morning." He said he was quite willing to do so. The next day I got the shocking news that he had died that very night. I never did get around to talking with him. This just proves once again that we cannot postpone opportunities. Maybe he did read the tract, and maybe he did trust Christ as his Savior. I probably should have talked to him right away.

Then there was another gentleman who seemed to be kind of a loner. He always sat by himself, but I was determined to go and fellowship with him. Of course, in our conversation I asked him just where he thought he was going to go when he died, and he came right out and said, "Well, I believe I'm going to hell," which was a shock to me. I asked him why he would say that and he told me that he had shot a man some years ago, and he didn't think that God could ever forgive him for that.

Of course, I told him that, yes, God forgives us completely, if we trust Him to be our Savior and allow Him to work in our lives. Yes, God will forgive you for that. It seemed like that sin was just seared in his heart and mind, though. Several days after that I asked him the same question and he said again, "Yes, I am going to hell."

I said, "Jim, you don't realize what hell is really like." And I showed him the Word of God in 2 Thessalonians 1:8, 9, and I said, "Look at this, where it says 'In flaming fire taking vengeance on them that know not God, and that obey not the gospel of our Lord Jesus Christ, who shall be punished with everlasting destruction from the presence of the Lord and from the glory of

His power.'" I said, "Jim, that is God talking and that is a very, very serious thing." He would just sit there as I witnessed to him and I really didn't feel I was getting through to him at all.

Then, finally, came the time when I was to leave the rehab center and I thought, *Well, I am going up and talk to Jim just one last time.* I went to his room and I said, "Jim, let me ask you that question again: if you died today, where would you go?"

Without any question or hesitation he said, "I would go to heaven, because I have trusted Jesus Christ to be my Savior." You can't imagine how thrilled I was to think that here was a fellow who had just really seemed to be hopeless, and he finally saw that God would forgive him. Now he was a child of God!

So we should realize that all around us is a mission field. For the most part, people are hell-bound, but we have this wonderful message of the gospel of grace. God commands us to share that message because we never know who God will bring across our paths for us to witness to. We should never miss an opportunity to witness.

Beginnings

LIFE BEFORE AWANA

It is very hard to understand what this world was like when Awana was just beginning to get started. We did not realize how far technological growth would take us. I thought everything was just fine, and did not feel that Awana had been neglected or held back in any way because we didn't use all the latest advancements in technology. I think you will enjoy this list, and find it hard to believe that we did not have these things in those days:

1. Television
2. Computers
3. Cell phones
4. Microwaves
5. Dishwashers
6. Air conditioners
7. Contact lenses
8. Penicillin
9. Polio shots
10. Expressways
11. Tape decks
12. Electric typewriters
13. Pizza

14. McDonalds

15. Artificial hearts

Here are a few other truisms of that time:

- Pot was something you cooked in.
- Fast food was only eaten during Lent.
- Grass was to be mowed.
- Five cents was the cost of a pack of gum or an ice cream cone.
- Rock music was a grandmother's lullaby.

AND THERE WAS NO AWANA.

If you could measure the technical advancement of our world and country since Christ was born until 1845, you could scale it as one inch. And then if you were to measure from 1845 until 1945, it would measure two inches. From 1945 until the present, it would be higher than the Washington Monument.

We forget what an amazing technological world we are living in today. Still, we have to come to the realization that all the knowledge of all of these brilliant men whom we admire so much because of all they have accomplished—with all of that put together, it would never take them one inch closer to heaven. So it is great to know that at Awana, we have the grateful message of salvation, which gives us that sure hope of heaven. We see how far Awana has progressed today and see all the various tools that we now have. We certainly do not have any reason to stay as we were at the beginning; rather, we move ahead fast and use all of these technical abilities and gadgets to get the gospel out to a world without Christ.

THE WORLD'S MOST AMAZING CHURCH: CHICAGO GOSPEL TABERNACLE

In my opinion, the Chicago Gospel Tabernacle was one of the world's most amazing churches. The main reason it was so amazing was the pastor, Paul Rader. He was one of the great men of the century. The Tabernacle was often called the "Steel Tent." It seated about 6,000 people. There were crude benches to sit on and sawdust floors with coal stoves on each side for heat. But God's presence was there. The enthusiasm each Sunday was like going to a World Series ballgame. The busses and streetcars hauled the people in by the thousands.

Imagine some two hundred in the choir, a band of fifty members, two grand pianos, and the second-largest organ in the city of Chicago. These were all part of this amazing ministry. Paul Rader had an unusual pastoral staff, and the musical staff included men like Merrill Dunlap, Lance Latham, Howard and Clarence Jones, Richard Oliver, and many others, who were very, very talented musicians and composers.

Many folks have said that Paul Rader was the founder of Christian radio in the city of Chicago. He had the first coast-to-coast broadcast preaching the gospel each week. The mayor, William Hale Thompson, was so enamored of Paul Rader that he had Rader on the first program that was presented from the radio tower in Chicago.

Why was the Chicago Gospel Tabernacle such an amazing church? I know of no church in the world that produced so much lasting fruit in such a short time as the Tabernacle. Paul Rader's ministry was approximately eleven years long. He went to be with the Lord when he was about sixty years old. Here are just a few of the ministries that were founded through the challenges of Paul Rader and the Tabernacle:

- Lance Latham, founder of the North Side Gospel Center where the Awana Clubs were born

Chicago Gospel Tabernacle

Paul Rader

- Clarence Jones, founder of the worldwide radio station HCJB ("Heralding Christ Jesus' Blessings")
- Paul Freed, founder of Trans World Radio
- Torrey Johnson, founder of Youth for Christ, "Songs in the Night" radio program, and Midwest Bible Church
- Paul Fleming, founder of New Tribes Mission
- Peter Dyneka, founder of the Slavic Gospel Association
- Oswald J. Smith, the worldwide missionary ministry of the People's Church in Toronto, Canada
- Charles Fuller, the famed evangelist of California and founder of Fuller Seminary, was led to Christ by Paul Rader
- Jerry Falwell, founder of Liberty University, says that Paul Rader had a great influence on his life

- George Ziemer, founder and pastor of the Wisconsin Tabernacle, was challenged by Paul Rader
- Howard Ferrin, founder of Providence Bible Institute
- Victor Cory, founder of Scripture Press
- Bill Dillon, Sr., founder of Sunshine Gospel Mission
- Bill Dillon, Jr., founder of Inner City Impact

What an amazing ministry, and what amazing men whom God used, and who were fully dedicated to Him. All around the world there are missionaries and workers in other organizations who were motivated by the life and ministry of the Chicago Gospel Tabernacle.

One of life's most memorable moments for me was when I personally met Paul Rader. Lance Latham, my mentor, asked me to pick Pastor Rader up at the hotel and bring him to our church to speak. I was just a teenager, and very frightened about what I could even say to this great man. I remember trying to rehearse to myself just what words I would say to him. Then came the moment when I was to pick him up at his hotel. I remember as he walked up to the car to get in, I was just awed by his presence. As he got into the car, his first words to me were to thank me for my thoughtfulness in coming to pick him up. Then, before I even had an opportunity to say anything, he asked me my name and whether I was a Christian. Of course,

Paul Rader's musical staff

Class at the Chicago Gospel Tabernacle

I was able to say, "Yes, by all means." Then I'll always remember him look-ing intently at me and saying, "You're real special to God and God's got a very special plan for your life if you'll let Him have it." He then asked me if I really wanted God to lead my life. I of course said yes.

In just a moment, my uneasiness with this great man vanished. I saw a true man of God who was one of God's humble servants and who saw that he needed to minister to me as a young teen. From then on, I couldn't wait to hear him preach and hear him on the radio broadcasts. I often asked myself where I would be today if it were not for the vision of Paul Rader, who influenced my pastor, Lance Latham, to start the North Side Gospel Center where Awana was born. We can constantly say, What if? What if they hadn't obeyed the Lord? Yes, I thank the Lord for the men of yester-year who blazed the trail so that I could have the ministry to which God called me.

LANCE "DOC" LATHAM: CROSSROADS

Many of you know that Lance Latham, who was pastor of the church where Awana was founded, was also my mentor. I was his youth director during those days when the Awana program was being built. I treasure so much the fifty years I was able to work alongside this godly man. I received an educa-tion that I could not have received anywhere else. I saw how he completely

Art and Doc Latham in front of the Awana Algonquin Building, circa 1970

trusted God in every circumstance of his life. He was brilliant, and yet he was the most humble man I had ever met. He was a tremendous musician who could have been very successful, from a worldly standpoint, in almost any musical career or area he wanted. But he chose the path that God wanted him to choose. He was a vital staff member of the Chicago Gospel Tabernacle where Paul Rader, the great evangelist, was pastor.

Rader's was an amazing ministry. It was probably the first mega-church. Latham had a vital part in the radio ministry, as well as the music ministry of the church, and he also acted as Paul Rader's personal secretary when Rader traveled around the world. From an external standpoint, you might have said Latham really had it made as a Christian, and would be the envy of other Christians. What else could he have asked for? But God was tugging at his heart to start a church.

There was a group of young people who were excited about going along with him in this new venture. The big question was where they should go. Well, God always opens the door somewhere, and they found an old, burned-out furniture store that had been vacant for a couple of years. They wondered if this space could be renovated into a church. There were many questions to be answered: How could they do this? Where would the money come from to make it happen? How could Latham earn some kind of a salary to live on, because there wasn't any money to cover this? But then, at that very same time, there came another challenging opportunity.

A new Christian radio station that was just beginning operations asked Latham if he would come and be the director. He was just made to order for this, and besides, that job came with a guaranteed salary. Then there came a second big challenge, in the form of an offer to be the associate pastor at the famous Moody Memorial Church in Chicago. How attractive both of these ministry challenges were! Here you can see Latham was at the crossroads of his life.

He chose to take on the difficult venture of starting this new church. Little did we know, back then, that this was to be the forerunner of the Awana Club program. If he had chosen one of these other ministries—a choice that no one would ever have questioned—there would be no Awana Clubs today. How I praise God for a man who was willing to follow God's leading in his life!

This is certainly a beautiful lesson for all of us. Life is made up of many decisions each day. Most of our decisions are small ones, but little by little, for all of us, as we make the decisions that the Holy Spirit places on our hearts, when we come to the place with the big decisions, we can have God's confidence in making the right choice. What a thrill it is to know that God's Holy Spirit can give us His definite direction when we stand at a crossroads of life.

THE TRUE GOSPEL MESSAGE (BY LANCE LATHAM—MY MENTOR)

As a young Christian, listening to a message on Sunday morning in a local church, I became increasingly perplexed. The preacher noted many interesting things in the Bible and then took time to explain the way of salvation. "In order to be a Christian," the preacher said, "you must be totally dedicated to the Lord, you must forsake all or you cannot be saved."

Is salvation then by commitment, by dedication, by hard work, by abandonment to the Lord? I asked myself. I heard it again as I traveled around and heard many different invitations: give your heart to God, give your life to God, ask Jesus into your heart, pray the publican's prayer, make Jesus Lord of your life, surrender all to Him.

These confusing messages and invitations spurred me to begin a pursuit of the true message. I increasingly heard a number of sermons to the unsaved which purported to be the gospel, but did not direct the sinner to

Christ's finished work on Calvary as their ONLY HOPE, and all too often did not even mention the Cross. The unsaved were told what they must do, what they must give God. They were told to give their health, their lives, they must "surrender all," they must make vows or resolutions to cut out all of their sinning and live for God. To our amazement, we heard one preacher using 2 CORINTHIANS 10:5 as proof of this way of salvation, saying, "Did not Paul tell us to bring every thought into captivity to Christ?" And Calvary is not even mentioned! The message is to all effects the same as that of the liberals: the total commitment.

The Awana movement is a challenge to return to the preaching of the gospel of grace. There is no other gospel! The gospel announces WHAT HAS BEEN DONE! The work is finished! The price of sin, your sin, was fully paid at Calvary! God asks the sinner to believe this amazing news! Works of flesh and obedience to law are not required, not asked for, and works of righteousness will avail nothing. If added, they will merely nullify the gospel! The great announcement and climax is ROMANS 3:28: "Therefore we conclude that a man is justified by faith without the deeds of the law."

The "surrendering all" the Word calls for is intended for believers only! It is addressed to "brethren" in ROMANS 12: "I beseech you, brethren, by the mercies of God, that ye present your bodies a living sacrifice. . . ." This is the grateful response God asks of those already saved. Harm has been done by laying this down as the condition or the price of salvation, which is in reality free. This is the opposite of the gospel.

What a glorious work Christ has done on Calvary, and what an amazing announcement that the ungodly as such, and only as such, are welcome to believe, to put their trust in this finished work. "For to him that worketh not but believeth on Him that justifieth the ungodly, his faith is counted for righteousness."

This message is truly the very heartbeat of the Awana ministry.

WILDERNESS CHALLENGES

The North Side Gospel Center, located in the furniture store, had a flourishing ministry—and then was asked to move. What a shock it was to know that in three months our site would have to be vacated; we thought we might never see many of these Awana clubbers again. We prayed and asked God to give us a temporary location. It turned out that a Masonic temple rented its facilities to us. That was an experience in itself! Then they began building a church.

At the same time, a piece of property was made available in Wisconsin to build a camp. Camping had been such a big part of Latham's ministry that this was a tremendous opportunity. At that very time, though, God was challenging us to start the Awana program. No funds were available, but we had seen many clubbers get saved and want to serve the Lord.

Paper Drives

Arriving in the new church building of the North Side Gospel Center was wonderful, because we now had a delightful large game room and had the original game circle painted on the floor. It was an excellent place, but part of the financial arrangement was that the church would not be supplying funds for Awana. We had to raise our own money for whatever we needed: for uniforms and awards, for the kids, or for whatever was needed. So many of the leaders were the ones that contributed to meeting these needs, to make Awana possible.

In those days, though, we were just developing our tests, and I came to the conclusion that the Lord's work had to be done a little bit better than that. As it says in the Bible, we should always strive for excellence and to make things better. *If only we could get these materials printed, it would be so much nicer,* I thought. But there was no way to get them printed, because we didn't have the funds for that. It was really thrilling to see God's plan develop; after all, He is the One who started Awana and He showed us how to make it all happen.

So, where were we going to get the funds from? I happened to notice in the newspaper that we could sell old newspapers by the pound, and that they were worth so much money per pound. If you brought the papers in, the scrap company would weigh them and then pay you for whatever weight you had. I decided to see what we could do to possibly get a little money to buy a press so that we could print our own handbooks. Well, the day came and we took the bus out to collect newspapers, but before that I had to challenge our clubbers. We had a lot of clubbers at that time who knew Christ as their Savior, and I remember standing before them one day and saying, "Now, listen, it is easy to say you love God, but I am going to give you a real test to see how much you love Him. We are going to have paper drives on Saturdays from here on in. Every Saturday, I want you to be here promptly at eight o'clock and we are going out and collect newspapers and fill that bus up and see how much we can get so that we can get a printing press to print our books." They responded beautifully.

It was a difficult job, as it was wintertime and very cold. We would go down into filthy basements and haul the newspapers out. It was not attractive at all. We looked at this as something that God was pleased with, though, and it wasn't long before we had enough money to buy an old second-hand printing press. I remember we purchased this press for about $200. It was not in very good condition, and besides that, we did not have a qualified printer to do the printing.

Another problem was that I did not know how to run a press, but God said to me, "You can learn by just talking to people and asking them to help." So I started talking to printers and, before I knew it, I was working the press along with my friend, Rich Wager, who was one of my co-workers then. That by itself was truly a wilderness experience. There were times in the early morning when the humidity was so high that the paper wouldn't feed properly.

We learned how to print the handbooks by printing the pages and laying them out on a table in order. But then they had to be collated into books, and we could not afford to send them out for this. We really had to pray and ask the Lord to help us to be able to get the printer to work so we would have enough for the clubbers who were coming in the afternoon to assemble the materials into books. What an encouragement it was in those early days that God laid it on the hearts of these clubbers to come right from school and help assemble books. That to me was a real sign that God was leading us. But here is something I want you to remember: God wonderfully laid it on the hearts of our clubbers, just as He had done with those who went out on the paper drives, and they said that they wanted to continue to be part of this project. They came in each day after school and walked around the tables collating our books.

That's how we got our first books, and they were so very precious because they had been printed by us and assembled by our dear clubbers. It is so great to see a ministry that God raised up to win kids to Christ, but the kids themselves had a great part in starting the work.

As I look back at that, I say praise God for how He put the plan together: to be able to get the money together, to get the press, and to get all of these books printed and collated. God is wonderful in getting His plan just the way He wants to do it.

Clubbers collating Awana handbooks

Yes, the paper drives were discouraging at times. We didn't have just one or two of them—we kept at it month after month for several years because it was the only income that Awana had at that time. Some of these paper drives were in the coldest days of winter, with snow and ice on the ground; others were in the heat and humidity of summer. We would go into dark, dirty basements of some of these houses and carry out loads of paper, put it into our bus, and then take it down to the scrap paper people. They would then weigh it and give us the money we needed to carry on Awana for the next week. Yes, those were difficult days, but as I look back on it I wouldn't trade those days for anything.

The paper drives paid the salary of our first employee. Uniforms, awards, and original handbooks were all made possible by Awana clubbers working for the Lord collecting newspapers. I praise God for the clubbers who were such an encouragement to me in those beginning days. God taught us so many lessons: to be patient and to remind us that He's the One who started Awana and that He was more interested in seeing Awana succeed than I was. That was a lesson the Lord constantly had to teach me, by the way.

One of the verses that I remember memorizing is EPHESIANS 3:13: "Wherefore I desire that ye faint not at my tribulations for you, which is your

First Awana leaders in the new uniforms; Art Rorheim is in the middle of first row

glory." It reminded me that God definitely plans some of these difficult times for us to go through to see how much we really love Him.

Chicago International Track Meet

Awana Team Breaks Eighteen-Year Track Record

One of the most exciting sports events that I used to like to attend was the National Daily News Relays held at the beautiful Chicago Stadium. Track men from all over the country would come and compete at these events. There were high-jump events, pole vaulting, relays, the famous "mile," and of course the two-mile races. Colleges from all across the country wanted to qualify to compete at these relays.

One of the special events that intrigued me was one called the "Midget Relay." This competition took place among four-"man" relay teams consisting of boys who had not reached their twelfth birthdays. Since the Awana Olympics had such a feature, I just thought, *Why couldn't we select a team representing Awana to run down at the Midget Relays?* I inquired and found out how to qualify to participate.

The park districts, the Boys Club of America, the Catholic Youth Organization, and many others were invited to come down to the University of Chicago field house to qualify. I submitted my application and we were invited to compete. I had never had any experience in coaching a track relay team, so I thought if I was going to learn how, I'd better ask those who *have* had experience. I found a Christian high school track coach who shared some things with me.

Then I contacted Gil Dodds, who at that time was the world's fastest miler. Gil was also a born-again Christian, and gave me some good tips about coaching. It was a very exciting time as we arrived to compete with the fifty or more teams that were there to qualify. Only four would be selected to run at the National Relays.

At the starting line stood five timers with their stopwatches checking our times. We were the next-to-last to run in this competition. We knew what the time was we had to make in order to qualify. I can assure you, it was an anxious moment as our team was running.

Finally, when they came across the finish line, the notice came from the judges that we had tied for fourth place. Therefore, there would be a playoff (actually, a race-off) between the two fourth-place teams. Our participants rested for about fifteen minutes and then stepped up to the line. What a thrill it was as our team beat the other team by about one-tenth of a second. That's how we qualified to run at the Chicago Stadium event.

We had three weeks to practice for this big event. I knew a Christian principal at a high school who allowed me to train the team by running in the halls after school hours. I learned that the key to a successful relay team is how well you pass the baton from player to player. We practiced and practiced until we had full confidence that we could do it perfectly.

Then came the big night at the Chicago Stadium. As you walked in, you could see that there were some 18,000 people in attendance. Al Melgaard was playing that fantastic organ. Best of all, the playing of the Awana theme song was a feature by itself. It was an utter thrill for our team to be able to go down into the locker rooms and mingle with the great track stars who were also competing.

Finally, the exciting moment came when we were told that our race was next. Eddie Gustafson was our fast starter. The gun went off and Eddie immediately took the lead on the first lap and had a beautiful handoff to our second relay runner. The third handoff was just as nice and then came the exciting last lap where we were neck and neck with the front runner. Then, at the last quarter lap, our runner sprinted ahead and went across the finish line as the champion. There were probably some 2,000 Awana people in the stands, just cheering for all they were worth.

Awana championship team at the Chicago Stadium; the runner third from left is now presidentially appointed Federal Judge Wayne Anderson

The track announcer, John Carmichael, made the thrilling announcement that the Awana Relay Team had just broken an eighteen-year record! Yes, that was an exciting race to win. But we know that the most important race of all is to run God's race for our lives so that we are faithful winners in God's sight. 1 Corinthians 9:24 says: "Know ye not that they which run in a race run all, but one receiveth the prize? So run that ye may obtain."

FAIRMONT FAIR

While we were still back at the North Side Gospel Center in the furniture store, God was beginning to develop the Awana program. It wasn't Awana at that time, but God was showing us some things He had to teach us.

Down the street from the church was the Liberty Theater. On Saturdays, I would often see the kids line up for almost a block waiting to get into the theater. In the privacy of my own heart I often thought, *Wouldn't it be wonderful if the day came when the kids would line up to come into our Pals Club?*

Well, we decided to come up with an idea to promote the Pals program. The plan was to have what we called the "Fairmont Fair." This was to be an event where we set up little booths, almost like a carnival, where the kids could come in and get some popcorn, or have their weight guessed, or throw darts, and just have a really fun time.

First Fairmont Fair

But then the question was, "How do we promote this?" I thought of a plan to go to the public schools where the clubbers attended and ask the principals if I could take two or three of our clubbers and go out early with the patrol boys to make some announcements about this special club program. I know what I did then would be impossible to do today, but they agreed. The plan was this. I had sandwich boards put on the clubbers, and all it said on each board was: "Coming Big Fair." They were to answer no questions; all they did was walk around the school and get up the kids' curiosity.

The second week they did the same thing, but this time the boards said: "Big Fair for Boys 8, 9, and 10 years old." All the girls certainly were discouraged and disappointed, but the day before the fair we passed out circulars telling them the circular would be their ticket to get into the fair.

Well, to our amazement, on the day of the fair, we had them lined up for a block waiting to get in! We had perhaps fifteen of our young ladies taking attendance and writing up the addresses and names of these new kids who came. We had 325 Pals attend that night.

We had a wonderful evangelist by the name of McGarahan speak and give the gospel and challenge these kids to serve the Lord. It was a wonderful day because many kids were reached that day that we never would have reached before, and we got into so many homes that we never would have had contact with if we hadn't had the fair. Actually, some of the kids who came to that fair ended up serving the Lord in the mission field.

One of the groups from the first Pals Club

So today, around the country, Awana has Fairmont Fairs or Fun Fairs or whatever the club wants to call them. We must remind ourselves that there is a "mission field" of thousands of kids around every church. The Lord tells us to not just put up a sign and try to get them in, but to go out into the highways and byways and *bring* them in and then watch them get saved—and also watch them develop into real workers for the Lord. That is truly the essence of the Awana motto, from 2 TIMOTHY 2:15: "Study to shew thyself approved unto God a workman that needeth not to be ashamed, rightly dividing the word of truth."

ORIGINAL AWANA CLUB

Many folks have wondered just what the original club was like. Let me share with you how God wonderfully taught us back then just what the ministry should be like. I did not have the experience to have gotten anything out of books, nor did I have any training. God had to teach me and lead me each

Pioneer Clubbers in uniform at Scholarship Camp, 1980s

step of the way. I look back and see how wonderfully God helped me to design the Awana game circle—I just loved to create new games! We were reaching kids by the hundreds. We did not have Cubbies or Sparks at that time, as they had not been started yet.

Today we know that most of the Awana Clubs in America have club meetings on Wednesday night. You might be interested to know that at that original church, we had club every day *except* on Wednesday. Monday night was the high school night, and there were probably about a hundred teenagers in attendance. Tuesday night we had Pioneers, the junior-high kids. On Thursdays and Fridays we had about 150 Pals, the eight-, nine-, and ten-year-old boys. Saturday was a good time for the Chums, who were the eight-, nine-, and ten-year-old girls who met in the morning; in the afternoon, our Guards, the junior-high girls, would meet. So this was the plan.

But really, if there was any secret to the success of those early clubs, it was the Wednesday night program. This was so important because it brought everyone together as a team with a plan, as everyone went visiting on Wednesday night. We tried to get an adult with a team leader to go out visiting in the clubbers' homes; sometimes we only would get into one home that night, but everyone who was on the visiting team came back to church where Lance Latham gave the Wednesday-night Bible study.

What a thrill it was when, during prayer request time, teenagers who had been out visiting would stand up and say something like, "Now pray for so-and-so because I now know why little Jimmy acts like he does because I saw what his home was like." Hearing the testimonies from these teenagers just thrilled all of the adults from the church, as they saw what God was doing through the Awana program. Well, there may have been some adults who wondered, *Why do we need all of those kids here?* and *Why do we allow some of them to mess up our floors and this sort of thing to take place?* Fortunately, there was just a small number of them, because they saw the fruit and the impact that Awana was making on all of these kids.

After Doc's Bible class, the prayer requests came forth. That is when we heard the prayers from the church people. As far as the Awana people were concerned, all of the leaders met with their directors, each having individual prayer time together. This was very important, because during that time they could pray for each of the clubbers in their club and pray about the many things that they were asking God for. That's why those prayer times were really, really special.

Awana board of directors, 1970s

Another thing that was important was that all of us leaders came to be able to recite sections of the handbook, so that we were ahead of the clubbers in knowing their handbooks. We all knew the verses as well as they did and it had a real impression on all of the clubbers. The leaders didn't even have to look at the books, because they knew the verses very well.

After that we would have a planning session and look back at what happened a week or two before and then begin to lay out the plans for coming weeks. The big affair that we had every year was parents' night for every club, and planning was taking place for that as well.

So you can see how important Wednesday night was. I say today that the strength of a club is only as good as this: How often do the leaders plan together and how often do they pray together? If prayer and planning time is something done just occasionally when they feel they need it, that club will never be successful for the Lord. The more often you pray and plan, I can assure you, God will bless and you will see fruits in your Awana clubs.

PSALM 126:6: "He that goeth forth and weepeth, bearing precious seed, shall doubtless come again with rejoicing bringing his sheaves with him."

UNIFORM MIRACLES

In those beginning days of Awana, God was constantly teaching us the Awana program, but there were so many other facets He had to teach us, too. We knew nothing about graphics, printing, developing an award system, uniforms, or about the many other things that go with motivating and furthering the program of Awana.

As the Awana uniform was being developed, part of the uniform for the boys' program was the neckerchief. We would buy the neckerchief material in bolts and I remember we took a big butcher knife and cut it on an angle. Many of our teams helped us with this. Then, after the kerchiefs were cut, they were given to my wife, Winnie, who sewed them and put an Awana emblem on them.

She faithfully enjoyed doing this for quite some time, until the task just grew too large. I remember the day she said, "Art, I just don't see how I can keep up with it." We had two children at the time and Awana was beginning to grow and it had gotten to be more than she could handle. Being in a quandary as to what to do, I must admit that I had to ask the Lord to help me. I went to the Yellow Pages of the phone book, wondering what to look for; I know you don't find "neckerchiefs" listed in the Yellow Pages! As I pondered, I remembered that the neckerchiefs were made of cotton, and I saw a place called "Cotton Goods." Well, I felt led to call them and see if I could get an appointment to meet with someone to talk about my problem.

I found that this place was down in the heart of Chicago's Loop. Realizing that what I had to present was really not much of a challenge to any supplier, I was absolutely amazed at what happened when I came to this large manufacturing company and went in to ask if I could talk with someone regarding my problem. Now this is one time that I know God wonderfully arranged things for me. Within ten minutes of my arrival, I found myself sitting in the office of the president.

Now this, you understand, is not the norm. Why he should invite me in, only God could arrange and understand. He was a Jewish man, but as he talked to me he said, "Tell me what your needs are." I shared with him my real heart to see kids won to Christ and that we were developing uniforms for the club. I told him that I had these neckerchiefs that my wife had been sewing but could no longer keep up with the demand. I told him I was wondering if he could help me get some made.

He looked at me with a smile on his face and said, "That will be no problem at all. We'll be delighted to take care of that for you. I am very interested in what you are doing. I think your cause is tremendous." Before I left he said,

Guards at the Chicago Gospel Mission

Chums in India

"I want you to know that if you ever have any other needs, feel free to call on me." Well, I walked out of there just fully aware that God had arranged this for me. Within two weeks he had my full year's supply of neckerchiefs, and it actually cost us less money than what I had been paying for the bolt of material alone. So God arranged that for us, too.

Then time passed and we had to track down a supplier for uniforms. There was a manufacturer in Wisconsin that seemed like the ideal source. I was still the director of Camp Awana, and directing the boys' camp, so I wasn't able to ride herd on this project very well. I asked this manufacturer if they would be willing to have these uniforms ready when I came back from camp in the fall. They said that would be no problem, they would have the uniforms all ready for us when we needed them.

When I returned in the fall, I found that no uniforms had been delivered. When I checked with the company, they just said, "We came to the conclusion that your order wasn't large enough and we couldn't be bothered with it." They hadn't even had the courtesy to let us know that they had made this decision. Hence, I was in a real quandary. I asked the Lord how these clubs were going to get the uniforms that they were depending on us for.

Then God seemed to remind me of the words of Mr. Lewis, this Jewish man at the cotton goods factory, who had said he would help us if he could.

I called him, wondering if he was even there. He said, "Come on down," and as I shared with him he said, "I believe I can help you with that, too. I have a friend of mine who, I think, will take care of all your uniform needs." And he did. Praise the Lord! This man became our uniform supplier and within two weeks we had our entire order completed. In the days to come, that man invested more than $150,000 in uniforms that he put on the shelves for us and we did not even have a written contract with him. He had such faith in us.

These are just some of the encouragements and God's approval in those early days—proof that God was more interested in Awana than Art Rorheim was. Yes, His approvals are wonderful things along the way, even when we don't recognize them when they are taking place.

SCRIPTURE MEMORIZATION

Roots

God has wonderfully blessed the Awana program far beyond ever anything we could have imagined when the program first got started. We believe there are two main reasons that God has blessed Awana. First, we know that He never promised that He would bless the Awana program, but He has promised to bless His Word. We feel that the number-one reason for Awana is to teach boys and girls, men and women, how they can be sure of going to heaven by putting their faith in what Christ did for them at Calvary. Yes, the gospel is what Awana has majored in.

Second, and equally important, is memorizing God's Word. In this computer-minded day in which we live, we often say that the Word of God is God's software. Our minds are without question the greatest computer that was ever built. We want to fill our minds with the Word of God. How did the Scripture Memory Program become such a vital part of Awana? Let me share with you the Awana roots from which it sprang.

My mentor, Lance Latham, was the founder and pastor of the church where Awana was born. But Lance Latham had a father who was also a pastor of a church in Chester, Pennsylvania. He strongly believed and practiced that Scripture memory was vital in the life of a pastor. He would never read the Scripture portion for his message. Each Sunday morning as he preached, he would quote it from memory.

He was anxious to train his children to see the value of memorization as well. Each morning he would get them up early and memorize a verse with them, one verse each day. At the end of the week they would recite it and at the end of the month they would again recite what they had learned. Through this system of disciplining themselves, Lance Latham, at the age of seven, was able to recite three entire books from memory.

Latham's father had a unique method of introducing new members into his church. Whenever they came in, perhaps twenty-five at a time, he delighted in giving each one of them a portion of Scripture—from memory, of course. Then an unusual thing happened. They had a revival in the town and more than 200 people were going to be joining the church. Now came the big decision: What was he going to do? Was he going to change his policy of giving each person Scripture? If not, would he read it to them, or would he simply set out to memorize Scripture for this special occasion? It was only two weeks away. He decided to memorize the additional Scripture. What an

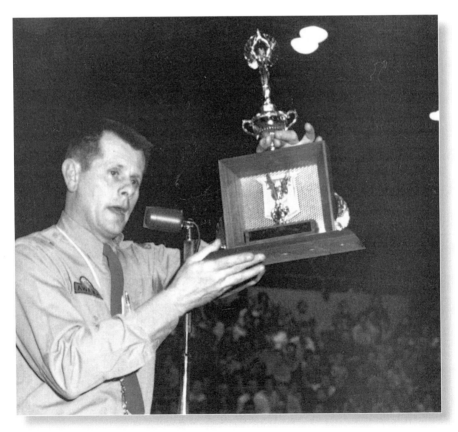

Art announcing the winner of the Meritorious Award for Scripture memorization at a 1960s Olympics

impressive event that was, to have more than 200 folks receive membership and all get a portion of Scripture from memory.

All of us at Awana treasure the roots from which we grew because of people like that, who blazed the trail in Scripture memorization. We need to have as a main goal in life to live the challenge of Awana's theme verse, 2 Timothy 2:15: "Study to shew thyself approved unto God, a workman that needeth not to be ashamed, rightly dividing the word of truth."

What a scripture legacy Latham's earthly father left us! To think that there are literally millions of boys and girls all around the world who have been memorizing Scripture because one man saw the importance of it and he challenged his son. I'm so glad his son challenged me to carry on the vital ministry of Scripture memorization.

Why Memorize?

Every Awana leader would probably say in unison that memorizing Scripture is at the very heart of Awana. Why is it important? Why should we emphasize that all clubbers and leaders regularly memorize Scripture?

Grace Baptist Church, California, 2000: One example of the thousands of children who have participated in Scripture memorization through Awana

The Bible has much to say about the benefits of memorizing Scripture. PSALM 1:2–3 promises that the person who continually meditates upon the Scriptures will prosper in whatever he does. A similar statement is found in JOSHUA 1:8, where the person who studies Scripture is promised success. David said, in PSALM 119:11: "Thy Word have I hid in mine heart, that I might not sin against Thee." David had memorized much of God's Word and stored it in his heart. This was his strategy for resisting temptation to sin. David also wrote, in PSALM 119:16: "I will delight myself in Thy statutes: I will not forget thy word."

Memorizing Scripture should be a priority in our lives. Lance Latham, my mentor, set a tremendous example through his dedication to Scripture memory. He persuaded me to discipline myself to memorize chapters of Scripture. I started with ISAIAH 53, the wonderful prophetic chapter that depicts Christ coming as the Lamb to the slaughter on Calvary's cross as full payment for all our sin. I didn't know any special memorization techniques, so I just disciplined myself each day to spend time going over ISAIAH 53. To my amazement, I had it memorized within a week.

All members of the Awana staff memorize and recite Scripture weekly. Some of the headquarters staff belong to a dedicated group that meets regularly before work to memorize and review several books of the Bible, along with their regular memory work. These are just ordinary people who never dreamed they could memorize an entire book of the Bible, but with consistent effort, they have learned to recite huge chunks of Scripture.

One of the keys to memorizing Scripture is accountability. Unless you set some goals and are accountable to someone for reaching those goals, you'll probably never memorize anything. The greatest thing you can do with your mind is fill it with Scripture. I want to personally challenge you to put your mind to work learning God's Word—why not start today?

Importance of Memorization

Every Awana leader would probably echo in unison that Scripture memorization is the very heartbeat of Awana. Why is it important? Why should we persistently insist that all clubbers, leaders, and pastors should be involved in Scripture memorization?

Your God-given brain is the greatest computer in the world. It's been said that it has 10 billion segments. However, the average person consistently uses less than 10 percent of its capacity. God wants us to fill it with His inspired Word. In computer terms, it's God's software and His software never crashes.

Four Reasons Why Many Christians Are Not Involved in Memorization

1. It's work.
2. It takes time.
3. It requires discipline and accountability.
4. It appears to be too difficult.

Reasons for Memorization

1. Memorizing Scripture can help one become a child of God (ROMANS 10:17).
2. Memorizing Scripture can help us grow and mature as Christians (1 PETER 2:2; 2 TIMOTHY 3:16, 17).
3. Memorizing Scripture can help give us daily guidance (PSALM 119:105; JOB 23:11, 12).
4. Memorizing Scripture can bring real joy and happiness (JEREMIAH 15:16).
5. Memorizing Scripture can help keep us from sinning (PSALM 119:9–11).

Awana conference at Moody Church, Chicago

6. Memorizing Scripture can help us answer the questions of others with authority (1 PETER 3:15).

7. Memorizing Scripture can help us in our witness to others (ISAIAH 55:11; JEREMIAH 23:29).

8. Memorizing Scripture can help us become approved by God and to rightly use His Word (2 TIMOTHY 2:15).

9. Memorizing Scripture can give you something worthwhile to think about when you can't sleep (PSALM 63:6).

10. Memorizing Scripture can help keep your mind pure and filled with wholesome thoughts (PSALM 19:8; PHILIPPIANS 4:8; 2 CORINTHIANS 10:3–5).

How to Get Started

1. Prayerfully decide to memorize.

2. Challenge someone to memorize with you.

3. Be accountable.

4. Select the passage.

5. Select the time and how long you will work on memorization each day.

6. Set a completion date for the passage you are memorizing.

Helpful Methods

1. Read the passage three times slowly.

2. Look for truth in the passage.

3. Always use the same Bible.

4. Visualize the words on the page.

5. Divide long sections into smaller sections.

6. Repeat each section over.

7. Visualize the first word of each verse in a chapter.

8. Repeat verses dramatically out loud.

9. Write the passage out.

10. Record the passage on tape.

Leadership planning, circa 1955

11. Repeat the passage with the tape.

12. Review, review, review.

Ideas for Club

1. Use Scripture memory games.

2. Select a verse of the month: Recite that verse at the flag ceremony and another verse for council time.

3. During council time, have each leader recite his or her favorite verse and explain what it means.

4. Use a blackboard when teaching a new verse.

5. Have leaders memorize the handbooks along with their clubbers.

More Ideas

1. Memorize a chapter rather than miscellaneous verses.

2. Memorize Isaiah 53, one of the choice chapters in the Bible.

Awana Staff Program

It was an exciting day in 1960 when Awana moved from the basement office of the North Side Gospel Center into a building of its own. It was just a double storefront building, but it was exciting because it gave us more room than we had ever had before. At that time we thought we would be set for years, at the very least. But the Lord had other plans, because it wasn't long before we outgrew that building. It was while we were at this building that the Lord prompted me to challenge our staff about getting into a regular Scripture memorization program.

One of the most vital structures of the Awana program is to challenge boys and girls and leaders to memorize God's Word. I became very convicted and felt that it was hypocritical for me to challenge others to do it when we, the staff at the Awana Headquarters, were not leading the way.

One of the first questions was: What should be memorized? Of course, we expected everybody to recite our theme verse, 2 TIMOTHY 2:15. Then there were other familiar verses, like EPHESIANS 2:8, 9; JOHN 3:16; TITUS 3:5; JOHN 1:12; and a few others that we knew, which were part of our clubbers' handbooks that we memorized. Then we decided that it would be nice to do an entire chapter.

I'd often asked a group of leaders to choose what they would consider to be their favorite chapter in the entire Old Testament. We know it is all God's

Leader training, Moody Church, Chicago, 1958

Word, but there are some portions that are more meaningful to us than others. The one chapter that we decided to memorize was ISAIAH 53: 1–12.

What a beautiful message it contains. It presents the gospel so clearly. Then, to remember that this is also prophetic, because it was written some seven hundred years before Christ was even born. It so wonderfully shares how He was to go as a lamb to the slaughter, and to be oppressed, and to be afflicted, and that He would not even open His mouth. How beautifully all this was fulfilled at Calvary for us. That was the beginning of our staff memorization.

Here we are, more than fifty years later, and, praise God, our entire headquarters staff still memorizes Scripture. In fact, it's a requirement for being a member of the Awana staff. Many have memorized entire Bible books. We're all just ordinary people who don't have unusual memories, but it's an indication that when we discipline our time in the right way, we can memorize God's Word and fill the computers of our minds with God's software.

It's one of the great treasures that every Awana employee has, to know that during the years they minister here they are constantly, week by week, storing the Word of God in their hearts. We know we should not only store Scripture in our minds, but also ought to allow the very truths of it to grip our hearts so that we can direct Awana in godly ways and be the personal witnesses of this great gospel with which God has entrusted us.

Training conference in California, 1995

Awana quartet would sing before Art gave a message. Left to right: Owen Talbot, Henley Holmbo, Ed Sherry, and Marvin Madson

Awana leadership often mentions that one of the great thrills of their ministry is to listen to young boys and girls reciting Scripture from memory. One of the highlights in that area for me was when I visited Bangladesh and heard some two hundred formerly Muslim boys and girls who were in Awana reciting Scripture to me for almost fifteen minutes. I just praise God for the leaders who have made memorizing the Word of God so real to them. If you have never taken on the challenge of memorizing chapters of God's Word, do it today and start memorizing the wonderful chapter ISAIAH 53. What a blessing it will be to your heart, as it is to mine.

In 1 PETER 3:15 is a challenging verse: "*be* ready always to *give* an answer to every man that asketh you a reason of the hope that is in you." That is one of the main reasons why we value Scripture memorization, because God places people to cross your path and you have to be ready to share His word.

I will always remember, back in the early days of Awana, when I would often witness to one of the suppliers who did the products for us. There was one by the name of Mr. Calner, whose company supplied all of the monograms that went on all of our uniforms. Mr. Calner was a devout Jew, and he was also one of the key leaders of the Boy Scouts International of America. We had much in common to talk about, as both he and I had a great interest in kids. We would often discuss what really was the difference between our programs.

I said, "We practically do everything the Scouts do and that would be just the beginning of Awana. The reason for Awana is that each kid can be

Awana staff, 1967

sure of going to heaven." And so I would witness to him. When you witness to Jews, you realize that they do not believe anything in the New Testament. That gave me an unusual opportunity at one time, when I did not know what to say to this man, and the Lord prompted me to recite Isaiah 53 to him. Well, I had not recited Isaiah 53 myself for at least six months, and Satan was more or less reminding me of that. I was just thinking, *Don't do it. You are going to blow it if you do that.* But God persuaded me to go for it and I did. I was amazed that I did not even miss a beat as I recited Isaiah 53. When I was all through, I looked him in the eyes and I said, "Mr. Calner, that's your Messiah," and he was stunned and did not know what to say. Finally he said, "I will have to go to my rabbi and see what he has to say about that." Well, we have been commanded by God to witness like that.

Mr. Calner then invited my wife and me to come to his home for a Passover seder, and that was an experience I will never forget. As we sat at their table, with yarmulkes on our heads, we were treated to a three-hour-long feast. They went through the procedure of the Passover, and it was very interesting and very detailed, with every member of the family present. They all had to partake in some way, but when they were all done, you realized that they had no hope whatsoever. They do not even have a false hope of eternity. It makes me sad to think how brilliant they were; but with all the knowledge they had, they did not have godly understanding. I feel it is so important to memorize the Word of God because you never know when God will call on us to be His representatives.

We have often asked, "Why has God blessed the ministry of Awana?" There are two main reasons: one is that we have majored in the clear presentation of the gospel; the other is that we have majored in Scripture memory work.

I truly praise God that the gospel and Scripture memorization are still the heartbeat of Awana today, and that for sixty years we've concentrated on these two things. I am so delighted, as we come each week and listen to all our staff members recite verses (and some even recite chapters) together, that the memory program is still going forward full force.

As I look back at people who helped keep the fire going in the memory program, I recall that one of those was our clubber who grew up in Awana, became an Awana missionary, and was also an assistant to me here at headquarters: Arne Abrahamsen. He was the one who directed the memory program for many years, and I want to thank him because he really prepared for each session that he conducted. He himself had all of the verses memorized so that he would not have to read them from his book. He recited them word for word, which made a real impression on all of us. When Arne moved on, he appointed Dale Klein, who has been a vital part of Awana for thirty-five years. Before he came on staff, he was on the board of directors at Awana and involved in Awana in Milwaukee, Wisconsin. Since he has been on our staff, he has spearheaded the memory program and has done a great job with real dedication.

We had a program called Sword Club (now Community 119) which is a special memory program for those who would like to go that extra mile. Praise the Lord, the memory program is also moving along, with many, many of our staff wanting to go beyond the standard memory program here at Awana.

So I just thank the Lord for the two key people who have been involved in keeping the Scripture memory program running so well at Awana: they are Arne Abrahamsen and Dale Klein. Praise the Lord for both of these dedicated men.

PROGRAM MIRACLES

Four Colors

Red, blue, green, and yellow are four basic colors in practically all graphics. Why were they chosen to represent the four teams that compete on the Awana game circle? I guess they could just as well have been white, black,

Art in his office at the Algonquin Building, circa 1975

purple, and orange. Actually, though, the color choices came about in a very unusual way.

If you had been back at that old furniture store that became the North Side Gospel Center in 1933, you would have seen that this store had had a second floor and an elevator that used to take the furniture up to the second floor. The elevator had been out of use for many years, but one day while I was looking down that elevator shaft, I saw an old trunk lying at the bottom, covered with debris. Because of my curious mind, I proceeded to get down into the shaft and see what was in that trunk. It was obvious it had been there for many years. When I opened the trunk, I was amazed at what I saw. Spotlessly clean on the inside, it was packed full of little red, blue, green, and yellow woolen beanie hats. How they had managed to get into the elevator shaft of a furniture store, only God knows, but it seems like God placed them there for a purpose.

As I saw those beautiful little beanie hats, I thought, *Could it be that this could be a part of our first Awana uniform?"* At that time we had no idea of what God had in mind for us in the years to come. My first thought was to make a little circle monogram with the word "PALS" on it for that age group. Then we got a T-shirt that had the word "PALS" on it and that was the first uniform. Of course, this was not an official Awana Club, because the Awana program and handbooks had not been created yet.

So, from that point forward, our game circle was red, blue, green, and yellow. We often jokingly say to Awana leaders who have spent a good portion of their life in Awana that their blood must flow red, blue, green, and yellow.

Game Circle Creation

Let me take you back to that original North Side Gospel Center building, which was just an old burned-out furniture store that was turned into our church. The first floor was the sanctuary and the second floor was where I held the club meetings. This was before the days of Awana, when God was teaching me some of the basics that would have to be used in the Awana ministry in the days to come.

I had probably seventy-five to a hundred boys in my Pals Club at that time, but I was having a very difficult time controlling them and running a successful game period. There was always confusion trying to get them quiet while I was giving them instructions for the next game. When I would say, "Please be quiet," I realized that not all of these kids had been taught that being quiet really meant being quiet. Some of them did not come from homes that operated that way, and they would wait for us to repeat it about three or four times before they would even begin to respond.

I realized that this system was never going to work if we were to have a successful game period. It was at that time, I believe, that the Lord gave me

Game circle, circa 1970

Game circle, circa 1980

the idea of the Awana game circle and game square. I remember painting the circle in red, blue, green, and yellow on the wooden floor and the square around it. Then I was ready to see if this was going to work.

I remember I had all of the kids gathering around in the game room as we normally would do without the plan. We played some simple games, like "Steal the Bacon" and others, but they really were worn out and the kids were not that excited about them. So I told them I was going to try something. "First of all, I will number all of you off and you will be either red, blue, green, or yellow. Your color will be who you are in the game time and you will line up according to the color on the game floor. When I blow the whistle I will count to five and I will give 100 points to the team that will quietly line up on their line perfectly."

So then came the big experiment: I blew the whistle and started the count. All of a sudden, I saw clubbers racing with great enthusiasm to their colored lines, and they all were already standing at attention when I got to five. I watched that and I have often said, "This was the first Awana miracle."

I could not believe what I was seeing. Then I thought I should try it again to make it even more exciting, so I said, "I saw that some of you had your feet over the line about an inch or two, and you have to be perfectly on the line, so let's give that a try again." I let them run all around the room, then I went through the same procedure and there it was, just as beautiful as could be. Each time we played a game, I just couldn't wait to walk out there and, with one blast of the whistle and a count to five, once again see what would happen. I still often say that this was the first Awana miracle!

How little did I know then that this was a method that God had chosen to be used all around the world, even in the jungles, as a method of reaching boys and girls to get their attention. Even in Bangladesh, which today is still a Muslim country, while I was there I saw how beautifully the boys and girls were running their circles. I have traveled around the word and watched many, many clubs. I had absolutely nothing to do with training them. Somewhere along the line they had received training and realized that discipline is an absolute as far as having a successful club. Discipline needed not only in the game period, but also all the way through council time and even during handbook time. You need discipline—and remember, kids love discipline even if they come from undisciplined homes. When they see consistent discipline, they see the joy it brings when everyone is doing the right thing. Yes, the game period was something that God wonderfully helped us design.

Discipline in our own personal lives will have a great impact on how fruitful our lives will be for our wonderful Lord.

Creation of Olympics

It was in 1955 when Rich Wager, our first Awana employee, met with me to plan the first Awana Olympics. We tried this experimental program first with the boys' clubs, Pals and Pioneers. The first four chartered churches would be competing. The first Olympics would be held on the game floor at the North Side Gospel Center, the birthplace of the Awana program.

Would this type of event succeed? That was our big question. I will never forget that first Olympics meet. People were packed in wall-to-wall. The air was charged with enthusiasm. The North Side Gospel Center Pal and Pioneer teams were the first Olympics champions.

Girls saw the exciting meet and insisted that the Awana Olympics were for girls as well as boys. When I asked them what Olympic games should be planned for the girls, they all said, "We want the same events that were played at the boys' Olympics." Olympic enthusiasm multiplied quickly. Soon there were three meets going simultaneously in nearby churches. It soon became obvious that the growth of Olympics would require a high-school gymnasium.

First Awana Olympics

Then came the concept of trying a two-circle Olympics. Many thought this would be impossible to control, and would lead to severe disorder and discipline problems, but the two-circle Olympics was unbelievably successful. Again, the number of Olympic teams multiplied. It wasn't long before four-circle Olympics were common. Awana leadership in Chicago and Los Angeles have conducted eight-circle Olympic meets with amazing success.

Spectators at the first Awana Olympics

Award given at the 1980 Olympics

Under the direction of the Awana missionaries, 233 Olympic meets were conducted during the 1994 season. More than 90,000 clubbers participated. During those early years of Olympics, a committee of trained officials spent more than fifteen years refining and perfecting the games. The entire meet has been designed and balanced so that it appeals to clubbers with various natural abilities and physical traits: the fast, the tall, the stocky, the muscular, the quick, and the agile. Yet no individual athlete can win an Awana Olympic award alone. Success requires a team effort!

Awana Olympians want to win and we encourage healthy competition. But the chance to win with a spirit of competition is only one of the many benefits of Olympics. Other benefits include:

1. Motivating clubbers to make progress in their handbooks so they can qualify for the team. As clubbers recite handbook sections, they are hiding God's Word in their hearts.

2. Enjoying fellowship with clubs from other churches. This is fun for clubbers and encouraging for leaders who meet adults with a similar interest in reaching boys and girls for Christ.

3. Showing the facility staff and spectators a strong Christian testimony through good sportsmanship in the games.

4. Enhancing church identity by team participation and the enthusiastic encouragement each team receives from supporters in the bleachers.

5. Reaching out to unsaved parents and other spectators.

Awana Olympics is truly an evangelistic opportunity. Every Olympic meet includes a "halftime" when a capable speaker presents the plan of salvation.

I will always remember an Olympic coach who stopped me on the gym floor just prior to a meet. She said, "I must share with you my testimony." She told me that two years earlier, she had attended the Olympics because her son was competing. "I was so impressed with the leaders and the good sportsmanship that was displayed by everyone. The gymnasium was full and I was sitting on the last row in the grandstand. Then they stopped the meet halfway through and said there was a very important message to be given by a special speaker. He said that knowing for sure how to get to heaven was the number-one issue in all of life.

"It seemed like he was talking directly to me. He said, 'I was a sinner for whom Christ died, and there on Calvary's cross He took my place and paid the price for my sins: past, present and future.' That night in the grandstand, among all those spectators, I trusted Christ to become my personal Savior.

Varsity Olympics

I didn't realize then how God would change my life with His joy and purpose for living. To think that now I'm an Awana girls' director, and I have the exciting privilege of sharing that life-giving message of the gospel each week with these precious girls."

Yes, Awana Olympics is an exciting athletic event, but that's not all it is. Olympics is a vital ministry, reaching out to a world of parents who are hell-bound and so desperately need to hear God's wonderful good news of salvation. Plan now to get your clubbers involved in the next Olympic meet!

Creation of Sparks

I have often pointed out that Awana is really one miracle after another, because I did not have the ability to develop so many areas of Awana. There was one area that I was concerned about and that was a ministry to kindergarten kids. I had never worked with that age group; I basically worked with the older groups, directing older high-school kids. Still, I knew that there had to be a ministry for that younger age group. Well, God had a plan to bring that about.

I was visiting out in California at one of our Awana training conferences and I happened to sit in a workshop when I had a free period. I was very impressed with the lady teaching that class—how well she did and all the

Art and a group of Sparks

enthusiasm she had! When it was over, I asked our missionary about her and commented on how well she taught. Our missionary said, "Aren't you aware of the background of this lady? Her name is Nora Whiteside and she had one tragedy after another take place in her life." She and her husband were anxious to have children and waited about ten years to have their first child. This child grew up in Awana and had just received the Timothy and Meritorious Awards. Nora and her husband were thrilled about this progress. Then, in a terrible tragedy, their son was slain by a teenager. Their precious only child was suddenly gone.

Then more tragedy entered into her life. Her husband, who was a brilliant engineer, did training in underground engineering. In one of his underground training sessions, there was a breakdown in communication, and he was actually covered over by a bulldozer and died. There she was, with her only son and husband both gone, yet you could see she was still praising the Lord that she could still witness for Him.

So I sat down and talked with Nora, and I said, "Nora, I'm sure that God has something for you and perhaps you might even become a missionary in California working with the girls' clubs." I mentioned that we were having a missionary conference training program at Awana headquarters and asked if she could come to that. I invited her to stay at our home so that she could see whether this might be something that God would lay on her heart to do. I remember so well the evening that the missionary conference was over. Nora was in our home sitting in our living room couch and I was talking to her about the conference, asking her what she thought. She said it was great. I asked her if this was something that God wanted her to consider and she said, "No, I don't seem to have a tug in my heart for that area."

Now here is where God reveals Himself yet again, doing things in His own marvelous way. I started talking about some ideas I had for Awana, not thinking of Nora at all. I told her that someday I would like to have a program for kindergarten kids. It just seemed to be part of the conversation, but I had no more gotten those words out of my mouth than I saw her eyes just light right up. She looked at me and said that is something that would really excite her and wondered if she could be part of something like that.

I said, "Nora, if this is something that is in your heart, why don't you consider coming in and together you and I will work on that?" Within a month or two, she was able to take care of her affairs there in California, and then came to Awana, where together we began to work on the new program. I was able to help her with the awards system, but as far as the actual program itself, Nora was the one God had given the ability to do that work. We had to name the program, so we thought we would open it up to all of our staff to come up with some suggested names. It was actually my secretary, Judy Ellingson, who came up with the name of Sparks.

You probably know how God has wonderfully used the Sparks program all around the world. I believe there will be millions of kids in heaven because of the Sparks program. What a delight it is to see how God takes and delights His people with His ministry and delights in seeing them respond. Today we are so thankful for how God has constantly challenged people to develop different parts of the Awana program.

Creation of Cubbies

I never thought very much about coming up with a program for boys and girls younger than kindergarten age, but there again I found God doing some things in His own wonderful way.

I was down in Phoenix, Arizona, speaking at the missionary conference and they had me stay with a couple whose kids were really Awana-minded. They had all grown up in Awana and had received their Timothy and Meritorious Awards, and the enthusiasm that Shelly Roden had was just great to see.

I remember that first morning when I got up for breakfast, she said, "Here is a new book that I just completed. I have done this for the 4-F program and it was written in regard to the characteristics of the very kids that would be in the group younger than the kindergarten kids."

I looked at that book and I said to myself, *Could it be that maybe this is something that she could do for us?* I said, "Shelly, what do you think? Would you be interested in developing this program?"

She just lit up and said, "Of course, I would be delighted." So it was that Shelly Roden started to develop the program. Shelly was also very gifted in music, and she is the one who wrote the Cubbies song. Now, we know that God has different ways of doing things and, of course, we don't always obey God in exactly the way He wants us to, either. I was interested in having Nora Whiteside, who had developed the Sparks program, work together with Shelly, but I soon found out that Nora was very cool to that idea. I guess it was her pride that made her feel she could have created the program without Shelly Roden. It is great to see how God deals with people who have open hearts, though, and one day Nora came to me and said, "I have been wrong in not being willing to have a part in the Cubbies program and I want to cooperate as much as I can to help Shelly with the program." So we can clearly see how God has blessed and blessed because He brought His people down through the years to do His work at His time.

Hitting the Mark

One of the very frustrating times in the early days of Awana was when we would constantly receive phone calls from people who wanted to get the program started, but needed a missionary to come and explain it to them. They were calling for help, but we were unable to respond. Then God once again encouraged us, by reminding us that He still was the One who started Awana and was more interested in it than we were.

I received a phone call from an Awana leader whom I had never met. He said he had heard that I was interested in making a film to promote the Awana ministry. I didn't remember that I had shared that thought with anyone but some of the few members of our staff. Nevertheless, I said yes, but added that I did not know how we were going to do it. He replied, "I believe I can help you. I'll be glad to give you a few weeks of my vacation because I'm experienced in this line. I had the privilege of working along with some of the Moody Science films."

It wasn't long before we met and he shared with me what it takes to make a 16-millimeter (mm) film. I had taken moving pictures for camp and many still shots, but I was not capable of making that kind of sound movie. He taught me that we would first have to get a script written, and then we would have to get the key people who would carry out the message we wanted to send forth.

To keep expenses down, we had to build our own movie sets in the basement of the North Side Gospel Center. We brought some of our furniture and drapes from home and were able to make it look like an actual living room situation. I was delighted when I contacted Jack O'Dell, the producer of the worldwide *Unshackled* program for the Pacific Garden Mission, to ask him if he would consider writing the script for me; he agreed to do so without hesitation. Within a week he had a rough copy for me and we sat down and talked about it again. In two weeks we had a completed script.

This film was to be a promotional film rather than a training film. It was to challenge churches into realizing that there was a tremendous need

Hitting the Mark *premiere, Lane Technical High School, Chicago*

to reach the boys and girls in their communities and that Awana could help them do so. It got to be quite a project. The film was not just shot on the set location; many scenes came from camp, churches, and other onsite situations.

In it all, God beautifully brought that movie together. It has probably been shown thousands of times around the world to awaken churches to their need to reach kids for Christ in their own neighborhoods. How little did we know then that God was going to use a 16mm film called *Hitting the Mark* to be our first Awana missionary!

One day, just before an exciting activity up at camp that I was directing, a call came from a man in New York who wanted to talk to me. Now, normally I would not take time at the beginning of a camp activity to answer a phone call, but I see where God just made sure that I took this call. The man said that his name was Leo Spencer and that he was calling from Owego, New York. He had seen the *Hitting the Mark* film and he said that this was exactly what they needed out there in New York. He said that he had been director of a camp out there and he would like to get churches to be able to get Awana started. He encouraged me to take a day and come out there.

Really, I did a foolish thing by making a date with a man whom I did not even know. I did not know his spiritual background, and at that point I should have told him to write me a letter so that we could pray about it to see if we could work out something. Rather than doing so, I let him persuade me to give him a date.

Well, God was in it, because I gave him a date and flew out there. He met me at the airport and took me out to his home to meet his family, including his five children. They were very little kids who just crawled all over my lap, which I thoroughly enjoyed. He told me how happy he was that I had been able to come. I had gone out there with the intention of giving him the materials and showing him how he could contact churches and their pastors, but it was interesting what happened next.

He said, "I work for IBM and tomorrow morning I will be going to work. But I have my car filled up with gas and here are the keys to the car. You can go to the churches and you can call and visit with the pastors." I could not believe that here he was, actually turning me into being the first Awana missionary. I was assigned by Leo Spencer!

I started to visit these pastors and get acquainted. I could see the heart that Leo had for this work, and as I visited, we stirred up interest. Before long he said, "Why don't we have a training conference out here and we can start teaching what Awana is all about?" I told him that would be fine, so we set a date. I remember taking a few of our staff members with me to do the training conference. We traveled for fourteen hours to get out there and I was terribly disappointed, because only about forty to fifty people showed up. I kept asking myself, *Is it really worth it all?* Somehow the Lord said just keep on keeping on, and it wasn't long before we had other conferences set up. I traveled with Leo and visited some of these churches and God began to bless. We saw a real interest take root.

It is amazing to see what God did with Leo Spencer, who was just an ordinary man who enjoyed working behind the scenes, getting others to do the ministry they could do better than he could—and to think that Leo became our very first lay missionary! I wish there was some way we could take a survey of how many churches Leo contacted. There are probably a thousand churches throughout the East Coast area that Leo had some contact with over the years, encouraging them to start an Awana Club. He truly had great influence on some of the Awana leadership out there, because ten couples there became our Awana missionaries.

We see how God blessed the ministry of the *Hitting the Mark* film. When we took that on as a venture, though, we had no idea of the outreach it would have in the future. That is what God does. He still says in JEREMIAH 33:3: "Call unto me, and I will answer thee, and shew thee great and mighty things, which thou knowest not." Yes, God has been showing us all the time.

Creation of Scholarship Camp

Many campers and leaders have asked, "How did Scholarship Camp come into being?" The first Awana Scholarship Camp was held in 1952. However, the very roots of the Awana camping ministry were grown many years before.

Let me take you back to the year 1926. The place is Paul Rader's conference grounds in Lake Harbor, Michigan. The location is right on the beautiful sand beach of Lake Michigan. Paul Rader challenged Lance Latham to start a camp for boys and girls. The camp was just a long dormitory building. It was located on the top of a sand dune, looking out onto magnificent Lake Michigan.

The facilities were limited: just a tennis court and ball field and, of course, the beautiful swimming area. Swimming was the order of the day for each day of boys' camp: to wake up as they ran into the chilly waters of Lake Michigan. The camp program wasn't fancy; the warmth of the godly leadership was the catalyst that held it all together. If you were to talk to former campers from that area and time, they would say the most impressive activity at camp was the two-hour Bible study led by Doc Latham. Today, a two-hour Bible study at camp is unheard of. But out of that camp came many camp leaders who have been ministering around the world. The name of that camp was "Chic-Go-Tab," which stood for Chicago Gospel Tabernacle. The Chicago Gospel Tabernacle was the amazing church of which Paul Rader was the pastor. This was also the church from whence came Lance Latham, the founder of the North Side Gospel Center.

In 1935, the Lord opened an unusual camp facility, in Michigan, that was called "Michawana." This was a brand-new camp built by the government, 240 beautiful acres with the most attractive cabins and facilities. These fantastic facilities were operated for some eight years by the state of Michigan. One day a notice came from the camp headquarters in Lansing, Michigan, that the camp would no longer be available to the many boys and girls who came from states other than Michigan. (Being a Michigan state camp, it was understandable why.) Later the camp was turned over to a fine Christian pastor by the name of Ray Bayne, who ran it for the next forty years.

Of course, this raised a big question as to where the Illinois campers would go. God had a plan. He opened up 123 beautiful acres of land in Wisconsin, just north of Milwaukee. The United States had been engaged in a war, so this was a difficult time to build a camp, with lumber and all the other necessary supplies selling at a premium. But Lance Latham, the pastor of the North Side Gospel Center, where Awana was born, had tremendous faith that God was going to do it. God wonderfully brought to us a former camper, who now had a lumber mill, who donated an entire carload of lumber to build the mess hall. A truckload of meat was also donated. God just wonderfully provided to make that camp a reality.

At that point, Awana Clubs were beginning to grow quickly, and I felt there was a need for a camp such as Scholarship Camp for the many achievers who had already gotten their Timothy Awards. The big question was, "Is such a camp feasible?" I could see that it would be for one state, perhaps, but by that time Awana had spread across the country.

Our first Awana employee, Rich Wager, was by then the director and founder of Camp Silver Birch in Wisconsin. Because Awana had made such an impact in his life, God led him to offer Silver Birch to all the Scholarship Camp campers who applied—free of charge. What an incentive that was. Now, with little faith, I began asking, "Where would these campers come from?" Certainly they wouldn't come from across the country! How wrong I was. Praise the Lord: at that first Scholarship Camp, twenty-two states were represented. Awana clubbers who had gotten Timothy Awards even came from the Bahamas, as well as states as far away as California.

That first camp was God's seal of approval letting us know that Scholarship Camp was a vital part of the ministry of Awana. It wasn't long before an Awana missionary, Gene Goertzen, asked me to come and teach him how to run a Scholarship Camp in California. That camp flourished quickly. Gene Goertzen began teaching other missionaries and soon other camps sprang up. Today our missionaries conduct more than forty camps across the country each year.

Scholarship Camp

What makes Scholarship Camp so different from the ordinary church camp? Scholarship Camp is basically a leadership training camp for young people. You see, to qualify to attend, all of the campers must have completed three Awana books. The first goal of the Awana Scholarship Camp is not the same as the regular church camp, the first emphasis of which is salvation. (Yes, occasionally some of our Scholarship Campers trust Christ as their Savior, too. Even though they have all this Scripture memorized, some had not yet personally trusted Christ. However, that is the unusual case rather than the norm.)

Scholarship Camp is a fantastic place filled with tremendous activities and with Awana leaders who have worked as leaders throughout the year in local clubs and have a real love for seeing these campers get the burden and vision to allow the Lord to use their lives. Today, in some of our teen camps, many campers can now receive a Citation Award, which is the completion of ten years of Awana. They will have memorized more than a thousand verses by that point. What a treasure they have put into their computer-like minds: God's software will be their treasure forever and ever as God uses His Word to speak to them and persuade them in the days that lie ahead.

If you were to ask the Awana missionaries to rank-order the missionary activities they consider the most effective, Scholarship Camp would probably be the top pick. Olympics, Bible Quizzing, and Grand Prix all fulfill specific needs in the ministry, we know. But Scholarship Camp allows leaders to be with the clubbers twenty-four hours a day for a full week, to assist them in making some of life's major decisions. Only eternity will reveal the true results of these major decisions.

CLUBBERS

My Car Ministry

I have found that the most effective ministry I had as a club leader was my car-pickup ministry. You may already be picking up your clubbers. If so, ask the Lord to help make your conversation with them spiritually encouraging.

This is a valuable time that you do not want to waste. I'm sure you enjoy delivering all those precious parcels home. But driving the last clubber home may give you the greatest opportunity of all to lead a young person to Christ. You have a captive audience in your car with that last child alone.

We all know so well that today's clubbers have bigger burdens than ever before. They need to share with someone who loves them. We read in 1 CORINTHIANS 13:12a, "For now we see in a mirror, dimly, but then face to face … ."

God allows us to see just a portion of the fruit of our labors now. But, praise the Lord, someday soon God will reward faithful leaders who have invested their time in the lives of boys and girls. Without Awana leaders who have a vision of winning the lost, boys and girls will perish in a Christless eternity. May the Lord give you a vision as you look at your clubbers each week. I thank God for the more than 200,000 leaders who each week are reaching boys and girls for our wonderful Lord.

The Exciting Car Ministry

One of the most exciting aspects of that original club was the "leader's car ministry." Every leader was challenged to realize that wherever he lived, whether it was five or ten miles away, the neighborhood in which he lived was his mission ministry. It was unthinkable for him to drive all the way to club just to put in his time as a leader; rather, we hoped each one would

Calvary Baptist Church, Pennsylvania, circa 1960

realize that in his own neighborhood were potential clubbers that he could reach. Most likely, if he doesn't reach them, no one else will.

The car ministry is far more than just providing transportation. It is a wonderful opportunity to minister to the kids as you are traveling back and forth with them each week to club. You build up a wonderful relationship with them that will stay with them their entire life.

Let me tell you about a young team leader who had just gotten saved. He was so excited by the possibility of picking up kids in his neighborhood and bringing them to club. He was such an exciting leader that he filled his car to more than overflowing; in fact, some of the kids didn't even mind traveling in the trunk. This, of course, was not something that was recommended at all, but I appreciated the enthusiasm this boy had.

This news of him overloading his car with so many clubbers came to one of deacons in the church. This deacon very kindly took him aside and shared with him that this was not a good image for the church, nor was it safe for him to have so many kids in the car. He could probably receive a ticket—or think of the tragedy if he had an accident with all of those kids on board. The leader appreciated the kind and courteous counsel he received from the church deacon, but he still was vitally interested in all of those kids he was picking up for club. I believe the Lord gave this new convert a challenging suggestion for this deacon. He said, "I want to do the right thing, but would you be so kind as to come with me as I pick up the kids next week and you tell me *what kids I should not pick up.*"

Now that was a challenging answer! Really, every kid needs to be picked up one way or another. The deacon of the church appreciated the heart this young fellow had for the kids and the Awana work, and I'm sure they found a solution to this great need.

Sometimes I think one of the most vital and effective parts of my own personal car ministry was picking up kids who could have come on their own; I wanted to have the opportunity to talk to them while I had them in my car. I remember so well one particular boy I picked up who was new. He had never been to club before and I was anxious to find out more about him. As we sat outside his home, before I left I talked to him and asked him a little about his home life and his parents. In the conversation, he mentioned that his great-great-great-grandfather was a very famous man. I was very curious about who he was referring to and he said his great-great-great-grandfather was Isaac Watts, the amazing hymn writer, who penned some three hundred precious hymns. This was the man who wrote the song

Chums, 1996

with lyrics that start: "When I survey the wondrous cross/on which the Prince of glory died,/My richest gain I count but loss,/and pour contempt on all my pride."

After he told me this, I said, "You are really blessed to have such a famous great-great-great-grandfather." As I continued talking to him, I found out that this boy did not know the Lord as his Savior. He had never trusted in Him, so as we conversed, I said, "You know, someday you're going to want to see your great-great-great-grandfather. I know where he is. He's in heaven—and wouldn't you like to be sure of that for yourself?" Right then and there, I shared with this boy God's precious gospel and showed him that he was a sinner for whom Christ died.

That was a very precious opportunity to lead a young fellow who was just ready to accept Christ as his Savior. There he was, just like a piece of ripe, low-hanging fruit that could be picked from a tree. What a joy to be able to give the gospel to him and show him how Christ had died for him, and that all he had to do was just put his trust in Christ and God would take him to heaven. Then he would be able to meet his great-great-great-grandfather and all of God's people and all of the Awana leaders who had gone on before.

It's because of opportunities like this that I cannot urge you too much to see the value of picking up kids in your neighborhood. Of course, in all of this you have to get informed permission from their parents so they know for sure where you are going, and also have confidence that you will take good care of their kids. But I can assure you that the car ministry will pay big dividends.

Personal Evangelism by Teens

In that original Awana Club at the North Side Gospel Center, there were some unusually dedicated leaders. Many of them were teens, but the challenge that they all were given was that wherever they lived, that was their mission field to cultivate for the Lord. And they truly did that.

Many of them who had cars would fill those cars up and bring kids to club. Of course, the fellowship they had even during the time of transportation caused the leaders and the clubbers to become a very close-knit group, and had a real impact on all of them. Also, taking the clubbers home at night gave real opportunities to the leaders not just to provide transportation, but

Teen Leaders' Conference, 2009

also to talk about things of the Lord and even challenge some of the clubbers regarding their own salvation.

The Mystery Trip for Teens

One of the joys I had as youth director at the North Side Gospel Center, in those early days, was that I also directed the boys' high-school department, which at that time was called *Pilots.* Mrs. Lance Latham directed the girl's clubs, called *Mariners.*

What a joy it was to work with some sixty to seventy of these boys, many of whom were also leaders in the Pals Club. We had some three gymnasiums that we were allowed to use for basketball each Monday night. Then once a month we would have a co-ed time with the *Mariners.* This was also very special.

One of the challenges we had for reaching our goal of sixty in our Sunday school class was a mystery trip. We found that the curiosity about where we were taking them was always effective. I had thought a great deal about what would really challenge teenage boys. The first stop on the mystery trip was actually a decoy, to tease them a bit: We went to a retirement center, which is fine for teenagers to go to if they have been told ahead of time that they are to go there to minister! But this was just a stop to make them think that this was the entire mystery trip.

However, the next stop was the county jail, where the chaplain of the jail was a born-again Christian. As our bus arrived, the big steel fence automatically opened up for us, and we drove in with forty teens. During this stop, they were very solemn as they toured the penitentiary. They saw the earthly consequences of sin and also some inmates who were on death row. They were all sure that this was the final leg of the mystery trip.

However, I had one more stop to surprise them with. I had made special preparations to take them to the county morgue. Now, the county morgue does not usually allow visitors, but I had persuaded them to allow us to go through. I clearly remember arriving in front of the morgue. The boys weren't really aware of what this building was, because of the technical name on the outside. When I went in to talk to the person on duty, he told me that the man I had made arrangements with was not there and that he knew nothing about the tour. However, he said that if I took the kids in and acted as the tour guide, he would permit me to do that.

All of a sudden I became as apprehensive and scared as I knew the boys would be. This caretaker said the vaults were down below, on the first floor, and I could take the kids down there. I remember the happy group of teens that walked into the building, just wondering what this was all about. As we began walking down the steps, we encountered an attendant who was preparing a body for shipment. I'll never forget how quickly everything became quiet; it was obvious that the boys were shocked at what they were seeing.

We then proceeded down into the vault where the bodies were actually in drawers. As I stood there with my group, I can assure you there was utter silence as I pulled out drawers with bodies in them. Many of them were suicide victims. It was the most effective object lesson I have ever given. As I showed them the evidence of sin, I asked them, "Do you think for one moment when these people lying here were your age that they could have ever dreamed they would wind up in the county morgue?" It gave the teens a fresh glimpse at the consequences of sin and the fact that it could happen to them. All of these teens are now grown and have their own families, but many of them have said that tour made a huge impression on their lives, one they will never forget.

GALATIANS 6:7, 8: "Be not deceived; God is not mocked: for whatsoever a man soweth, that shall he also reap . . . . For he that soweth to his flesh shall of his flesh reap corruption; but he that soweth to the Spirit shall of the Spirit reap life everlasting."

PARENTS

As I grew up in a Bible-believing church, I often heard missionary speakers. Somehow or other I had built up the idea in my mind that the only valid mission field was one that was on foreign soil. You could not be a missionary unless you traveled to a foreign country, I thought. I was definitely not aware that God told us that the world is the mission field. Our mission field can be the house next door, the people we meet on our jobs, those we go to school with, and even the casual acquaintance that God brings across our path as we travel on an airplane or bus. The people God puts next to you are part of His mission field for you.

We know that some other religions and sects, and even cults, can teach us the value of home visitation. The Jehovah's Witnesses and the Latter Day Saints (Mormons) have had stellar success in reaching people for their cause this way. We are told that Jehovah's Witnesses pass out more than seventy tons of literature every day. A Mormon missionary has to memorize more than 135 pages of material before he is qualified to even visit in a home.

Yes, the home is a prime target for visitation and reaching people for Christ. In the early days of Awana, I established Awana Parent Nights for each one of our clubs. The main purpose of these nights was to reach the unsaved parents of the clubbers. For months, each club would work on preparing a presentation for that night. They would recite the Scripture in unison. Leaders would recognize clubbers' achievements. It was also an opportunity to thank the parents for sending their children to Awana. Most of all, though, it was an opportunity for the pastor to present the gospel to those parents.

Was visiting these parents successful? Yes, it was. We know that all parents appreciate people who are doing something significant for their children. This is true today more than ever in the past. Especially with today's one-parent homes, they appreciate anybody who gets on their team to help them with their children. In those early days there were no Cubbies or Sparks. We had Pals, Pioneers, and Pilots as the three groups for boys, and then there were the Chums, Guards, and Mariners for the girls. Each one of these clubs had its own Awana Parent Night. All the leaders would covenant together that, in the weeks prior to their Awana Parent Night, they would visit the home of every clubber who had attended club that season. It was amazing to see the response we got. Very seldom were there fewer than 100 parents in attendance who had never been in the church before. My pastor and mentor, Lance Latham, as he walked into church on those Awana Parent Nights, would often say, "I smell tobacco," meaning that he surmised there were non-Christians in the group with which he would be sharing the gospel message. Through the years, thousands of parents heard the gospel for the first time at those Awana nights in the North Side Gospel Center where Awana was born. Praise God that many of those clubbers who were on those programs are now serving the Lord worldwide as pastors, missionaries, camp directors, and Awana leaders.

Recruiting Parents

One of the most important features of the Awana Club in a church is that it is an avenue or entry point for reaching the kids' parents for Christ. The main method of reaching those parents is through the regularly scheduled Parent Nights for each department of Awana.

Every club would have its own Parent Night. The club would put on a program and try to minister to the children's parents. We would use a memory program in which clubbers would memorize Scripture at their flag ceremony and at their council time. When new clubbers came in, they, too, would become part of the memory program. We would challenge all of the kids to have their uniforms ready, because, as we pointed out to them, Parent Night is just like the World Series of Awana. All of the parents will be there and awards will be handed out and you will be on display. Every club prepares for this. It is a real motivation for the clubs to do a really good job to impress the parents.

At the beginning of every club season, I would challenge each of my department leaders to prepare for their Parent Night. However, the preparation for Parent Night also included several weeks prior to the event. I requested that they keep their schedules clear because they were going to visit every clubber who had been in attendance during the year so that they could personally invite the parents to the special evening.

We sent a little circular home with each clubber to let them know that the leaders would be coming to visit, so when we arrived we were not exactly strangers. We sat down and shared with each clubber's parent how delighted we were to have their child in our club and as part of the Awana program. We told them that we were going to have a very special night that we encouraged them to attend. By coming to Parent Night, they could get a better view of what happens at club and could meet the leaders; we hoped it would be a real inspiration for them.

We found that after this type of visitation, on Parent Night we would often have in the church more than a hundred people who had never been in the church before. What an opportunity it was for my pastor to give them the gospel! Then, after the program was over, we would always have a time of fellowship with refreshments. We challenged all of the Christians of the church to be part of this ministry so that they could have the opportunity to sit down with these parents, welcome them, and let them know how much we appreciated their coming. It really became a wonderful method of reaching the parents. I could go on and on telling you how many parents were reached with the gospel and how many entire families were won for the Lord. Some of them even became missionaries.

At the Parent Night programs, there were various things to do. We would often take a lot of pictures during club nights and show slides for the parents so that they could see their children participating in the activities. Then we would have Scripture recitation, with sometimes a hundred or more clubbers on the platform. The parents were always thrilled to see their children reciting Scripture. We would introduce all the leaders who were part of the program, so that the parents could see and meet the leaders who were investing in their kids' lives.

This was a thrilling new adventure for the parents, as they could seldom imagine what their children had been doing at Awana. How exciting it was to see some of these very parents become special people in the church and become real soul-winners themselves. It was all because they were reached through our Parent Nights, so I cannot overemphasize the value of that special night.

BUILDING MIRACLES

North Side Gospel Center

It's hard to believe that the entire Awana headquarters was originally an eight-foot by eight-foot office under a stairwell in the North Side Gospel Center where Awana was born. As Awana began to grow, additional facilities

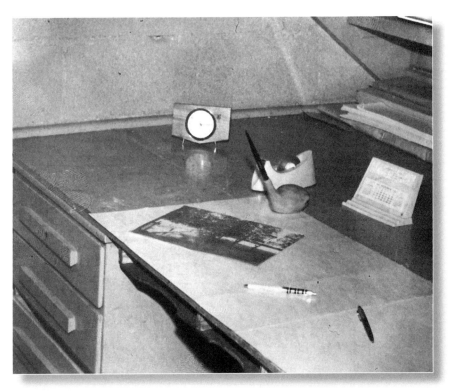

Birthplace of Awana

were needed. It wasn't long before Sunday school rooms had to be used to handle some of the shipping needs, and then, when we got a printing press and started printing our books, we had to have a printing room. But there our little office was, and we were using just about literally every inch of it. Finally, there came a time when I just had to sit still and realize it was absolutely impossible to continue our growth in that space, because there was no more room.

Well, the Lord always has His plan, which we are not always aware of, and it was God who prompted me at that time to just get into my car and drive around to see what might be available. As I drove around, I saw a building—an old storefront—that looked quite attractive, but I thought it was way more space than we needed. Besides, how would we ever get enough money to purchase something like that?

Praise the Lord, we had some godly men on our board of directors: Lance Latham, Burt Dobbert, Howard Hawkinson, and Linc Carlson. When I presented this possible location to them, they felt led by the Lord to consider

Original North Side Gospel Center

it. In fact, they thought we should purchase this building, at a price of $43,000. There was just one hitch in this plan: We probably had only about $10,000 total in our bank account.

Then God gave us the idea to see what we could do to purchase that building with interest-free loans. When the North Side Gospel Center was built, people loaned the money for construction to the church on an interest-free basis. So I thought, *Let's see if we can have a banquet and perhaps we could present something like this.* So I got hold of a school with a large cafeteria and advertised that we were going to host a banquet. I was amazed at the response; so many Awana people wanted to come that we ended up with more than a thousand people attending our banquet. There were fewer than ten people on our Awana staff at that time and we wondered how we could possibly produce a banquet of that size. We would have to do all of the cooking, and all the preparations would have to be done by our own staff!

North Side Gospel Center, birthplace of Awana

It was then that my dear wife, Winnie, said, "I will take on the responsibility for all of the cooking and arrange all of it. And I will get the people to do the serving."

I was really amazed to see how that all took shape and fell into place—and when we presented our needs to the people who might extend interest-free loans, we were thrilled at how well they responded. They were so generous that we were able to purchase that building. I remember that our speaker for that banquet was Clarence Jones. He was the founder of that fantastic radio station, HCJB, in Quito, Ecuador, that sends out the gospel in eighteen languages each day. He was a real inspiration to all of us to press on and watch God do the next step.

The Belmont Building

We purchased that first building and fixed it up, and what a thrill it was when we moved into our own building! I was so happy to see all of that room we were going to have, but I must admit that I had sort of a guilt complex because that building had more room that we really needed. I didn't know how we could justify the size. When people came in to tour the facility, they would ask why we had gotten such a large building and paid all that money for it.

Well, little did I know that in just about eight years, we would be in the same dilemma. We were going to have to leave that building, because not

Awana headquarters, Belmont Avenue, Chicago, circa 1962

only were we completely filled up there, we were also renting garages in the neighborhood so that we could use them to store some of our supplies. So we came to the place where God said, "You've got to move on." Just what do we do? God had to reveal to us His plan for our second building. Praise the Lord for these dedicated men: Arne Abrahamsen, Dale Klein, and Don van den Akker.

God started His plan with us by having a former clubber, now a real estate man in Rolling Meadows, Illinois, give us a call. He thought he had a piece of property that might be something we could place a building on. Well, we were encouraged, but thought that Rolling Meadows was way too far away to think of locating our headquarters building there. We had so many questions. Where would the employees come from? How could our present employees travel that far? It seemed like there were a lot of roadblocks to keep us from going there, but all the time God said, "Keep pressing on, keep pressing on."

The Algonquin Building

Finally, we decided to build this building, even though it seemed financially impossible—but God is One Who likes the challenge of the impossible. We went ahead to draw up plans and then have the cement work done. Another former clubber we knew came to me and said, "Art, I will make a deal with you. I will put in all the cement work that you need and I will put it in for $5,000 less than the lowest bid you can get. And you can take years to pay me." We couldn't resist that offer, so we went forward with his plan. He was an excellent builder and did beautiful work on the foundation and all the other cement work.

Then one day God did yet another wonderful thing. I was still directing Camp Awana at the time and I was up at camp and in came this young man who had put in the cement, Jack Skaathun. He said, "Art, my mother talked to me last week and she said, 'You can't give Awana a bill for that. You could never pay Awana for the impact that it has had on your own life.'" He continued, "Well, I have come to the persuasion that my mother was right and you will never get a bill from me." I was just amazed to see how God was right now doing His work.

Within a couple of hours of Jack's declaration, another camper whom I had not seen for many years came in. He said, "God has blessed my business and I would like to give $2,000 toward the new building." All of this happened in one day and so I just said, "God, I know You are really in this building plan." Then, as we began to build and get the framework up, one day a van stopped by and the man in that van said, "You probably don't remember me, but my name is Ken Pearson. I was part of Awana and was reached through Awana about fifteen years ago and it has really changed my life. It was because of my contact with the gospel back there in those days. Now I see you are building a new building here and I would be honored if I could have a part in doing all the painting and the interior decorating for

Awana board at the Algonquin Building, circa 1970

you, as that is my specialty. Would you allow me to just display a little of the love of what God did for me by letting me take on the project of the interior decorating of your building?" To say I was overwhelmed would be putting it lightly. In my heart I was just praising God to see Him do a miracle that we could never have planned for.

I could go on and on about how many other volunteers came in to help us build that building, but when it was all done, again I wondered, "How can we justify this building? It is so much more room than we really need!" But it wasn't long before we had filled up this building, too. We didn't have enough room for both offices and shipping, so then we had to think about another building.

The Tollview Building

God had so wondrously blessed us with all our previous buildings that we just knew He had another building waiting for us. Just a few blocks from our present building, located off the expressway, there was a vacant building for sale. There was also an adjoining property that we could use to very easily add on to that building, which would give us the additional space that we didn't have in our own building. This vacant structure became what we called our "cram-plan" building. While the additional space was under construction, all our staff moved into the existing building, which was not much larger than the building we had just come out of. Many people had to share offices with another staff person. Everyone had such a wonderful

Tollview Building

spirit, and there were no complaints, because they knew this was God's plan. Also, it was interesting for all of us to see the progression of the work next door to us. Each day we would go out there and see what additions and progress had been made.

One of the interesting things about this site was that we would have a new and upgraded shipping center. In our previous locations, we had had to walk around with carts and go from bin to bin to pick up the items for shipping. Now we would have rollers that we could use to send the items down to the next items to be picked. This was a far more efficient way of working than to have to hand-pick each item.

One of the nicest pieces of equipment that was given to us was a beautiful board table that was about twenty-five feet long. This was given to us as a gift from a cabinet maker, who told us that there were a few slight defects that they would have needed to fix or have redone for their original customer; however, to us it was a wonderful gift. There was no way we could ever get the table in through our regular doors, so we had to hoist it up and place it where our missionaries would be meeting. Because we did this before the roof was put on, it was easier for us to get it into the building. We took some beautiful pictures of all our missionaries sitting around this table at our missionary conference.

Our dedication was an exciting day. Outside the building, we put up stands for everyone who would attend this event. We had the mayor of Rolling Meadows speak to us; another of our special features was Audrey Benmuvhar, who was a ventriloquist. She did a nice presentation, which was a real blessing to all of us as we listened to her share some of the things that were going to happen in the future at Awana. This was a precious time because we saw Awana adding many more missionaries, which we desperately needed.

It was also in this building that the Adopt-A-Club plan was started for foreign missions. God opened many doors in these foreign countries while we were in the Tollview building. Nevertheless, it was not long before this building too was overflowing, and God once again had to show us where we should go from there.

"A Penny Saved Is a Building Built"

After three building programs in just twelve years, everyone at Awana needed time to rest. But six years later, building number five was in the works. With a projected price tag of $4.1 million for the new headquarters in Streamwood,

1980s Penny Drive

Penny Drive

Awana would have to raise more money than all the previous building campaigns combined. The centerpiece of this fund-raising effort was to be the "Penny Drive."

The Penny Drive has a track record of success that makes it appropriate for even big projects. I want the church at large to see how the "little ones" can play a big role in the life, ministry, and support of church growth and world evangelism.

March of 1989 was designated as "Super Penny Drive Month." The headquarters staff inaugurated the fund drive by wheeling in a contribution of $5,894.02, or nearly 600,000 pennies. In the next six months, the fund-raising efforts grossed $205,000 or more than 20 million pennies.

Clubbers were as committed to the project as anyone. One boy saved $72 worth of pennies in one year. Another group of children raised $587.95; the deacons' board at their church was so impressed that it voted to match the amount.

In May 1989, the 117,000-square-foot Streamwood facility was completed.

The Bode Road Building

Once again, God was wonderfully reminding us how He had provided for us in the past and that we should really have faith and trust in Him once again to see what He would do. We did quite a search while looking for property to build on, but we found that property was very, very expensive in our present area. We did find a piece of property that was in an excellent location, but would cost us more than a million dollars. We were just about ready to

Bode Road Building, Streamwood, Illinois

sign the contract, when God once again, in His wonderful way, guided us and provided another way of getting property. We saw a little ad in the newspaper in Streamwood that there was property for sale. We looked at this site and immediately all of us felt that this is what God would have for us. First of all, it had eleven acres of land and was in the most beautiful location, with a park district on three sides so there would be no buildings crowding us. The best part was that it was less than half the price we had been planning to pay for the other piece of property.

Then we searched for builders that would be able to construct a place that would meet our needs. We searched for about six to eight months and had various building contractors come in. They presented drawings and even models of what they could build so that we could choose. Finally the Lord laid on our hearts the conviction that this one particular building was the one we should select—and how we thank the Lord for the structure of our present building! It has been so adaptable that as Awana has grown, it has been possible to readjust different areas to meet our needs. It has been wonderful for us to see what could happen.

One thing that I asked for was a training center where we could have rooms like regular motel rooms, so that we could have people stay overnight right on our premises where their training was being conducted. We did not think our finances would be able to handle such a load, but I persuaded the others to at least put the basic structure in place. We didn't have to completely finish that part of our building project right away, but if we put in the basic structure, plumbing, and electrical, then we could trust the Lord that in the future we would be able to finish it. We planned for three floors and we just knew that God was going to provide that for us. The first year we did manage to get the first floor in, and the second year we got the second floor completed, and just continued until it was all finished. Now we have all three floors to the training center complete and how we wish we could have three more floors, because now many, many times we completely fill all our rooms.

It took about one year to complete this beautiful building. When we had our dedication service, Jerry Falwell from Liberty University came to be our keynote speaker. From then until this present day, we have seen God keep increasing and increasing our growth until our space here also got filled up and we knew we could no longer handle the shipping in that building.

Penny Lane Building, Schaumburg, Illinois

The Penny Lane Building

So, the sixth building God brought us to was a building in Schaumburg, which was formerly a shipping center for Motorola. With our new shipping center on Penny Lane, we just see that God wonderfully provided us with the most up-to-date shipping center you could ever want.

Here we are blessed with our sixth building, and thanking God for taking care of us and helping with all of these buildings to get the message of the gospel out to the world. We are so thankful that we are all a part of God's wonderful program in ministering to a lost world. Praise the Lord for what He has done in all of our buildings. We have been truly blessed by His many, many provisions.

The Tony Castillo Story

It was in 1933, the year of the World's Fair in Chicago, that the original North Side Gospel Center was born in an old burned-out furniture store that was renovated into a church. The first floor was a sanctuary and the second floor held the club rooms. It was in this building where the Awana game circle was created. Hundreds, maybe even thousands, of kids ran around that game circle and enjoyed the many, many games that were played on it.

The clubbers who came out of that humble-looking church included eight fellows whom God used to create camps that are still reaching kids for

Tony Castillo

Christ today. I am inclined to think that perhaps a million kids have been reached through these eight different camps.

I could go on and on sharing the miracles that happened in this church. However, the time came when the building was sold and we moved on to another church, where the Awana program actually started.

One day, I was doing a bit of reminiscing and wondered, *Is that building still there where we had all of those activities?* I decided to take a trip down to the city and, sure enough, there was the building, still standing. It had probably been about twenty-five years since I was there last. I looked to see if I could find the owner, to ask if I could go up to the second floor where the game floor was located, just to see if the game-circle floor was still there.

A liquor store had been built next to the building, and I soon found the owner of that liquor store ordering some of his merchandise. I showed him a picture of the *Awana: God's Miracle* book, which had a picture of his building. He looked at that picture and said, "Yes, that is my building."

I asked if he would allow me to go up to the second story and take a look at that game floor. He was very agreeable, and we walked up into that old building, which had been used for a lot of things since the church left. I looked at the floor where we had had the game periods, but was discouraged and distressed to find it had been turned into a nightclub and that a dance floor had been built on top of the original floor. There was no way I could see that game floor. Somehow the Lord seemed to say to me, "Don't give up.

You have to see if that floor is still there." I boldly asked the man if I could drill a hole in his floor, and, surprisingly, he agreed. As I drilled the hole, believe me, I was thrilled to see that original floor! I began to think what a treasure that game floor would be for leaders who had been part of Awana for a long time, and was sure that they would each love to have a piece of wood from that original game floor. So, I asked the owner if there was any way I could take up that original floor from under the current dance floor and replace it with another new floor.

It was then that I saw God do a miracle. As I shared with him what I wanted to do, I gave him $500 as a token to see if he would let me do it. He said, "You know, I really need the money at this time, but I would like to be part of what you are doing for kids."

So there we were some weeks later, with carpenters who had originally been clubbers and had run across that same floor as kids, and they enthusiastically began picking up that floor, which had been there for a hundred years. Large spikes held the floor together, but we eventually got it up. Then we took the flooring and cut it into pieces, to be sanded down and made into awards. We planned to present those awards to some of the clubbers who had run around on that floor many years ago. We have shared those pieces of flooring many, many times.

But the greatest thing was yet to take place. I thought of Tony Castillo, the former owner of that original building, and gave him a call. I said, "Tony, how would you like to come and see what has come out of the original Awana building, to see what God has done with what was founded right in your building? You can bring your wife and your girls and along with my wife, we will have dinner together. Then I will give you a tour of our building." He excitedly accepted the invitation.

Well, he came with his family and I started to take him on a tour of our present building. His eyes wide open, he asked, "Did God do all of this?"

I said, "You are right, Tony, this is the evidence of what God can do." After we had toured the building, I took him up into my office and we sat and we talked. I said, "Tony, do you know why Awana was born? It was born just to show kids around the world how they can be sure of going to heaven, by just putting their trust in Jesus Christ. Tony, would you like to be sure of going to heaven?" God had prepared his heart, and right there in my office, Tony Castillo trusted Christ to be his Savior. We were all so thrilled. We found out later that his wife was a believer and had been praying for him.

It wasn't long before Tony and his wife got involved in a church that had Awana and became Awana leaders.

Then another marvelous thing happened. We had wonderful Awana clubs in Venezuela, and a conference for Awana pastors and leaders was taking place there, with some seven hundred people attending from all over Venezuela. Many of them were walking miles and miles to get there and, of course, the conference was all in Spanish. I would need an interpreter and thought maybe I could get Tony to step in; he was Cuban and knew Spanish very well. I asked him if he would like to go down there with me. He excitedly accepted and so down to Venezuela we went. I can remember that in front of all of those people, I said, "Tony, you have never publicly given your testimony and shared how you are sure of going to heaven and that Christ died for your sins. How would you like to do that right now?" Tony got up and with his beautiful Spanish language and with a big smile on his face, he shared the joy he had in his heart by knowing Jesus Christ as his Savior.

What a joy it was to have Tony give me that wood off that original game floor, but the greatest prize of all was Tony. If you ever come to the city of Chicago, you can see that Tony is involved in a church. He has a lot of musical ability and is able to play several instruments, and there he is heading up the music in an inner-city church.

It is great to see what a change God wrought in Tony's life, but there are still many people in our cities who are hell-bound; it's those people we need to witness to and reach them for Christ. God is calling on us to be willing to give that wonderful message of salvation to everyone we meet. What a joy it is to lead someone to the Lord!

The Original Game Floor

When we had the opportunity to take up the floor of the original building where the Awana game floor was created, we were delighted to be able to cut that old floor up into about twelve-inch pieces and make what we call a Steadfast Award. This award was handed out to leaders who have really been faithful for many, many years. It is thrilling to go to conferences and see so many people who have been leaders for twenty-five and thirty years. We were just so honored to be able to give each of them a piece of the original floor.

I was out in California at one of our conferences and many of the leaders there received these awards. Our creative missionary, Gene Goertzen, decided to use his piece of wood to raise some money for one of our missionaries. He held an auction where everyone could sign up for how much they would give for this project—and, praise the Lord, $1,000 in missionary funding came in from just that one piece of wood!

We think of our faithful leaders with such tremendous gratitude. There was one particular leader who came from the Salem Bible Church in Salem, Michigan. Claire Dickerson is ninety-seven years old and she is a Sparks leader who still walks to club each week. It is an inspiration to many to see a leader who still has not given up. Claire is not even thinking about retirement.

We thank God for the faithful leaders who serve God in their local churches. May our goal in life be steadfastness, faithfulness in serving our wonderful Lord, so we can look forward to hearing Him say, "Well done, thou good and faithful servant" (MATTHEW 25:21).

B.B.S. DEGREE

Back in those early days, we had to use many volunteers because we did not have the funds to pay people to do any of the assembly work for us. One of the fun times at the game period was a game that required beanbags, so at first my wife Winnie would sew the beanbags, along with the neckerchiefs, for us. Later on, we found a retirement home that was willing to help us.

A born-again Christian nun who took on the task of sewing our beanbags was just thrilled to have a part in Awana. As we talked to her, she said, "Well, I was Catholic all those years and I found that in the Catholic religion, you weren't really important unless you had some kind of a degree behind your name." Then she told me that she never had earned a degree until she started working at Awana. That remark really got my curiosity up, so I asked her what degree she could possibly get in Awana? She smiled and replied, "I got the B.B.S. degree." Still uncomprehending, I then asked, "What degree could that possibly be?" She proudly told me that it was the "Bean Bag Sewer" degree.

I was so thrilled to hear that. I thought that today a lot of us get degrees, but I think the degree that God is most pleased with is the B.B.S. degrees, earned by people who do their work because they love the Lord—that is the degree God gives them. Most of all, some day He will reward us with eternal rewards because we are faithful in doing what God calls us to do.

CHAPTER 3

Camp

CAMP AWANA

My first experience with going to camp was as a ten-year-old boy. At midnight on the appointed day, hauling my duffel bag, I climbed aboard the *Saugatuck,* which was a paddleboat that was to take us campers to Muskegon, Michigan. We traveled all night and got there at eight the next morning. The camp, there on the shores of Lake Michigan, was just one long building divided into cabins. This was my first experience of being away from home.

I didn't know anyone and I was very homesick. I ate too many green apples and got sick. I was there for two weeks and vowed that I would never go to camp again; however, God had other plans, because the next year I went to camp for an entire month. How little did I know then that my camping ministry would continue for more than fifty years!

The first camp was called Chic-Go-Tab. God then provided a government camp near Grand Rapids, Michigan, with 240 acres of beautiful campgrounds; that facility was called Michawana. We worked there for eight years, until that opportunity was withdrawn. We thought that we might be without a camp facility then, but God wonderfully provided a 123-acre piece of property on a delightful lake, which we bought for $15,000, and without question that was God's provision.

Lance Latham, my mentor, was responsible for making all the big decisions during this "wilderness time." There was not a building on the entire piece of property that could be used for camping, but Doc had great faith,

Doc Latham at Camp Awana, late 1980s

and he said, "Let's trust that God will provide facilities for us." We had eight months before camp was to begin and all of these things had yet to be provided, so that was a step of faith that I will never forget.

One of our former campers owned a lumber mill in Kentucky, and donated an entire trainload of lumber—enough to build the entire mess hall. Week after week, we saw God provide, not only materials but also volunteers to help us build the camp. It was my responsibility to enlist these volunteers to bring all of this about. This was a new experience for me, as I had no building background, but God wonderfully provided in spite of my limited abilities in these areas.

The first year, all of our "cabins" were Army tents. (Within a couple of years, though, the tents were eliminated and cabins were built to accommodate about 250 campers.) I can remember Doc Latham calling on people to pray that the camp would be ready when the campers came up there. One week before camp was to start, we didn't even have half the tents up, but again God provided volunteers who came and worked all hours to make it happen.

But there was even a greater problem. It was the week before camp and there was no water. I remember that all the carpenters who were working on our mess hall got together on their knees and asked God to send water. Just two days before the camp opened, the water came forth, and what a time of rejoicing that was for everyone! When the campers arrived, there was only one water spigot available for all the campers to wash up in, but since it was a boys' camp, they did not mind too much. It wasn't long before the facilities were completed.

Because I was responsible for the camp program in addition to the buildings, I became heavily involved in God's camp training for me. I had to remind myself, "What is the number-one purpose of camp?" We know we have to have the facilities for the kids to have fun and good times, but the main reason is to make sure that every boy and girl who comes to camp can put their trust in Jesus Christ, and thereby have the assurance and hope of heaven. And then, of course, to see them trained in the Word of God, so that they could be approved workers for the Lord in the days to come.

CAMP DISCIPLINE

Everyone who has been to a camp knows that camp is supposed to be fun—and some of the most fun times are in your cabin when you should be sleeping but you really carry on conversations for half the night. Most of the campers are meeting friends for the first time, so that is understandable. Of course, as the campers get to know each other better, their conversations would carry on night, after night, after night. I soon observed that I had a major problem: These very campers, whom I was very determined to reach with the gospel and train in the Word of God, were sometime falling asleep in Bible class the next day. I knew this had to be corrected or we would lose sight of the real purpose of camp.

I thought of the basic principle that we had for running the game circle. When we count to five, we expect everyone to be silent. This system, when it works (as it almost always does), can change the entire discipline program of an Awana Club, so I thought it should also be used at camp. I asked myself, "How can we incorporate this into the camp program?"

The buildings and cabins of the camp were spread over some fifty acres. I had a good sound system installed everywhere in camp so that everyone could hear any and all the announcements that were made. Camp was run with music. The first thing in the morning, we had some quiet music to gradually arouse the campers from their sleep, and then shortly after that came the reveille bugle sound. By that time all the campers should have gotten out of bed. Then we held a short exercise time to help everyone wake up. After the

Flag ceremony, Scholarship Camp, Camp Awana

campers were dressed, we played the music "Sweet Hour of Prayer." That was the signal so our cabin leaders with their campers could have a time of prayer and commit the day to the Lord.

After our prayer, we would play "The Star Spangled Banner"; during this music, the campers would head up to the flagpole area for the flag ceremony. This was not just a suggestion: When the last note was played, everyone was to be lined up at the flagpole area in perfect silence. When this is practiced properly, it is amazing how simple and effective it is, and how much the campers and leaders enjoy it.

The first morning at camp, we would teach the campers the importance of the American flag and how to respect it. The Stars and Stripes were used at each meal to bring the campers to the mess hall in perfect order. We would have a message about the flag at that time. Then the bugler would play to the colors and everyone gave a right-hand salute. We recited the pledge to the flag and we would sing "My Country, 'Tis of Thee." At the end of the flag ceremony, another march was played and everyone quietly, without talking, would march into the mess hall and stand around their tables. After prayer, everyone knew it was time to fellowship and enjoy our meal time together.

UNUSUAL CAMPING TRIP

While I was directing Pals in that original club at the North Side Gospel Center, God wonderfully gave us hundreds of kids. We had promised them a special camping trip if they reached their goal. They did it with enthusiasm, so we planned for an overnight camping trip, with eighty Pals, to the Dells in Wisconsin.

As director, I did my utmost to plan it well so that we wouldn't have things go wrong. The weather was beautiful on the day of the trip. I had small motor boats for the campers to use that their pup tents would fit in. We traveled down to this beautiful little island. There we had a nice campfire and put up our tents. To see all these little eager-beaver Pals so enthusiastic about what they were doing was just a thrill.

Well, the time came for them to get into their tents, and we said it was time to get some sleep. They were most cooperative. How little did I suspect what was going to take place then!

About a couple of hours after they were in bed, I saw a little bit of lightning, and then there was wind and thunder. Little flashlights went on in all of the tents. I knew what was going through their minds: They were somewhat scared. It wasn't long before more than a little thunder came through. As the rain came down, the wind swept furiously across the island, and every pup tent blew over and fell to the ground. I heard eighty clubbers just about crying because they were desperate and didn't know what to do. There was no shelter at the island, so with the leaders, we loaded the kids into the boats and got them back to the mainland, where we all sat in the bus all night waiting for the sun to come up the next day. That was a long night. It was quite an experience to sit there with everybody soaking wet.

As we arrived back on the island the next morning to retrieve our belongings, I went to pick up a tent that had fallen and to my amazement, and perhaps near-horror, I saw a Pal who was still sleeping, never even realizing that we had all gone!

Looking back, we realize that in today's world I probably would have been accused of child abuse; perhaps there would be headlines about the neglect that I showed. But God spared us from that—and that little Pal has been a missionary for more than thirty years, serving the Lord as a Bible translator. What a joy to see the fruits of the Scripture seeds that were sown years ago.

Driving home with the clubbers that next day was a discouraging time because I wasn't anxious to meet the parents and tell them just what had taken place. But while I was driving along, everybody in the bus sleeping and tired, a little Pal piped up and said, "Mr. Rorheim, last night was a special night to me. At the campfire I trusted Christ as my Savior." All of a sudden, I realized that the entire trip had been worth it, because one little Pal had become a new creature in Christ. Since that time I have talked to many of those campers, who are now family men, and they look back at that as one of the highlights of their club experience. We really never know the impact we are making on clubbers as we spend time with them and take personal interest in them.

CAMP AWANA CONSTRUCTION CHALLENGE

Building Camp Awana from its infancy, when there was nothing to it but a piece of property, was an eventful process, and we knew that 150 campers were to arrive in about 8 months. What a challenge it was! Fortunately, World War II had just ended, so we were able to get tents and other Army surplus supplies to help get the camp started.

One of the main things that you need at camp is a good truck. At that time, there were no funds to buy a vehicle. But one day, I received an interesting call from a lady who told me she had a straight-eight Buick—one of those really big Buicks—that had a very good motor in it, and she had a little church built on the back because she used it to go around and pick up kids for Sunday school. Well, she said that since it had not been used for many years and it just stayed in the garage, she would like to give it to us to use up at Camp Awana.

I was not sure just what we could do with a piece of equipment that was so old. However, I went over there and I got this Buick car that had fenders on it almost like a tank, and big wheels. I took a battery along and got it started and started down the street with it. I didn't realize that there was not enough water in the radiator, but all of a sudden the radiator cap flew off. It was like a geyser shooting up in the air. I drove a little farther and suddenly the horn began to blow, and I had no way of turning it off. So I had to stop and lift the hood and pull some wires to keep the horn from constantly blowing. I managed to finally get it back to the church, all the while wondering just what we could do with that old piece of equipment.

Then I thought, *It has a good motor in it. Is there any way I could get this up to camp?* It was wintertime and very cold, so we decided to see if we could pull it up to camp behind our bus. Now, this car had virtually no brakes; in fact, it probably hadn't had any brakes for a long time. I put on one of those big winter army suits, and sat in that car as we were pulled by the bus. One concern was if the bus stopped suddenly: there were no brakes for me to stop the car with, and I would go plowing into the back of the bus. It was certainly a very precarious trip, but we made it up to camp. We had a good mechanic who checked it out for us and we took the "church" off the back and made a platform on it instead. That old junker turned out to be a wonderful truck for us at the camp.

Just a short time later, we found out that there were prefabricated cabins that the Army had used, which we could get for just a couple of hundred dollars each. They would be coming up from Florida, and they would ship them all the way up to Fredonia, Wisconsin. Now, the only vehicle we had was that old truck with a flat platform on it. Just think: That old piece of equipment, which we initially never dreamed would turn out to be a useful truck, hauled twenty-four cabins to their locations, where they were constructed on site.

We could practically write a book on how that truck just seemed to operate and do the job when needed until we could afford to get a full-size camp truck. So, praise the Lord for His providing for us in this very unusual way.

Tepee at Camp Awana built by Art

CAMP AWANA STORIES

Camp Teen Challenge

During the forty years that I directed the activities of Camp Awana, I found that if you are going to reach and teach these kids the things of the Lord, they have to be happy campers and have fun. We also know that fun at camp comes in many different ways.

We had a beautiful lake where we held many activities, and we had track tournaments with overall competition all through camp to see who could get the most points and become the all-around camper. Of course, to be all-around campers, the kids had to have a virtually perfect score in their Bible work. After directing the camp for many years, I saw kids who had originally attended as just seven- and eight-year-olds, but were now in high school, having come up through the camp program year after year. They expected that we would have something new and exciting for them each year that they came to camp.

That year I was determined to do something that they had never seen before. All of our camps were either all girls or all boys. This time it was an all-boy camp. Just before the high-school kids arrived at camp, I got one of our sharp women who worked at camp to devise an exciting little challenge for these kids. I asked her to be in the cabin when the high-schoolers arrived and introduce herself as the new cabin leader because there was a shortage of men leaders this year. Furthermore, she should assure them that "we are going to get along just fine," and that the bed up on top there was hers and to

Camp Awana girls' leaders, 1960s

please not "mess with my hairspray and makeup." As you can imagine, these kids who had been up to camp all those years were just stunned, stopped in their tracks. They could not believe what they were hearing—but not a word was said.

Then, to challenge them even more, this lady leader said, "Let's come up beside the cabin and I would like to have a nice picture with all of you boys for a keepsake." You can imagine what faces were in this picture! Finally, she asked them all to get back into the cabin and told them that she was going to pick up her suitcases and that "then we will start off having a wonderful camp together." I could only imagine the conversations that went on in that cabin while she was gone.

The one thing the campers did not know was that I had a hidden tape recorder that was picking up all of their comments. Their comments went something like this:

"Wait till my parents hear about this, that a lady was in our cabin ..."

"Just think what my folks will think—they don't even sleep in the same room together, and here I am with this lady in my cabin . . . "

The remarks went on and on in this same vein. Little did they know how I was going to have some fun with them.

The mess hall at camp was always a great place for activities. This year, I had each cabin stand up while I played those comments for them, which of course was very embarrassing, but everyone laughed and had a great time. The next interesting thing we did was to pull the same trick on our eight- and nine-year-old boys, to see how they would react. We could not believe how different it was! They were not opposed to it at all. They said things like, "Oh, we are going to have a mom in our cabin with us and she will probably make our beds for us, and that is going to be just fine."

These were just some of the fun activities that the kids never forgot!

Turtle Races

Another activity that the campers enjoyed tremendously was the turtle races. Camp had many, many turtles on the property, and the kids would (naturally!) start catching them. When a kid found his turtle, he would take it down to the handicraft room and paint it with the kid's own lodge color, and also put his name on the turtle's back. The big feature was the turtle race: We would take all the newly painted turtles down to the water park, where we had a little squared-in pond. We attached a helium balloon to each of the turtles, took the turtles out into the middle of the water, and released them. How interesting it was to see their balloons, which remained above the water while the turtles were below the water and couldn't be seen. The one that reached the shore first was the winner, so we all cheered wildly as they got closer and closer to the edge; eventually, one of them would crawl out so we could determine the winner. That was another one of the fun activities that the campers enjoyed.

Kite Marathon

The kite marathon was also quite a special feature. In those days, the kids loved to make their kites as well as to fly them. We had this marathon contest for which we used purchased kites that were all the same size; then we challenged the campers to see who could put a kite in the air first with about a hundred yards of string. So that was the first contest, to see who could get his kite up first. The next part of the contest was to see how many kites were still in the air that evening. If a camper's kite was still in the air, he won the privilege of staying out all night in a pup tent, tending to the kite—and

Scholarship Camp

believe me, they thought this was the greatest! Because their kites were way up in the air and could not be seen after dark, during the night they would pull on the string to see if there was still a tug. This kite marathon was a real hit with the kids.

UFOs

Many years ago, we went through a period of time when it seemed that people were constantly talking about "unidentified flying objects" (UFOs), meaning flying saucers or alien spacecraft. People claimed they had seen them and believed they came close to Earth and had seen people, but we all felt this was just imagined. Still, a lot of people were utterly convinced that UFOs were a real thing.

So, while we were at camp, we thought we would have some fun, with the teenagers especially. We were able to design something with a clear plastic bag, which we tied up at one end and fixed so we could inflate it with a little bit of camphor that would burn. On a nice warm night when the breeze was just exactly right flowing over camp, we would light these things and release them so that they would gradually go over the camp. The campers looked at those things and said, "Those must be UFOs." They just kept passing over the camp, and when the camphor dissipated, they disappeared, of course. That was just another one of the fun camp features that, as the kids have grown up, they talked about: "That was something that we did not realize you had done, but we enjoyed it so much."

Tree Hut

Another camp feature was a tree hut. My son, Kenny, was always very adventurous. He and another buddy got back in the woods—we didn't know where they were—and during the afternoon hours, they built themselves a tree hut, way in the top of one of the tallest trees. When I found out about it, I realized it was really quite dangerous, and I thought I would either have to join them and put up something a little safer, or else do away with the project.

I decided to get some previous campers who had become regular carpenters to come and build an excellent tree hut way up in that tree. Then, of course, I had to devise a safety measure: a harness to put around the campers, in case some of them got scared halfway up, so that we could still help them and so there would be no problem with anyone falling. They got to go up in the tree hut in the early part of the evening, play games, and at night they would have their devotions before bedtime. The fellow who was their leader was Art Anderson. Just about the first night we used that hut, we had one of the worst storms we had ever had at camp. There was lightning and thunder and rain—and can you imagine what went through the minds of these kids, as this was the last place they ever wanted to be in such weather?

In the morning, with a walkie-talkie system from the mess hall, we asked them, "How did things go up there last night, since we had a rather bad storm?"

The counselor said, "Well, an interesting thing happened. I didn't realize we were going to have a storm, so I thought I would read something about trees, over there in ECCLESIASTES 11:3, 'If the clouds be full of rain, they empty themselves upon the earth; and if the tree falls toward the south, or toward the north, in the place where the tree falleth there shall it be.'"

Can you imagine what must have gone through these campers' minds as they went through that awful storm? Still, it was such a memorable experience that those kids never forgot it for the rest of their lives.

Doc's Bar

Lance Latham, whom everyone called Doc, was a very athletic person in his college days. He was on the school athletic team and majored in the horizontal bars, which you often see male gymnasts perform on in the Olympics. Doc was a rather frail person, but he had very strong arms and could do many flips on that bar—so much so that everyone really enjoyed watching him perform.

Up at camp, one of the ministries he had was working with the teenage campers on the bar at his home. His home was just a little shack up on top of the hill and outside his home were the horizontal bars. This was a real attraction to all the teens. Doc used an award system of pins for the teens' accomplishments as they progressed in the various bar activities. That was a real special feature of camp for all the high-school kids.

Everyone in camp knew that Doc had the horizontal bar. One day, we asked all the campers, "Be sure to send a card home to your parents so that they know you are having a good time." We happened to notice this one card that an eight-year-old boy had written. He said, "I am having a good time up here, but there is also an old man that lives up on top of the hill here and he has a bar." That was real cute and everyone at camp knew

Art's leaders, Camp Awana, 1948; Art and Doc, middle front row

what he was talking about, but we also had to make sure that we explained to his parents what kind of a bar it was. It certainly was not a liquor bar that we had up there! But it was a cute little note that came from the heart of this camper sharing with his parents about camp. Yes, the old man did have a bar.

Tragic Fire

At Camp Awana in Wisconsin, after a delightful day, we were sitting in our chapel singing, hearing testimonies, and listening to a tremendous message from the Word of God. But as our meeting was coming to a close, we saw through the windows smoke and flames in the distance.

Of course, we were curious to know what was taking place, so a few of us got into our cars and headed toward the area where the fire and smoke were coming from. As we got closer, we saw what had happened. A dear, hard-working farmer had just filled his barn with hay and straw and had just completed milking some thirty to forty head of dairy cows—and his barn was ablaze. When we arrived and saw this barn, the heat was tremendous. We had to stand quite a distance away just to keep from getting burned ourselves.

What a tragic sight met us as we looked through the silhouetted windows of the blazing barn. We saw cows that were desperately struggling, with their tongues hanging out, not knowing what to do. They were only a few feet from the door, but, as we know, cattle have a hard time leaving when they should. I couldn't help but equate that with humans: It is the same with salvation. So many people are so close to trusting Christ as their Savior, but they never quite get there. Down through the ages, millions will have had the opportunity, but will spend their eternity in Christless graves.

Today we hear very few messages on hell, but we know hell is just as real as heaven. As we read in 2 THESSALONIANS 1:8–9, "In flaming fire taking vengeance on them that know not God, and that obey not the gospel of our Lord Jesus Christ, who shall be punished with everlasting destruction from the presence of the Lord, and from the glory of his power."

I have often thought that I personally need to allow this to grip my heart and to give me a greater concern for all with whom I come in contact. They are either hell-bound or heaven-bound, and we have the precious message that makes the difference. The day is coming when they'll realize the error of their ways and spend eternity without Christ.

Then, as I saw the face of the farmer who had stored all his goods in the barn, and as I saw it all go up in smoke, it reminded me afresh (as it says in COLOSSIANS) that we should set our affection on things above, not on things

"Teach" Latham's leaders, Camp Awana, 1947

Campers, Girls' Scholarship Camp, Camp Awana, circa 1965

of the earth. Things that are seen about us are temporal and limited, but the things we do in the name of Christ are for eternity.

Lightning Strikes

It was an exciting day, because all the Scholarship Camp kids were going to come to Camp Awana for the first time in their lives. This was the second Scholarship Camp that we had ever had; the first one was held at Silver Birch Ranch in Wisconsin.

It happened to be a rather stormy day when they all arrived. We were trying to get them into the mess hall before the rains came down. I was also quite anxious to get them into their cabins, where they had never been before, but now I had them in the mess hall, where I was speaking to them and encouraging them, and telling them what a wonderful, wonderful time we were planning for them at camp.

As I stood there, I noticed that it was getting darker and darker and the rain was coming down really hard. I had just finished my little speech and

Scholarship Camp, California, circa 1990s

walked away from the microphone when, all of a sudden, there was a crash of thunder and lightning, and flashes of fire actually came right out of the microphone! The lightning had struck one of our trees about half a block away, and that tree went into a cabin and set the cabin on fire. The lightning surge then traveled another thousand feet into one of our other buildings and burned out the electrical in that building. The third strike was in the mess hall. Now, as I look back at that experience, I realize how close I was to having something very serious attack my body.

After all of this was over, we had to find a way of rebuilding that cabin, because many campers were scheduled to be housed there. These campers were placed temporarily in another cabin while we figured out what to do. But the Lord wonderfully brought builders up there, and it was just a matter of a little time until we had that cabin ready again. These are times that we all will always remember, but we thank God for the blessings of Scholarship Camp.

Unusual Dilemma

One of the big joys of my life was the ministry God gave me in directing Camp Awana, along with my mentor, Lance "Doc" Latham. One of the big features of the year took place every Labor Day. We would have all the high-schoolers and the young people come up for a weekend at camp. It was packed full. They all had to register weeks ahead of time to make sure they were on the list for camp. It was such a precious time of fellowship and spiritual training for these young people.

Well, I was responsible for all the maintenance up there, as well as for helping those who were running the program. One year our cook came in to see me and said, "Mr. Rorheim, we have a very big problem. The sewage is running down into our storeroom where we store the food. What can we do?"

Well, I am not a plumber, so I said, "God, you've got to help me." I got some of our key workers together and they went out to dig up some of the septic lines—and they worked, and worked, and worked. At that point we had no running water. If we didn't settle the problem soon, the camp would have to close. There is just no way to operate under those conditions.

Soon it was midnight and, believe me, I was praying hard, saying, "God, what do I do?" Then a car came driving over the hills at Camp Awana. It was one of the campers coming in late. He came up to me and asked where he should bunk. I said, "Well, what is your name?"

He answered, "Jim Atler." I repeated *Atler . . . Atler,* and I told him there was a John Atler that was up here when we first built the camp, who was a plumber and did all of the plumbing for us. To my surprise, he said, "That is my dad and I took over his plumbing business." All of a sudden I realized, *God, did you send someone here to help me?*

At that point I shared my dilemma with him. He asked, "Where is your septic tank?" and I went out to the septic tank with him. It so happened that we had a big compressor there that we used to hook up to our paint cans to spray the cabins, and it was standing right there. Jim said, "Is this thing working?" When I said yes, he asked me to start it up.

We had a large hose connected to that compressor. Next thing you know, he said, "If you don't mind, would you get down into that septic tank?" Let me tell you, with the dilemma I was in, I would have stepped into just about anything, including a septic tank. I got down in there and he asked me to connect the hose over the other entrance. Once that was done, he was going to start up the compressor.

He started it in no time flat, and it was just like a bomb exploded. Everything broke loose and I was covered from head to toe with all of that waste. I had never experienced anything like that in my life. Well, I got out of that tank and I made the fastest run of my life down to the lake to get myself washed up. When I came back up, I told Jim, "If there ever was a time that I had mixed emotions, this was the time, because I was as happy as could be with what took place, but probably as discouraged as could be with what happened to me." *Praise the Lord!* At the very moment I needed help, He sent the right man to take care of my problem.

Around the Globe

THE NEW TRIBES MISSION: FIVE MARTYRS

It is exciting to fellowship with Paul Fleming, the founder of New Tribes Mission. I never met a man who had such a passion for reaching the lost in foreign countries. He just felt that everyone, preachers and lay folk alike, should pack up and go to the countries whose people have never heard the gospel, and that everyone in America, if they really cared, should share the gospel.

It was the beginning days of New Tribes Mission, of which my mentor, Doc Latham, was also one of the co-founders. The first five missionaries going out on behalf of New Tribes were going into the jungles of Bolivia. They were named to go because they were not reaching people in the cities, so they were going back into the jungles where no missionaries had ever been before.

I remember these first five came to our church, the North Side Gospel Center, and gave their testimonies. One of them was an executive at Chrysler Motor Company in Detroit, and probably had a six-figure salary. However, each one of them knew that they had been called of God to go to the mission field.

What a thrill it was, in those early days of the North Side Gospel Center, to hear their testimonies. The very next morning, all of their gear was packed into our church bus and they were driven down to New Orleans, where they were to board a ship that was ready to take them to Brazil.

*First Awana missionaries, circa 1975. First row: David Jamerson, Dale Gerard,
Leo Spencer, and Gene Goertzen; second row: Denton Reilly, Wally Warfield,
Don Bunge, Art Rorheim, and Bob Mayer*

Everyone was talking about what an exciting time it was as these five men
set out for New Tribes. They had not been there for many months, searching
to reach the cannibal peoples with the gospel, when we received the word that
they had all been slain by the natives. What a tragedy!

Still, it was tremendously inspiring to see five men who loved God so
much that they were willing to give their lives for the cause of the gospel.
When they set out, how little did they know that in just a very short time,
they would be giving their lives and arriving in heaven as God's martyrs. To
some, it looked like Satan was having a real victory, and that New Tribes would
be sure to fail since the first five were martyred. Instead, God just seemed to
use this to light a fire under a whole lot of people to get on the team and be
part of New Tribes and go to the foreign mission field.

As I look back at that time, I remember it certainly spoke to me. Even
at that time, I asked, "God, do you want me to go the mission field?" It wasn't
long before I was sure that God wanted Awana to have a world vision heartbeat, and I will forever thank Him that he opened our Awana eyes to reach
out to a lost world.

Carry the Vision

❧ Make it *your* business to reach every life you can, in every way you can, for this important work of world evangelization. There is no better time than *now*, for tomorrow you may be in Heaven. Those *you* would have challenged will be idle still, and the heathen *you* were going to reach will still be on their way to Hell.

❧ Start your day with believing prayer. Ask the Holy Spirit to guide you and to prepare and empower you. Dig deeper into the Word of God. Get out and witness to the lost. Challenge the saved. Write letters and pray when there's no other way.

❧ See to it that *all* available challenging material or other spiritual helps are provided for everyone you know. *Pass on* the message that God has used to awaken you to your responsibility.

❧ Pray for your co-workers, for missionaries, for unevangelized fields, for those in spiritual leadership, and for more Christians who will catch the world vision.

❧ *Eat, live, drink,* and *sleep* your job, for it's the biggest business in the world. If you have caught the vision, *carry it!* May it be so catching that those you reach will carry it to others who in turn will reach others also.

Paul Fleming

GOD'S PROVIDENCE

One of the joys I've had in Awana has been traveling to many countries around the world to visit Awana Clubs there and meet people of different cultures. Yes, some of them have different skin color, their food is challenging, and their way of life can be radically different. But we are all God's children!

Each time I've gone to a foreign country, the Lord has constantly reminded me of one solemn thought, and that is, "I could just as easily have been born here." Apart from the sovereignty of God, which allowed me to be born here in America into a Christian home and to have a Bible-believing church that has challenged me and taught me the ways of God, I could just as well have been born in the jungles of Africa or South America somewhere, worshipping an idol or a witch doctor.

So God has challenged you and me and the church with the Great Commission in MARK 16:15: "Go ye into all the world, and preach the gospel to every creature." At one time, I had to ask myself, did I really have a foreign

Awana Missionary Conference, 1980s

missions heart? I really didn't. God had to get me under great conviction until I was able to say, "Yes, Lord, I will go to any place in the world if that's where you want me to be." It was then that God showed me clearly that the Awana ministry was the world that He wanted me to be involved with.

There are some things that seem to be very unfair, and I believe that God is very concerned about it. There are more than 7 billion people in the world, and of those 7 billion, only about 10 percent speak the English language. It seems, then, when we talk about reaching out to a world and we find that 90 percent of all church funds are being distributed to this 10 percent that speak the English language, this means the other 90 percent of the world receives only 10 percent of the finances of Christians.

I'm told that in the United States we have more than 200 versions of the Bible. It's sobering to realize that a good portion of the world doesn't even have one page of the Bible in their language. Every person in the United States has the opportunity to hear the gospel if they really want to. With the thousands of Bible-believing radio and TV programs that are aired weekly, everyone can hear the truth if they want to. Then again, we realize that a big portion of the world has never even heard *of* the gospel, let alone heard the gospel itself. God has commanded us to go and give it to them.

Awana Missionary Conference

Art and Winnie, fiftieth anniversary of Awana; blanket made by the missionaries

It is reported that the world population increases by about 200,000 every day. About 150,000 go into eternity each day. What a tragedy to think that the majority of them are without Christ. God says, in REVELATION 20:15, "And whosoever was not found written in the book of life was cast into the lake of fire."

I know the reality of hell is something that has to grip my life more than it does. I've been told that there are almost 4 billion people in China and the Asian countries. If we were to stand at a given point and we had them begin marching eight abreast in front of us, they would continue marching forever and that line would never stop. Suppose we were to see that line of people marching over a precipice to their deaths? We'd say, "How tragic!" As tragic as that is, that's only a physical death; when we think of the spiritual death without Christ forever and forever, how much more tragic that is! This tragedy needs to grip my heart and yours, as God calls us to be His messengers to get this marvelous message of Christ to a lost world.

CANADA

I remember, many years ago, meeting one of the most enthusiastic Canadian leaders I had ever encountered. I was so surprised to hear that he was a full-time doctor of chiropractic. He was determined to help the churches

Mrs. and Mr. Bill Allison, Chairman of Canadian Awana, with Winnie and Art

in Canada get their Awana supplies through Customs, so he made his doctor's office a supply center for Canada. It was not long before God provided a beautiful building in Fonthill, Ontario, Canada.

Then God called Phil Whitehead to be the executive director and Bill Allison as the chairman of the Canada Board of Directors of Awana. Then Awana missionaries responded to God's calling. More than 400 churches there have been reaching kids and parents with the marvelous message of God's gospel of grace.

Praise God, more than a million lives have been taught God's Word and are heaven-bound. We thank God for the faithful, steadfast, Canadian Awana leadership.

Canadian Adventure

After speaking at a banquet one night in Florida, I received a treasured surprise gift. I was approached by John Pattan, a man I had never met before, who told me that God had laid on his heart to give Awana a beautiful fishing lodge. He said that he had one of the most beautiful, scenic places in Canada on the Aguawa Canyon and Montreal River. It was only accessible by train. Now, the largest tour trestle train bridge in Canada stops at the Awana train station at the entrance of this wilderness Canadian camp.

On one of my train trips to camp, I made a mistake and got off at the wrong station. I then had a very serious problem. My only way to reach camp was to walk, carrying my two suitcases, across the huge trestle bridge that

Awana's Canadian headquarters

spans the Montreal River. There was no other way to reach camp. My big concern was, "What if the train comes while I am out on the trestle bridge?" There was no way I could get off or step to the side: I would, without question, be hit by the train.

Finally I proceeded on my daring walk across the bridge. The railroad ties between the tracks were all I had to walk on. As I cautiously stepped from one railroad tie to another, I found myself getting a little dizzy and I thought I was going to fall and not be able to get up. While sitting on my suitcase, I cried out to God to help me and after a short rest I continued walking to the end of the bridge. Shortly after I got off the bridge, the train did come, and I cried out to God saying, "Thank You! Thank You! Thank You! for once again sparing my life."

I am fully persuaded that God sent His angels to protect me yet again in one of my foolish adventures; PSALM 34:7 says, "The angel of the Lord encampeth round about them that fear him, and delivereth them."

VENEZUELA: MY FIRST JUNGLE EXPERIENCE

I was raised in a fundamentalist, Bible-based Christian church that had a heart for foreign missions. Although I heard many godly missionaries speak, their messages didn't seem to impact my life.

As I became executive director of Awana in those early days, I felt that the only ministry that Awana could undertake was to reach boys and girls here in America. Then God sent across my path one of the most godly missionaries I believe the world has ever seen: Paul Fleming, who became the founder of New Tribes Missions. You could not talk to him for more than five or ten minutes without hearing his heart burden about reaching the lost in foreign countries. He was very anxious for me to catch the vision, so in a very exciting but practical way, he asked me to go on the missionary plane with Doc Latham down to the jungles of Venezuela.

Flying over the jungles was a very exciting experience. With my head next to the pilot, I took pictures of the jungle. I saw some smoke coming out of the treetops from the native peoples' fires, and I could not help but think, *This jungle is filled with people who never heard of the gospel and are hell-bound. We must reach them.*

Soon it came time to land our plane in the jungle. No plane had ever come in there before, so they had no runway, but they had cleared off a space by taking the trees down. When we first flew by, there were animals all over in the cleared area. Finally, the plane landed, and this was quite exciting because the natives had never seen anything like it before. They gathered around us to see this "big bird," as they called it. I was willing to

Art and Doc cooking in Venezuela, 1950s

Leaders' conference in Venezuela, circa 2000

just get down there and mingle with them and it wasn't long before I had my movie camera out and was taking pictures.

While I was taking these pictures, God spoke to me and said, "Why don't you get these kids to get involved in a game period, because they have never played games before?" Well, that was quite a job, because I didn't have any equipment with me and I couldn't speak their language. I really didn't think that this could be done. More and more the Lord spoke to me: "Just try it and I will help you do it."

I needed someone to translate for me, so I asked a fellow who knew a little English to help me. I asked him how he became a Christian and he told me the most interesting story. He said, "I was desperate and I just thought there was nothing really in life that was worthwhile. I was drifting, traveling through the jungles, and I came upon this missionary station. There I met the missionary who seemed to take such a personal interest in me and show me from God's Word how I could be sure of going to heaven. That way was only if I trusted Christ to be my Savior and that God had an exciting plan for my life. From that moment on, I knew I was different and I had a joy that I had never experienced before."

I asked him who that missionary was, and to my surprise he told me the missionary's name was Wally Warfield. Wally Warfield was one of my closest friends while I was growing up; he went to camp with me when I was just ten years old! He became the second missionary from the North

Side Gospel Center, and with his new bride he went down into Brazil. After quite a few years, he had to return because of health reasons, and then he became our first foreign missionary director for Awana. So it was such a blessing—and just think, I had to go all the way to Venezuela to hear this beautiful story of my dear friend Wally.

I went down into the bush and got some sticks that we used for the four corners of the Awana game area. Then I found some sharp sticks and I scratched out the circle on the riverbank. We invited all the kids to come for the game time we were planning to have.

I was so surprised when not only some of the kids showed up, but the whole village came as well. I lined up well over a hundred kids on this big square, and they were all looking at this white man in the center of the circle, wondering what he was going to do. I too was wondering what I was going to do!

I realized that this was completely different from game time in the States. For example, competing in those games I had thirteen- and fourteen-year-old girls who already had husbands. I started with some of the simple, basic Awana relay games. I had hardly gotten started when I saw the kids' eyes light up and big smiles appear on their faces. The enthusiasm that was there was electric. Right then and there, God reminded me that kids are the same all around the world: They respond to people who truly love them. I knew right then and there that God had something more for me in the foreign field.

After the game period was over, I had an experience I will never forget. A little boy named Buano, who was about eight years old, was incapable of playing in a game with us. He wasn't born with a healthy body; he had half a leg removed from one side and there he was with a cane and just a little loincloth that was all he owned. I am sure he did not weigh more than sixty or seventy pounds. He came up to me with a smile on his face and said, "Mr. Rorheim, I know Jesus Christ as my personal Savior and some day He is going to give me a new body just like His."

What an awesome testimony from a little boy who had nothing in this world—but I was stunned by the knowledge he had and that he had trusted Christ as his Savior. His faith was more profound than all the great minds that put spaceships on the moon and all the tremendous technology of today; all of the knowledge that they have is not worth a snap of the finger compared to this precious little boy's. Praise the Lord for the missionary

Art with Venezuelan clubbers

who was able to get the gospel to him, so that he understood it and truly believed. I believe someday I'm going to see Buano up there in heaven and he is going to be clothed like all of us, as we will be clothed in the righteousness of God. That was a precious moment that I will never forget.

It was a real shock to hear that on the very next trip, when that plane flew back into Venezuela, it had crashed and everybody on board had died. I knew the two pilots very well; they were Cliff Martz and Ben Weatheral, who were very capable pilots. The crash was caused by of a lack of information. The attendants on the base that the pilots would normally talk to by radio had called it quits for the day and had gone home. So, those pilots were more or less flying on their own, and that was the reason for the crash. I thank God how He wonderfully saved Doc Latham and myself, because it could have been us in that crash.

I knew that God wanted Awana to get involved in foreign missions, but I was in a quandary because we had nothing in Awana that a person could use in that environment, no uniforms or awards that would fit in a jungle setting. As I flew home, I knew that I needed to depend on God. I prayed, "Now, God, you have to show us what to do." I began talking to some of our missionaries at home, and I started taking a few trips to foreign countries, and little by little God showed us how to communicate with the different cultures. Now Awana is in more than 110 countries all over the world, and the kids in those countries are being reached with the gospel. A lot of work was done to translate books into all those languages. Awana is now reaching into China; it is just amazing the doors that God is opening for Awana. So God has challenged Awana to obey the Great Commission to go into all the world and preach the gospel to every creature. May we be obedient to fulfill the ministry that He has called Awana to be a part of.

LIBERIA

I've had the blessed opportunity of traveling to more than fifty countries of the world to see how God has blessed the Awana ministry. One of the first countries that God blessed with Awana was Liberia. One of our former camp leaders, Walt Kroemeyer, was a tremendous missionary in Liberia. He and his wife lived with the people. They found a young Liberian boy whom they led to the Lord, and then nurtured him with Scripture, and mentored him through Bible school, and saw him become a pastor. Then God wonderfully allowed him to become the Awana missionary to Liberia.

An Awana headquarters building was built there and named the Latham Building. Then tragedy struck, as three forces of rebels began fighting against one another. They took no prisoners. They killed everybody they came in contact with. The beautiful ELWA radio station there in Liberia was completely destroyed.

Here is a copy of the letter I received from John Gaye, describing the tragedy of what took place in Liberia:

> One day the rebels entered the city with their purpose to kill everyone. My daughter and I started running away. She went another direction and I started to Sierra Leone where my wife and children were. The rebels have lots of checkpoints on the way. Dead bodies were lying on the way through. I was walking together with my friend when we got to the last checkpoint.
>
> We were arrested and our hands were tied behind our backs. My friend was standing and I was kneeling down. One of the rebels came behind my friend with a machete and cut off his head. I was the next to be killed. One rebel hit me with his gun butt on my face and two of my teeth were knocked out. I was kneeling down saying, "Lord, I'm coming home." But right then one of the rebels remembered me as the Awana missionary and told his friend rebel not to kill me. Praise God he let me go and gave me a pass.

This man was my Awana leader in the club before, but I did not recognize him because he was wearing a mask on his face. The rebels caught my daughter Elizabeth, and they beat her and raped her for five months continuously. She finally was able to run away from them. The rebels even gave her a gun to kill someone, but she refused to do so. She told them, "My father said I shouldn't kill anybody." The rebels told her to stand by and watch as they cut a pregnant woman open with a bayonet in front of her.

I often look at many of the pictures I took in Liberia and realize that maybe half of the people in them are now with the Lord. But I do praise the Lord for the faithful leaders who gave of themselves unselfishly to win hundreds of kids to Christ there in Liberia.

John Gaye and My Introduction

I can remember so well looking forward to going to Liberia, because John Gaye, our missionary, was there waiting for me. He said he had many pastors whom he wanted me to see. I wasn't sure just what-all he was talking about. I remember the day we landed in Liberia. Getting out of the plane, I couldn't believe the weather. It seemed like it was 110 degrees with high humidity. I realized immediately that I was going into a drastically different climate.

The real anticipation of this trip, as it is with all of the trips I have taken, is: Will all the luggage make it to the destination? If you ever want your heart to sink, it is when you stand there at the luggage belt and see all the luggage come through and realize that yours is not part of it. Here you are in a foreign country, without any of your clothes or supplies, and then you need to be able to communicate with someone of authority in another language. It is quite a project just trying to find people who will listen to you, because they don't really seem to care at that point. I had done all that I could do to let them know that my luggage had been lost.

Then came along our Awana missionary, John Gaye, saying, "Art, we are going to have to hurry. There is a pastors' meeting out in the jungle and they are expecting you to be there." In Liberia, they do not have newspapers or any way of communicating other than by radio, and they had announced that I was going to be there.

We traveled for about three hours and finally arrived at this hut, as I would call it. It wasn't very large and it had a bamboo roof. I went into a room that was packed full of people; you could cut the humidity with a knife, and the odors were something that I had never experienced before. But the joy and welcome that were displayed were really a blessing to me. They wanted me to speak for a little bit, which I was able to do and communicate because so many of them understood English. Then, to show their appreciation for my coming, they presented me with a gift: a big, heavy, beautiful robe. When they put it on me, I thought I was in a sauna bath. I thought, *How in the world can I ever function with this robe on me?*, but I was very courteous to them and I let them know that I liked the robe.

Then they said they were going to have a supper for us. I saw the women with big bowls getting rice together. Of course, they were mixing it with their hands. They had their babies next to them and they would stop in between mixing, change the diapers, and then continue with the rice. Well, I didn't think that I was going to enjoy that supper very much, but then again, you have to be courteous. There in Liberia, everyone sits down on the floor to eat, but they were kind enough to find a chair for me. There they were, all eating their rice, and they all were eating with their hands. This was my first experience seeing people eat like that, but somewhere along the line they realized that I could not do that very well, and they found a fork for me. As I looked at the rice—and I like rice very much—I noticed these fish eyes, which was their delicacy, that they had put on top just for my benefit.

The love and the joyful spirit they had were so refreshing, even though my physical being was not feeling very well. I could not wait until the service was over and I could get outside, but when I got outside the temperature was still well over 100 degrees. I wondered where I was going to get a shower, or if I could at least go down to the river so that I could wash off, but I found that none of these options was available to me. Remember, I had no clothes to change into, so this was really a challenging experience. I lived in the clothes that I had on for some three days, and I'll have to say that I kind of looked and smelled like the natives by that time.

Our missionary, John Gaye, said that they had a very special club out in Samay, and that since they were planning a big program just for me, we were going to have to leave. It was going to be about an eight-hour trip through the jungle. Again, it was a challenging experience just riding in their vehicles, which seem to be held together with wire at best.

I remember that when we arrived there, I could not believe what I was seeing. There was practically an entire village sitting there on the riverbank, waiting for me to arrive. I really could not believe it. It was hot, but there they were, and as I arrived they stood up and cheered. I was so delighted that I was able to be there. Then they told me that they had a program that they had been planning for me and wanted us to follow them. I followed them into their bamboo hut, which was their church building, and I sat there wondering just what were they going to do.

Now this was out in the jungle, and their commander, a man by the name of Jerome Siakor, led this group in song. Just where he had learned all of these techniques and how he was able to lead them so well, I don't know, but I was just amazed as they started to sing, and they sang with enthusiasm. It was song after song after song, and what a blessing it was just to hear them sing.

Then they said they wanted to share their program with me. I wondered what this was going to be. They started off with two children who were about Pal and Chum ages (eight-, nine-, and ten-year-olds), who were going to show how they had memorized their Scripture. They felt that when you memorize Scripture, it should be used to lead people to Christ, so they had two of these children have a dialogue between each other, one taking the

Club leaders in Liberia

place of an unsaved person asking questions and the other one beautifully reciting the verses to persuade him that this is what God had to say. How delighted I was to see that!

They went to the next stage, and that time it was the Pioneers and Pals. They did the same thing and it was even livelier by far. This went on and on and on. One would play the devil's advocate and the other was the one who said God had the answers to it all. The last one was the high-schoolers and they did the same thing. I sat there and thought, *I have never seen anything done so beautifully in all my life in all the clubs that I have seen down through the years and in the States.*

After the program, they took me around to see the various huts where the people lived and they showed me a little bamboo hut that I was to stay in. It had nothing but mud floors and just a little bit of a cot that I was to sleep on, which I was very ready to do.

As the days went on, they shared many, many things with me. They shared that they were from a tribe that the enemy rebel tribes did not like and that their lives were in jeopardy. I knew that the rebels could very easily come in and slay them—but these people displayed such beautiful faith. That night, they said they would have a campfire, and even though it was really hot, we went up to the campfire. There I sat and saw them all walking around the campfire singing and praising the Lord. They went from

Game circle in Liberia

one song to another and on and on and on. I was so tired that I left about midnight, but they did not leave. I'm not sure what time they stopped, but I truly enjoyed all the devotion and the heartbeat they had for really trusting the Lord.

Tragedy

Some time later a tragedy took place. It was some months later that we got the news that the rebels had gone in there with their guns, not to take any prisoners but to kill everybody they could. With all the candor of this club, Jerome Siakor and his family received some notice that this would happen, and they, with all their family, went into the woods, leaving the village with just the things on their backs that they could carry out, and they headed toward Ghana, which is quite a distance from Liberia. They were in flight when the rebels came in and began to assassinate all of these villagers. Many of them fled into the jungle, but many of them were unable to leave because they were elderly or they were children. All of them were slain.

Jerome Siakor and his family kept faithfully moving through the jungle, eating whatever they could find to eat, and made their way through to escape. It was maybe a month before they got into Ghana. Now, what a joy it is to know that Jerome Siakor is currently the missionary to Liberia! It may seem strange, when you realize everything that took place and caused him to have to flee, but when everything quieted down, his heartbeat was to go back to Liberia. He went by himself and found only a little shack without electricity. Practically everything had been destroyed. The Awana headquarters building that we had built—the building that John Gaye had lived in—had been completely destroyed as well. Nothing was there, but he wanted to get the Awana Club started again. Months later, little by little, he started to reach other people who had Awana clubs and they got one started . . . then another one, and now there are about sixty churches in Liberia because of one man's faithfulness, who was willing to pay the price to get Awana started.

Prior to this, I was looking forward to an Olympic meet that we were planning to have in Monrovia (the capital of Liberia). Participants were coming in from many different areas, and it was so beautiful to see them starting to arrive. Many of them walked for miles and miles to get there. I have a picture in my office that I took there; I treasure it, and I often look at that as one of my "tragedy pictures." It shows all of them happy and competing, having a wonderful time. I remember the Monrovian pastor who gave a beautiful message to everyone there, and then when I look at that picture I realize that perhaps half of the people in it are now in eternity. I think about some of the kids who were there. Did we get the gospel to them? Did they really believe the Word of God? God only knows if that happened, and it makes us realize once again that we need to take advantage of every opportunity we have to present the gospel, because we may never have that opportunity again.

So, despite the many tragic things that took place there, Liberia holds many, many precious memories for me.

Arrest

I had just gotten my new video camera and I made my way into Liberia all by myself. Two of my friends who had traveled with me, Arne Abrahamsen and John Deck, were back at the base. They did not feel that they had to go along with me and so I went by myself.

I went right into the heart of Monrovia. It is just a jungle of people, cars with horns blowing, and markets everywhere. You cannot understand how people can live in conditions like this. It was very, very warm, but I thought, *Here is my opportunity get some pictures.* I saw a Liberian policeman and I asked if it would be all right to take his photo, and he nodded that I could go ahead.

So there I was, taking pictures and feeling that I had gotten some really excellent ones. All of a sudden, I heard some sirens blowing and I saw some policemen pulling out their guns—and they were coming toward me as if I were Public Enemy Number One! They were shouting at me, and kept shouting, and I did not know what in the world had really happened. Of course, they were asking me what kind of a spy I was to shoot pictures and then, with guns drawn, they took and bundled me into their police car. There I sat in the car as I was arrested by the policemen, wondering what was going to happen to me now. I am glad that I did not know the mindset of the Liberians, the way they would kill someone for nothing at all. Anyway, there I sat, hot as could be, when the Lord did something wonderful. God's timing is astonishing: There I was in the police car, and one of the Awana leaders happened to be going by; he saw me in the police car, and

Arnie Abrahamsen and Art

of course he was very, very disturbed. He went and got a couple of other leaders and talked with these two policemen for about forty-five minutes to persuade them to let me go. After probably about an hour, they opened the door and allowed me to go.

I was so thrilled to get out of there! It was also a miracle that they did not take my camera equipment away from me. I look at that incident as one of my real Liberian miracles that God protected me in once again.

MOSCOW

One of my most exciting foreign trips was the first trip I took to Russia. I remember as I got on the 747 to head over to Moscow, I was quite anxious to see what Russia was actually like. As I was sitting there on the plane, in came about twenty-five of the sharpest-looking, best-dressed men I have even seen together.

I was rather curious, and I began talking with them. I found out that they were Mormon missionaries. I also learned that the Mormon church had a missionary force of 26,000 volunteers. Each volunteer spends 20 hours a week going door to door and memorizing more than 130 pages of materials to prepare for dealing with potential converts. I privately wondered how many missionaries Awana would have if that were a prerequisite to become one of our missionaries. It was obvious that they were devoted and had a passion for a religion which, we know sadly, is not centered around Calvary.

As our plane landed there in Moscow, I expected to see an exciting-looking airport. I could not believe how run-down the airport was—to think that this was the prime airport for Communism! As I was driven down the street, I realized that there were no advertising signs; because everything was owned by the government, there were no private enterprises to promote anything. I also noticed, as I was riding in the taxi, that practically all of the vehicles had broken windshields. Having something repaired was almost impossible.

Of course, touring the square with the communist emblems and seeing the buildings there made me realize that I was in anti-God territory. But then my attention was drawn to several soldiers who were marching back and forth in front of a tomb. As I looked closer, I found this was Lenin's tomb, and they were honoring this man.

We know the history of Lenin: He was the most vicious murderer of all the Communists—and to think that here they are honoring this man. I could not help but think that if Lenin were to come back and appear with me at that tomb, what do you think he would say? Would he be interested in people honoring him? No, I don't think so; the plea from his heart would be: "Oh, I'm in eternity. I am in hell and what I would give to be able to do my life over again, to realize that all of the religion that I had of hating God and any of the things of God and how wrong I was." I just could not help but think how blessed I was to know the truth and to know that I am heaven-bound.

REVELATION 20:15: "And whosoever was not found written in the book of life was cast into the lake of fire."

INDIA

I was with our Awana missionary in India and had gone through many experiences during the day. I was very tired—exhausted, in fact—but I was going to have to travel to get into Delhi for my next visit. They wanted to be kind to me and let me take the train where I would be able to lie down and maybe sleep, or at least get some much-needed rest.

Well, as you travel to the train station, you see many tragic families all over the place, inside the train station and even outside. It is terrible because they have no homes, and your heart just goes out to them.

They told me the train was supposed to arrive at midnight, but they were not sure if there would be anything available for me at that time. When the train pulled in, our missionary told me to just stay there and he would check it out for me. It was about fifteen minutes later when he came back and said, "You are very fortunate because there is one bunk open for you. So come on in and bring your luggage." After I entered, I noticed it was very warm, but I was so glad just to get in there and get into what I thought would be a nice air-conditioned train.

As I walked into the train, it was actually very scary. It was just a dimly lit hall, and as you went through, there were doors that led into these little cabins. Finally they stopped and pulled open a door and said, "OK, this is your bed"—and what a shock it was. I found out that the cabin was for four people and there were already three men in there. It was completely dark, no lights at all, and they told me that the top bunk was mine. I got up on that bunk and could not believe what I found: There was a small place to sleep, but it was on a piece of plywood. That was my bunk . . . and to think that I was going to collapse there for six to eight hours on my way to Delhi! That was an experience that I will never, ever forget. There was no air conditioning and the heat was absolutely unbearable.

I also wondered to myself, *Who am I actually staying with? I do not know who these men are or how trustworthy they are, but there You are, Lord. I am in the midst of a situation that You have allowed me to be a part of and I am just going to trust You that You are going to take care of me.* I have used the expression, "I think I spent a week on that bunk in just one night." I know it was only six to eight hours, but it seemed like a week. I just never thought that the train would ever arrive.

As I look back, the Lord wonderfully took care of me, and we had a wonderful time in Delhi as I visited with our missionaries there. As I think today of the more than 1,500 churches that are in India, that is just another miracle to see what God has done since that day, which was more than twenty years ago.

Daring and Scary

I was lying on my bed one night in a hostel-type facility in Delhi, India. You will never fully understand what Delhi or India are like without having been there personally and experienced the culture. Poverty is everywhere. People, animals, and unwanted children sleep along the streets.

As I lay on my bed about 2 o'clock in the morning, I could hear the Muslim chanting over the loudspeakers from the big Muslim temple just a few blocks away. As I typically do whenever I'm in a foreign country, I kept thinking, *I could just as well have been born here.* Here are all these people who are hell-bound and don't know the Savior.

There was no air conditioning in that hot room and some of the odors were not too friendly. In my frustration, I decided to get up and do something that perhaps could have been very unwise. I took my video camera and walked toward the temple to see if I could possibly get in and see where all this chanting was going on.

The streets were dark and there were people sleeping everywhere. I must admit it was a very scary walk. The temple had a large wall built around a full square-block area. I saw a small door in the wall and tried to open it. Believe it or not, it was open and I walked in. Immediately a Muslim priest greeted me. You can imagine what was going through my mind as to how he was going to accept me. Not knowing the language, I indicated with my video camera that I would like to take some pictures. To my amazement, he smiled at me and indicated that I should come with him. He took me to another room of the temple where he sat me down and told me to take off my shoes. Then another priest came to meet me and put one of the Muslim skullcaps on me. He indicated that I should follow him.

As I walked through many of the dark corridors of the temple, I wondered what I had gotten myself into. It wasn't long before we approached what you could call their "holy of holies": a large gold door that the priest opened and told me to go in. Then he led me right up to where the priests were doing all of their chanting over the public address system throughout the city. He indicated to me that I could take pictures of the priests as they chanted. There were also parishioners in this holy-of-holies atmosphere who had crawled up hundreds of steps on their knees through a long corridor to be there.

I looked into the faces of these dear, sincere people for whom Christ died and was overwhelmed with the thought that they did not know the truth. They never had the opportunity I had to hear the Word of God shared with them by godly people. Quite often, as I wake up in the middle of the night these days, I think of hearing those chanting sounds coming from the Muslim temple there in India.

ECUADOR

Quito, Ecuador, is an interesting city located some 8,000 feet above sea level. This is the town where Clarence Jones decided to set up the transmitters for Radio Station HCJB. That was almost seventy years ago, when he accepted the challenge that God had given him. From that location, in perhaps twenty languages, they are broadcasting this precious message of the gospel around the world every day.

Another interest I have in Quito is that my granddaughter and her husband and our three great-grandchildren are there as missionaries. My granddaughter directs the Awana Clubs there. On one of my visits to Quito I had the privilege of flying down into the jungles of Ecuador. There is an outpost in a little village called Shell. From there we flew into an even smaller village. I walked through the jungles with another missionary. The mud seemed to be over our ankles and we had a difficult time just standing upright.

Finally we reached the river. There we were met by a native who had a dugout canoe. Dugouts are what these craft really are: dug out of a log, narrow, and apparently very easy to tip over. I carefully got into the canoe, just trying to protect my camera equipment lest we tip over and lose it all. This was truly a jungle area. We paddled up the river for some time and finally the natives stopped and told us to get out on the riverbank. As we stood there, we were told that this was the exact place where the five missionaries were slain by the rebels whom they were trying to reach for the Lord by giving them the gospel. I couldn't help but think, *Here were five men who really loved the Lord, so much that they were willing to give their lives for that cause.* They knew before they went into the jungle area that this was a possibility, but they were willing because of their love for their Lord. Then, what a shocking experience it was to learn that the native who had paddled me up there was also one of the killers—who is now a born-again Christian and is now rejoicing in the Lord.

Then we met Dayuma, who was the young girl who came out of the jungle and became the liaison to the missionary wives to help them reach the natives who were responsible for killing their husbands. What a testimony it was to see these five women who did not give up when their husbands were killed; instead, they were willing to stay to reach the tribe that their husbands had given their lives for.

Art with Dayuma, translator from Ecuador

It was a real thrill to find that just a short distance away, there was an Awana Club that was reaching the kids in that area. A tragedy had also recently taken place there: The husband of the director of the Awana Club was a missionary pilot and had been killed a few weeks earlier in a plane crash. His wife had been receiving pleas from her folks to come back to America now that her husband was gone. Here she was with three children to raise, but she said, "God has called me here to reach the children of Ecuador and I trust God will use me all through this country." These are some of God's great and beautiful people who had a real impact on my life.

GHANA

It was probably in the late 1960s that I met a man by the name of Noah Quarshie. He was from Ghana, and he came up to me and said, " I just saw these Olympics and they are amazing. We have to have that in Ghana. Would you come and run them for us, if we get Olympics?"

I said, "Of course, I will be glad to do that, but you do not have any clubs there." He responded by saying that he would get clubs there. So he asked for samples of the books and also samples of the Olympic books, and I thought very little more about what he had had to say, not thinking that anything would ever materialize.

Game circle in Ghana, circa 1980

About a year later, I received a phone call and the voice on the other end said, "This is Noah Quarshie and you promised you would come if we have the clubs and we have the clubs." He assured me over and over that he did. Well, I had made a promise, so I thought I had better honor it and respond to him.

I had the surprise of surprises when I flew into Ghana, got off the plane, walked through the concourse, and got outside. There greeting me were about thirty Awana leaders singing the Awana theme song for me! I could not believe what I saw. And then I saw Noah, with his smile from ear to ear, and he said, ""We've got wonderful things happening and tomorrow we are going to be having the Olympics. In the meantime, everybody is excited because I have you on the radio program for one hour. And in the Olympics, we are going to have a band that will be leading all the teams over to the Olympic area. We have the Secretary of State that will be there and we will give him some recognition as well."

He went on and on and I protested, "Now wait a minute, how is this all going to happen? We have no missionaries here and we did not have anyone here that had ever seen an Awana Club in action. How is this going to happen?"

They took me over to his church where all the teams were planning to congregate, and one team after another showed up. They all had beautiful,

Clubbers in Ghana

big signs with the name of their church. Then the band arrived, and they started a parade down the main streets, proudly marching and singing. I have a video that I enjoy showing, as this really was a miracle. We finally got to the area where the Olympics was to be held. Fortunately, I had two of my able assistants, Arne Abrahamsen and John Deck. They were familiar with the Olympics and they were there ready to help run the Ghanaian Awana Olympics.

All of the participants lined up beautifully and when the flag count was given, there they were in perfect silence. When the games were given, I thought, *How are they going to play these games, and who taught them these games?* Arne announced the games and they started one of the sprint races. They continued going through the Olympic games and you would have absolutely thought that they had played those games all of their lives. What a beautiful job was done.

I asked to see one of the team's churches. They took me out into the jungle and when we got out there, I saw that a beautiful Awana circle had been dug out—right there in the dirt, the entire circle!—and there they put on a game demonstration. It was done just as well as anything we had ever done here in the States. Then they took me into the church, where they would be going through the handbook time, and we saw the handbook sessions.

Ghana Olympics

The kids were taking it all in and the leaders acted as if they had prepared for this for their whole lives. I could not believe it!

They also took me into the council time where they were to give the message, but prior to the message, they all sang songs, and they sang beautifully.

Ghana Olympic winners

The leader had a beautiful chart up there and he gave the way of salvation. It could not have been more clear or more outstanding, and I thought to myself, *Praise God!*

There are leaders who are going to continue and just keep on making things happen for the glory of God. I dare to say I marvel. God had to do a miracle there, because as I talked to the leaders, I asked, "How did you learn all of these things?" They told me they took the leaders' manuals and practically memorized every step in them. It just made us feel so good to think that our manuals were written so well that they could put on an Olympic and Awana game program as beautifully as they did just by studying our books. Yes, that was really a God miracle.

SOUTH KOREA

Of the many countries that I have traveled to, the country of South Korea has always particularly fascinated me. The people are so friendly and their food is very delicious. When you sit down in a restaurant, you find a food warmer in front of you on the table. No other country has so many selections on the table to choose from. Their kids are happy and very smart and learn very quickly.

It was more than twenty years ago when I first visited Korea to present Awana. They were very willing to adopt Awana into their culture. However, it took many years before the Korean leadership caught the vision to reach out in the country to get the churches to see the spiritual vision to reach their children with the Word of God.

Then Billy and Deborah Lee caught the vision and became Awana missionaries. They used all of the Awana uniforms and the award system. It was thrilling to see what a couple can do to train leadership and then light the fire to do a job for God. It was obvious that God's hand was upon them in the Awana ministry, as it grew rapidly.

Later I was invited to a special Awana game celebration in honor of my ninety-first birthday. Billy knew that one of my favorite chapters in the Bible is Psalm 1, the passage that we have shared in the Angola prison to the inmates as well as to many churches across the country. To my big surprise, he had challenged the leadership and the clubbers to recite to me there in this arena. There they stood, perhaps some two or three thousand of them, and in unison recited Psalm 1. What a thrill that was for me!

Billy Lee, Awana director in Korea, with Art

As a special tribute to me, I was presented with one of my life's most precious gifts: a handwritten Korean Bible. Thirteen hundred Korean leaders had beautifully hand-scripted each page of the Bible. It was beautifully leather-bound into six editions, each one handwritten in its entirety from GENESIS to REVELATION. It is truly my most treasured gift, and I have it displayed near my desk in my office at Awana International headquarters.

I will forever thank God for the love of Billy and Deborah Lee and the Korean leaders who gave me my most precious earthly gift. I just say, "Thank You, Lord, for the many godly people who have come across my path."

CULTURAL SURPRISES

Japanese Delicacies

It has been my privilege to travel, on behalf of Awana, to more than fifty countries around the world. As you visit these countries, you can't help but marvel at the handiwork of God as He has created these various distinct cultures. Not only are their languages different, but their foods and their ways of life are also very different. In fact, food is usually one of the challenges of traveling.

On one of my trips to Japan, I experienced a rather humorous time in a restaurant. We know that in these latter years, Japan has become famous for its sushi, which of course is raw fish. Now, I have never had an appetite for that. But while sitting in a Japanese restaurant, my eyes were opened wide when I saw the waitress bring a large, two-foot-long, live fish for someone to eat at the table next to me. It wasn't long before the fish, which was very uncomfortable, flipped and jumped off the table—only to be picked up, cleaned up, and brought back. It wasn't long before I, too, was to receive one of those surprises.

One of the Japanese missionaries really wanted to treat me to the finest food in his culture, and he had selected two fish in the tank we passed on the way in that were to be delivered to me. Now, these fish are actually filleted, but it doesn't seem to affect their livelihood. Their tails still wiggle and their eyes move, and I can assure you that this was not one of my favorite delicacies.

Indian Delicacies

Now let me take you to India. I had the privilege of having the missionary there take me into a quaint village. These people live in such a small world that when I arrived, they practically looked at me as a priest or a god who had come to visit them. They were so thrilled that they had to sit us down and serve us their best delicacies. It wasn't long before a fancy little cup was presented to me with some sort of material inside. I can assure you, the odor by itself frightened me. But all the eyes of the family were watching intently to see how well I was going to enjoy this.

At times like this, I really pray that the Lord will help me to be polite and be able to keep the food down and be able to digest it. Well, by faith I took and slurped this food down, really wondering how long it would stay down. I'm so glad I did not know what I was eating until afterward. I was told that this was their special delicacy that they only give to special people. Perhaps you have seen native women sitting around a large pan, chewing on the roots of trees. After they have chewed them for a while, they will take and spit them into this pan. Then all of this is fermented until it is ready to be eaten. Yes, I've encountered many other uncomfortable foods, but they all are incidental to this one.

Indian Train Ride

I'll never forget the all-night train ride I took while I was still in India. I was to meet the train at midnight at the station. I had never been to a train

Art in India

station like that, with people and entire families sleeping all over. When the train stopped, they had to check to see if a place was available for me. The missionary who had suggested the train wanted to be kind to me, and felt I should have a place to sleep rather than have to sit up all night. We went through the train and finally they said there was one spot open. As I walked down the corridor of this train, with hardly any lights, it was really scary.

The conductor opened a door and said I was to stay in the little cabin there. I walked in and found out there were three other people in there sleeping already. One of the upper bunks was to be mine. As I climbed up, I found out that the "bunk" was nothing more than a piece of plywood. The train had no air conditioning, and this was to be an eight-hour trip. I really wondered whether I could hold out that long. The scary feeling of not even knowing who was in the room with you and then the tremendous heat made me very glad to come to the end of the train ride. Praise the Lord, I had no ill effects.

20,000 Indians

While in India, I had the opportunity to speak to about 20,000 Indians, entire families who were sitting there, in an evangelistic effort. The missionary

Art and Winnie in the Philippines

there had asked me if I would speak to them and I spoke through an interpreter for about forty-five minutes. Then I was expecting the meeting to have a benediction and come to a close. How little did I know the way they do things in India!

After I got through speaking, another speaker got up and spoke for forty-five minutes, and I was sure that then the meeting would end. It was extremely hot, and the people were all just sitting on the ground; it looked so uncomfortable! There were little children and babies sitting there, and I just couldn't believe that they were as patient as they were. Then, after the next speaker finished, the evangelist got up and I thought, *He's going to take and finalize it.* Well, he must have spoken for close to an hour, but the people were all still patient. He made an invitation and many of those in the audience came forward to trust Christ.

After the meeting was finally closed, I was amazed to see about fifty of these Indians line up to talk with me. I couldn't understand why it was so important to speak with me. They had something in their hands. It wasn't long before I realized that this was something I had never encountered before. These people had evidently been taught some biblical truths and they had some very serious physical problems. They wanted me to pray with them and

Preschool children, South Africa

anoint them all with oil. Well, that was a challenge that I have never, ever experienced before or since. I must admit I had to get the assistance of the evangelist, who was an Indian, to handle this for me. I praise the Lord for the seriousness of these folks in dealing with their illnesses in a scriptural way.

When we think about India, with its some 300 million children, I can't help but wonder how they are going to be reached for Christ. We're thankful for the Awana missionary, who is doing an excellent job. But I often wonder how some of these Indian women even exist when I see the poverty they live in. I see how early in the morning these dear women are sitting with some of their meager wares to sell, maybe with a child in their arms. I could be there late at night and they would still be there. I wondered how they could physically handle that.

Something that really bothered me was to see women involved in the construction of a large building. This building was composed of cement forms. I saw about ten dear women; they looked like they didn't weigh much more than 100 pounds, but here they were lining up with tubs on their heads that would be filled with concrete. Then they had to walk at least 100 feet with this concrete on their heads and then it was to be dumped. I saw them doing this all day long. I just couldn't even see how they could stay alive. I couldn't

Africa, near the Cape

help but think how blessed we are when we think of the comforts that we all have and we realize that we didn't choose the place of our birth. We could have just as well been born there.

Every time I go to a foreign country, I just thank the Lord that He allowed me to be born where I am now, and to be able to hear the gospel. But He also challenges us to have a heart to reach these people around the world with the precious message of the gospel of Jesus Christ.

Art and Winnie in Cairo, Egypt

Winnie and Art while visiting an Awana Club in Hawaii

Art's rock collection, gathered from all over the world, displayed in his office

The Rorheims near Mt. Rainier, Seattle, Washington

People

INTERESTING PEOPLE I HAVE MET

Apart from my mentor, Lance Latham, Paul Rader, the pastor of the Chicago Gospel Tabernacle, was without question the most unusual man I have ever met. His ministry at the Chicago Gospel Tabernacle was an inspiration to me and perhaps thousands of others.

Chief Whitefeather, the grandson of the famous Sitting Bull, was also a very interesting man. God blessed him with an unusual voice, which earned him an opportunity to sing for the Queen of England. He was also the man who named all of the buildings at Camp Awana.

William R. Newell, the writer of the beloved hymn, "At Calvary," was a tremendous theologian and Bible teacher. Perhaps of all other people, he taught my mentor, Doc Latham, the most about the clear message of the gospel of grace. Visiting him in his home in Deland, Florida, was a thrilling experience.

Meeting President Bush was indeed an exciting experience. He was most friendly and cordial and willing to listen to me as I shared with him the ministry of Awana.

Merrill Dunlap, the piano partner of Lance Latham, also a product of the Chicago Gospel Tabernacle and a close friend of Paul Rader's, was a tremendous musician who has written hundreds of beautiful hymns. He was also an accomplished pianist. He's been a real friend for many years.

Clarence Jones, the founder of radio station HCJB, is one of the most brilliant men I ever met. I valued so much the times he would come and visit me in my office and counsel me regarding the future of the ministry of Awana.

His brother, Howard Jones, was also a vital man in my life. Howard was a brilliant musician, but also a tremendous camp leader from whom I learned so much.

William Pettingil, one of the authors of the Scofield Bible, was also a man I appreciated meeting in the beginning days of the North Side Gospel Center. He was a tremendous Bible teacher. He had a real impact on my life.

Dr. Dave Breese, a real friend who grew up in the Awana program, also made a huge impact on my life with his love for the gospel and the amazing Bible knowledge that he taught me. He is the one that made that heart-searching film on the gospel, *Blessed Calvary*.

I also very much appreciate James Scudder, pastor of Quentin Road Bible Baptist Church, who always focuses on the gospel of God's grace. He holds a two-day conference each year, bringing people from all over the world to just ponder this primary question: "What is the clear message of the Gospel?" What a real inspiration and a great friend he has been to me over the years.

I also appreciate Paul Fleming of New Tribes Mission, who had such an impact on my life by challenging me that Awana must extend to foreign missions. He was such a mission-minded person himself that he influenced everyone he came in contact with.

Having enjoyed sports all my life, I enjoyed meeting a few famous sports figures. Randy Huntley, the catcher for the Chicago Cubs, had a real interest in the ministry of Awana. I also enjoyed spending some time with Ernie Banks, the All-Star shortstop for the Chicago Cubs. To be able to talk with Arnold Palmer, the legendary golfer, was also an exciting time. It's great to see these days that there are so many true believers who are witnesses for our Lord in the sports world.

I remember talking to Mickey Rooney, the Hollywood star. I was told he was a born-again Christian. When I asked him when this took place, I was amazed at the answer he gave me: He said he had always been a Christian!

There's only one thing we all are, and that is sinners. Until we put our faith in Christ and trust Him as our sin-bearer, we never have the assurance of salvation. But the joy of every Christian is to know that someday we're going to meet the King of Kings and Lord of Lords, who has loved us and redeemed us and is planning eternity for us to enjoy. Without question, the greatest friends in life are our Christian friends and those who pray for us regularly.

"DOC" LATHAM

One of my dearest friends is now with the Lord. He was the inspiration I had for Awana and he was also my pastor for more than forty years. He was truly a father figure to me. The angels, I'm sure, rejoiced at Doc's reception.

Because I worked with him for so many years, he made a greater impact on my life than did any other man. When I was still a teenager, he entrusted me with the ministry of leadership. Then, some years later, I served with him as youth director at the North Side Gospel Center and as his assistant as camp director.

In 1950, Doc encouraged me to accept the challenge of becoming executive director of the newly formed Awana Youth Association. I could not have handled all of those responsibilities without the example and guidance of this disciplined man, who always put God first in everything.

I valued his guardianship down through the years. He challenged me to make Scripture memorization the foundation for the Awana program, because of his strong conviction that to know the Word one must memorize it. Doc motivated me to memorize eight chapters of Romans in one month. It was a real challenge I had never had before, but I respected him so much that I took on the challenge and I thank the Lord to this day for that great opportunity to memorize God's Word.

Latham's favorite verses of the gospel were ROMANS 4: 4 and 5: "Now to him that worketh is the reward not reckoned of grace, but of debt. But to him that worketh not, but believeth on him that justifieth the ungodly, his faith is counted for righteousness."

Doc was also an example of love and concern for others. He was never too busy to take the time to talk with any boy who crossed his path, and he also challenged everyone to get involved in memorizing God's Word.

No one will ever play the piano with the same rhythm and touch that Doc had. But, instead of pursuing a professional music career, he devoted himself to a ministry of working with children and grandchildren around the world.

With Doc we have a legacy in Awana, a legacy that we must guard and continue with zeal and purpose. Ours is the task of winning other boys and

Art with Teach and Doc Latham, North Side Gospel Center, circa 1970

girls and their families to Jesus Christ, and to accomplish this we must discipline ourselves and study to show ourselves approved unto God. We must be the workmen who are not ashamed, rightly dividing the word of truth.

Just before the Apostle Paul turned over the reins and the baton of his leadership to his favorite son, Timothy, he warned him of a few things. From his heart he said, "Oh Timothy, keep that which has been committed to thy trust." In other words, Timothy, don't fall by the wayside, don't get off on a tangent and forget the main thing and let the tangent become the main thing. Also, in 2 TIMOTHY 2:3, Paul says, "Thou therefore endure hardness, as a good soldier of Jesus Christ."

Paul also realizes that there is something else that is so very important. 2 TIMOTHY 1:6 says, "Wherefore I put thee in remembrance that thou stir up the gift of God, which is in thee by the putting on of my hands." In other words, you have this treasure of all the things that God has given you— but it is so easy to allow it to become less than a vital part of your life. You should take time and ask God to stir it up, to rekindle it, so that your passion for the lost will be vibrant and you will not become just an ordinary Christian. That certainly is a challenge that we all have in Awana: that we will remain true to the Word of God and constantly be in a place where we can stir the hearts of Christians in this dark world, and that we will be bright shining lights for our wonderful Lord.

Christian camping was also a big part of Doc's heartbeat. For more than forty years I had the honor of being a co-director at Camp Awana with him. Thousands of campers will be in heaven because Lance Latham and his wife, Virginia, were willing to share the gospel and disciple campers to give their lives to serve the Lord. Doc truly was a trailblazer for God in spreading the gospel.

PAUL BROMAN'S AMAZING MINISTRY

If I were to name the three men who impacted my life the most, they would be Lance Latham, my mentor; Paul Broman, missionary to Japan; and, of course, my own father. Though I consider Paul Broman one of the most amazing men I have ever met, most people here in America would not even recognize his name.

About fifty years ago, Paul Broman was sitting in a New Tribes missionary candidates' class in California. The teacher of the class was my mentor, Lance Latham. Doc, as we called him, felt it worthwhile to take time out of his busy schedule, week after week, to come to the New Tribes missionary candidate school to teach them all a clear presentation of the gospel. Paul Broman, a young man in this class, did not at first see the gospel. He felt that Lance Latham was in error and he wanted to share his opposite opinion. However, Doc was not interested in arguing with him.

Some weeks later, in the same type of class, while Doc was teaching out of the fourth chapter of Romans, Paul said it was like a light from heaven came to him, and he saw clearly the gospel of God's grace. It thrilled him so much that he had to get up out of this class of about one hundred people and go down to the riverbank and cry for joy for more than an hour.

Shortly after this, he felt called of God to go to Japan as a missionary. When he arrived there, his main goal was to start a school which he would develop for cast-off kids—kids whose parents didn't want them. He wanted to teach them, first of all, how they could be sure of going to heaven, and then to give their lives as missionaries for the Lord. All this took place more than fifty years ago. After arriving in Japan, he married a Japanese lady. They began adopting these cast-off kids and also had ten of their own. Eventually they wound up with twenty-two children; all of them had Bible names and today all of them are grown and are missionaries all around the world. Almost all of them speak three languages fluently: Japanese, Chinese, and English.

They now have two of the finest schools in all of Japan. Their excellence is so well known that all the elite, affluent people of Japan want their children to attend these schools. To avoid partiality, he has to have a lottery system to decide who may come. In a country that is basically Buddhist, they still have a wide-open door to give the gospel and teach the Word of God in the school. They also conduct one of the largest tract ministries in the world.

I camped with them for a week and saw their work firsthand. At five in the morning, we got up and had prayer together in a little tent. Then, after a breakfast, as we all sat on the floor, we were challenged from the Word of God and out we went into the city to distribute tracts and talk to people about the Lord. I never saw anyone more thorough in giving out tracts. All of us agreed that God would hold us responsible if someone slipped by without getting a tract. They also have many sound trucks, which they drive up and down the streets to give the gospel. This, of course, could never be done here in America. They also have personal tape recorders with speakers on them. That allows them to give messages that may be only thirty seconds long, but this way they know people will listen to them if they keep it short.

Paul's sons are very brilliant men who have developed a computer software company. God has likewise blessed this. They now sell more than a million dollars' worth of computer software each month and have five computer offices. One of them is a large building right in China. This gives them a real entrance to reach the Chinese people.

They probably have some three hundred missionaries around the world whom they are able to support from the profits they get from the school. Still, you can't help but admire Paul Broman's humbleness after God has blessed him so. He raised all these children in a small home where there was almost no furniture. They didn't even have an inside toilet. He did this purposely so that when they went to the mission field, it wouldn't be too big a shock for them. Praise God, today they're still living the same way. In 1 CORINTHIANS 3:12, 15, we read of God's award ceremony. He says, "If any man build upon this foundation gold, silver, precious stones, wood, hay,

Paul Broman with Art

stubble . . . If any man's work abide which he hath built thereupon, he shall receive a reward." Those are God's classifications. I'm inclined to believe that Paul Broman is building on this foundation some beautiful gold, silver, and precious-stone work that is going to last for eternity. Thank you, Paul, for the godly example you've been to me personally.

Paul in Japan

My first visit to Japan to visit Paul Broman was probably about twenty years ago. While I was there I worked with these amazing people, and found out that they really hadn't gotten involved in much Scripture memorization. And so I challenged them that they must get involved in Scripture memorizing, and not long after that—Yes!—all of their staff began memory work.

When I arrived there on my next visit, I was asked to have breakfast with one of the staff members there, who had three children who wanted to recite some Scripture to me. They were somewhere around three, five, and six years of age. I thought that maybe they would get through John 3:16 and maybe Ephesians 2:8–9, and so I was anxious to hear what they would do. After breakfast these three little ones stood in front of me, and I will never forget how thrilled I was. They beautifully recited Psalm 1, Psalm 23, and then they also did Isaiah 53, and all without missing one word. The next time I went to Japan, I found out that these same three had memorized

PSALM 119, which has 150 verses in it. I couldn't believe what I was hearing. They knew that PSALM 1 was special to me, so they said they wanted to recite that again to me—which they did, reciting it in English and Japanese, and then following with Chinese. I couldn't believe how flawlessly they were able to do this.

This just shows what can happen when you have parents who know the importance of bringing their children right to the Word of God and set their minds on learning with them. What a thrill it was for me to be able to stay with them and to see as a family how much they wanted to serve the Lord.

When I was there, I met a fellow by the name of Joshua Broman. He was only five years old when they went to Japan and he remembers that I recited ISAIAH 53 to him. Now he is a man in his thirties and has a family and God has really taught him so many, many things. He is a brilliant photographer and video producer and has produced some beautiful videos. While I was there, I learned that because of his knowledge, he had been selected to take over and develop a new film called *Kingdom Come,* with a budget close to $100 million, which will be shown in theaters all around the United States. And to think that this little fellow now is a producer!

In addition to that, he and a couple of his brothers also developed a software company. The thrill of it is that all of this money goes right into carrying the gospel out. They are living in some very modest homes, even though they could afford to live in some very elegant homes because they have legitimately made all this money, but they only want it to go to serving the Lord. I am looking forward to being able to see this film, *Kingdom Come.*

It has been a real thrill for me to have a small part in a ministry there in Japan, which is one of the most difficult countries in the world to reach for Christ because they have a Buddhist background. God is using his servants there in the most wonderful way.

HACK WILSON: MY BASEBALL HERO

As a boy I was always fascinated with sports. I enjoyed going to any sporting event. It didn't make any difference whether it was baseball, football, hockey, or tennis, I just enjoyed any sport that was well done. I can remember as a boy, the Chicago Cubs was my team. I practically worshipped them, as so many did, although I very seldom, if ever, got an opportunity to even watch them. This was before the days of television, so about all we could do was read about it in the papers. However, I would save my pennies and when I had accumulated enough, I would go down to watch the Cubs play. I would only have enough money to sit in the bleachers, but I was very happy being there. I even went alone because my friends didn't have the money or they didn't care for sports as much as I did.

The idol baseball player of that young boy in the centerfield bleachers was the center fielder for the Chicago Cubs, Hack Wilson. Hack Wilson held the record for the most home runs in the National League; he had hit fifty-six. I can remember the excitement that filled me every time he got up to the plate, especially when he hit a home run. The entire grandstands went up in a roar, including me. I often thought how great it would be if I could just change places with Hack Wilson. If I could just be him, all my joys and desires would be taken care of. To be famous like him and have the people cheer for me as they did for him would be wonderful.

Well, the years went on, and I watched many other players whom I enjoyed, and Hack Wilson soon retired from baseball. I remember some years later, I read in the sports section of the paper that Hack Wilson, this man who had been my idol, so to speak, had just died penniless as a drunkard in a skid-row room. That story made a real impact on me, because it made me realize how limited and limiting these temporal ambitions can be. To my knowledge, Hack Wilson never trusted Christ as his Savior and most likely, if he didn't, he is in hell today. Yes, he believes now and knows the truth, but it is too late. He would gladly come back and be a "nobody" believer and be able to spend eternity in heaven. But his eternity is sealed forever.

Yes, we're reminded in Scripture, in COLOSSIANS 3:2, "Set your affections on things above, not on things on the earth." I remember getting a ball autographed by the Hall-of-Fame pitcher, Bob Feller. Here's a man who, in his baseball days, pitched two no-hit games; perhaps 95 percent of all baseball pitchers go through their careers without ever having even one no-hit game. I thought what a famous man he was, but as I stood there watching him autograph my ball, I wondered if he was a believer and was heaven-bound. Because with all of his temporal glory, he, too, could be bound for an eternal destiny without Christ.

ANDY PAFKO: ALL-STARS
CHICAGO CUBS PLAYER

Now I want to take you back to my childhood days, when I was just a nine-or ten-year-old boy and a real Chicago Cubs baseball fan. I would look forward to the day I could save up fifty cents to sit in the bleachers of Wrigley Field to watch the Cubs play ball. One of my heroes then was Hack Wilson, who held the home-run record many times. Another amazing ball player was Andy Pafko, who was the left fielder for the Cubs. He wound up on the All-Star team and played against the famous Joe DiMaggio of the Yankees.

I found, many years later, that Andy had just retired and that he was going to come and be part of an Awana golf tournament, and I was going to be able to have him on my golf cart. I was delighted to think that he would be with me for all nine holes on the golf course. Now, as I look back, and after I left him, I realized how miserably I had failed, because I didn't witness to him about Christ. I failed inasmuch as I didn't even give him a tract explaining how he could become a Christian. God convicted me of this, so I thought, *I am going to try and arrange another opportunity to meet with him again.* I kept in contact with him, but because he was a busy man whom everyone wanted to see, it was very difficult to set up a time when I could get him over to Awana so that I could have another chance to witness to him.

Then one day, I saw in the newspaper that the famous Andy Pafko had died. Now his life was over and, yes, I had many, many regrets. Why didn't I witness to him when I had that opportunity? Did he go to a church of some kind, where the gospel was preached, and had he ever trusted in Christ? These are things I will never know, but I know that God spoke to my heart. I had failed, but from there on in, God challenged me to be a better witness for Him in the future.

HUBERT MITCHELL:
MISSIONARY HEARTBREAK

One of the joys I always had at our home church was that Lance Latham would bring in missionary speakers to challenge our hearts. One of the missionaries whom he brought in quite often was Hubert Mitchell. He was a man who touched your heart each time he spoke.

He shared with us about a time when he was in the field. He, along with his wife and two children, were down in the jungles and had been working faithfully with a tribe down there, and they felt that they were making progress in reaching the tribe members with the gospel. While he was there, his wife became very sick. We all know what a burden it is when you are back in the jungles with someone who is ill. Where do you go for help? At that point he was trusting the Lord to heal his wife, but she slowly got worse. He and his children just kept praying and praying for God to heal her, but there, out in the mission field, his dear wife died.

He said that one of the most heart-rending things that had ever happened was, "I had to dig a grave for my wife with the natives." They made a casket together, with his children watching the preparations for her burial right there in the jungle.

If there was ever a time you might ask yourself if God was listening, this was it. We all go through times when it doesn't seem like God is listening, but He always does. He always answers with what is best for us. Hubert Mitchell had that kind of a heart, to recognize that he was not just a victim of tough luck or bad circumstances; he knew that God was in this.

The most beautiful thing of all of this was when he came back to the States with his children; you might think that he could have had even a little bit of bitterness in his heart, but he was so far from that. Then out came this song that he helped to write, "He Giveth More Grace":

> He giveth more grace as our burdens grow greater,
> He sendeth more strength as our labors increase;
> To added afflictions He addeth His mercy,
> To multiplied trials He multiplies peace.
>
> When we have exhausted our store of endurance,
> When our strength has failed ere the day is half done,
> When we reach the end of our hoarded resources
> Our Father's full giving has only begun.
>
> Fear not that thy need shall exceed His provision,
> Our God ever yearns His resources to share;
> Lean hard on the arm everlasting, availing;
> The Father both thee and thy load will upbear.

His love has no limits, His grace has no measure,
His power no boundary known unto men;
For out of His infinite riches in Jesus
He giveth, and giveth, and giveth again.

—Annie J. Flint (with Hubert Mitchell)

What a beautiful heartbeat that comes from a man who has gone through some real testing from the Lord.

RICH AHLQUIST: AWANA'S FIRST TIMOTHY AWARD WINNER

During the "wilderness days," as we called them, when God was teaching us and there were so many things we had to trust Him for day by day, one of our greatest encouragements was a young boy named Rich Ahlquist. He would not only faithfully come and help us on the paper drives, but he was constantly prodding us to get another test written that he could pass. So God even used a young clubber to challenge us to not get satisfied, but rather to constantly progress in getting the handbooks done. How little did we know at that time what God had in mind for Awana.

Rich Ahlquist was a typical young Pal who was invited by a friend of his to come to Awana. That was really in the beginning days of Awana, when the achievement tests were only mimeographed sheets that we handed out to the clubbers. Rich was blessed with an energetic personality that everybody loved. He was kind, but he was also an excellent athlete. I had the privilege of having him as one of the campers in the early days at Camp Awana. He was especially gifted in swimming: In the swimming tournaments we held at camp, it was very common for Rich Ahlquist to win the all-around swimmer award in his age group. He was enthused about all the activities that took place at camp. I guess you'd have to call Rich Ahlquist one of those model campers that we wish we had more of.

Rich loved the Awana Clubs at the North Side Gospel Center so much that after school, he would come to be with us as we were preparing the Awana handbooks. He enjoyed being part of the collating team that put the books together each day. Still, he was also constantly asking when we would get the new tests ready, because he was already up-to-date on all the

Richie Ahlquist

memorizing that had been presented to him. Whenever we would run off a new test, Rich was there to get a copy of it and take it home. In a few days he would have that one completed, too.

Yes, we called Rich one of our real encouragers in the beginning days of Awana. He became a junior leader in the clubs and before long, which is typical of so many clubbers, he felt the time had come to go to college. We hated to lose his influence with all of us, but he said goodbye, we prayed for him, and wished him well.

Some time later I received a telephone call while I was at camp. It's one I'll never forget. I was told that Rich, being the tremendous swimmer he was, was standing on the pier in Lake Geneva and signaled to all of his friends there that he was going to dive in and swim 150 feet under water. This was more or less a usual thing for him, but he couldn't have known that that would be the last swim he would ever take. What a traumatic shock it was to me to have one of our key teens taken home in the prime of life. I was asked to have a part in the funeral. After the funeral I was asked to come and visit with his parents. Their sorrow was evident, but as they sat across the table from me they said, "We want to give you a copy of Rich's last term paper he wrote at college. We went to the University of Illinois where he attended and asked them to give us everything that he had written or put his name on. This was his last term paper."

The title of it was "My Greatest Decision in Life." In it he went on to share how one night he came to a Pals Club meeting and there he heard the gospel and put his trust in what Christ did for him and accepted Him as his Savior. He described how, when he went home to tell his folks, they told him it was just an emotional experience and that he would soon get over it. He continued by saying that ten years had passed and it was not an emotional experience. Christ was more precious to him today than ever before and he wanted to serve Him the rest of his life. How little did Rich know that the rest of his life was just a few months.

Yes, Rich's life had a huge impact on all of the leaders and clubbers alike, but perhaps most of all, he made an impact on his own parents, who then trusted Christ as their personal Savior. In times like these, we must claim ROMANS 8:28: "All things work together for good to them that love God, to them who are the called according to his purpose."

PAUL WYMA: CAMPFIRE TESTIMONY

One of the many joys I had during my forty years ministering as camp director were the beautiful campfires and testimony times. Camp is such a great place where clubbers make decisions to serve Christ and even go into the mission field.

I remember so distinctly, once when I was leading a time of testimony time around a campfire, one fellow by the name of Paul Wyma got up. He was probably only about thirteen years old and he said:

> I remember when my folks were missionaries and my dad was a missionary pilot. I remember they were back in the jungles with some of the other New Tribe missionaries and they had a real heartbeat to go back in there to meet with some of these tribes that have never, ever heard the gospel before. I remember my dad as he met with the other two missionaries and they prayed together before they went into the jungle. They said, "This trip will probably take us about three weeks, so you will have some idea of when we will be returning." And of course, every

day we would pray and pray, "Please God, take care of my dad and the other missionaries." It just seemed like such a very long time for them to get back.

I remember so well when one night, my mom and I had just retired in our little hut we had, we heard some footsteps and rushed outside and sure enough, there was my dad. He just wrapped his arms around us and he just cried and cried and cried. He was so happy to see us, but he shared with us what had really ripped his heart out. "We were down in the jungles with these people and they were very friendly to us, but they were led by spirits they feared. When people got sick, they felt that they were in favor with the spirits if they would bury them alive. There I saw them put people into the graves who were still alive, and just to see them put the dirt on them and see them die was sad, but the saddest part was to see them die without Christ. There I was and I knew the gospel but I did not know the language and to think I could not even talk to them about Christ."

That made such an impact on me that I told the Lord that I want to be a missionary, too, and I want to go down into those tribes.

I had not seen this fellow for probably thirty years, but one day, I was at the New Tribes headquarters there in Sanford, Florida, and I saw him. I recognized him and yes!, he had been a missionary and now he is directing a great part of New Tribes Mission.

It is so great to see young people who can listen to the Lord when He talks to their hearts and helps them to pursue the ministry He has called them to.

WALT KROEMEYER: CARVING LIVES

Let me take you back to a beautiful Awana camp in Michigan. We named it Michawana just because it was located in Michigan and also named it for Awana. It was a gorgeous camp, owned by the government, with 240 beautiful acres of land. There were cabins that were made virtually entirely of logs, with only four campers to a cabin, which is very unusual. It was our privilege to have this camp leased to us for a very small amount of money for eight years.

That time was during the war years, the Second World War was taking place. I can remember the day that the war came to a halt. We were up at Camp Michawana and everyone was celebrating.

One of the key leaders of that time was a young man named Walt Kroemeyer. Walt was a handicraft instructor and a very talented man. He had the campers involved in many beautiful leather projects, where they made wallets, Bible covers, and many other craft items. Walt had them all involved in many activities, but he himself was a uniquely talented wood carver. I remember that one day he stood in front of all the campers with a large log. He looked into the eyes of the campers and said, "Do you know what is inside this log?" Of course, no one had the slightest idea what he was talking about, and then he said, "There is an elephant in here and I am going to prove it to you."

What he was going to prove was that each day, during his free hours, he would sit with his knife and carve and carve until he had the most beautiful elephant carving you could ever imagine—and it all came out of that tree, just as he had promised the campers.

God laid it on his heart to go to Liberia with his dear wife to be a missionary. There they lived back in the jungles with the natives and while they were there, a little boy trusted Christ as his Savior. Walt saw real potential in that little boy and they nurtured him and got him into a Bible school where he got some training. After he grew up, he became the pastor of a church there, and then it was not long before he became the Awana missionary to Liberia.

He began getting many Awana Clubs started there and it was a precious time. I had the privilege to run our first Olympics in Liberia. Some time later, a real revolution took place. There were three groups that were striving to get leadership and they were ruthless; they would shoot and kill everyone they came across. More than half of our Awana leadership was slain during that period. A letter that I received during this time (reproduced in the "Liberia" section earlier in this book) is a tragic letter, but precious for the fact that the writer's life was spared.

In my office at Awana headquarters, I have many treasured gifts that I have received from all around the world, but the one that sits alongside my main desk is a beautiful carving from my friend, Walt Kroemeyer. It is not only an elephant, but also a beautiful desk that was hand-carved just for me. So I say thanks to Walt Kroemeyer, who was not just a gifted handicraft person, but a real model Christian. He was a hero of mine because he was a missionary who walked the walk and talked the talk and produced fruit for our Lord Jesus Christ. Today Walt and his wife are both in heaven, and I truly look forward to seeing them again some day.

BOB BARRON: CLUBBER TO LEADER

Visiting clubbers in their homes is a vital part of the Awana ministry. Through it, we not only show caring compassion to the clubbers, but we also are provided with an opportunity to reach unsaved parents. We never know which visits will make an eternal impact.

Almost as if it happened yesterday, I remember a dear old lady walking up to me with a scrap of paper in her hand. "Mr. Rorheim, there's an address on this piece of paper and I want you to go visit this home."

I was somewhat taken aback by this demanding lady, yet I wanted to do the right thing. I smiled at this dear lady and assured her that I would follow up on her request. While walking from my car to this house, I thought about what the old lady had told me. The mother was single, worked as a nurse, and was raising her three boys, two of whom were twins. The visit went well, and I invited the boys to our Pals Club, an offer they immediately accepted.

Bob Barron

How could I have known what spiritual giants I would find in that home! Bob Barron was saved when he was eight years old, and quickly grew in the things of the Lord. When he was just a fifteen-year-old, he came to me and asked if he could lead a Sunday school class. I saw his enthusiasm and I could not turn down the heartbeat that he had for the Lord. It wasn't long before I saw how he was touching the hearts of the Pals. Years later, when our club began to grow, we had 150 Pals and we needed two nights for just the Pals, Thursday and Friday. Then I thought, *Who could I get to run the Pals on Friday nights?* How could I ever think of having a boy who was only seventeen years old directing an entire club like that? But I did, and I was amazed at the ability that God gave him to have a successful Pals Club.

Some years later Bob became the youth pastor of the North Side Gospel Center. He then served as a youth pastor for fifteen years in a church in Milwaukee, and later on he became a Christian education teacher at the Moody Bible Institute. Later, he served as a member of the Awana board of directors for several years. He also had a real passion for foreign missions and did a lot of traveling.

Then the Lord said, "Bob, it's time for you to come home." It was really a tremendous loss for all of us to see him leave, but we knew that he left a real legacy behind for all of us who dearly loved him.

I often wish more visits could have ended like that first one with the Barron family. All three boys ended up attending Pals, where they trusted Christ as their Savior. Mrs. Barron worked at Camp Awana for more than thirty years as a camp nurse, and what a blessing it was to have her there to deal with all of those needs at camp.

This story reminds us how important just one decision can be when you may not even feel like doing it at all. That one visit can affect many, many people. Just to see the wonderful fruit of obeying God constantly reminds us that if we really, truly love God, we will obey Him, during these times and all others.

RICH WAGER: AWANA'S FIRST EMPLOYEE

The year was 1933; Chicago was celebrating the Worlds Fair. However, in the midst of these festive city activities, God was planning a ministry that would reach around the world with the precious message of the gospel. This

Rich Wager, first Awana employee

ministry began in an abandoned furniture store that had been ravaged by the Great Chicago Fire.

The heartbeat and the calling of this amazing ministry was Lance Latham, who was working alongside Paul Rader at the amazing gospel witness, the Chicago Gospel Tabernacle in Chicago.

The beginning of this new ministry was a small group of young people who were most challenged. The first floor of this two-story building was renovated to become the sanctuary, and the second floor became a clubroom to attract the kids in the neighborhood with the gospel.

Even though I had no formal Christian education or training, I was honored to be selected as the youth director of this challenging new ministry, which was named the North Side Gospel Center.

I remember the day that Rich Wager, as a young lad, came to club for the first time. He came from a home with an alcoholic father, but the excitement and friendliness of the club leadership immediately won his heart. To describe Rich Wager best, you would say his batteries were always fully charged, and if you rated his enthusiasm on a scale from one to ten, he would be given a twelve. He had the mark of leadership from the very beginning and in every activity he was determined to win; losing only made him more determined to win the next time. Win or lose, he always had an enthusiastic smile on his face that displayed his leadership to his clubber friends.

After he trusted Christ to be his Savior, he grew spiritually faster than any clubber I ever saw. As a teenager, in addition to being a junior leader, he also had a burden to have his own Sunday school class. God blessed him with teaching skills from the very beginning. What a beautiful sight to see him mentoring the kids he was teaching.

In 1950, the Awana program was developing so that it could be available for other churches to use as a ministry to their neighborhoods. I knew that if the program was to grow, God would have to send leadership to make it happen, and God answered our prayer by bringing Rich Wager beside me as our very first employee. Together we shared a desk under a stairwell at Awana's first headquarters/office. Rich directed the eighty-member Pioneer Club at the North Side Gospel Center, while I directed the high-school club called Pilots. Churches were now coming from everywhere to see the new clubs in action.

Rich and I acted as a "think-tank" together, as we would challenge each other to develop the Awana program. No funds were available, and the test for the clubbers was all we had, but Rich said that we must strive for excellence, and we must get a printing press of our own so that we could print our own books.

To raise money to buy a press, we gathered the clubbers together every Saturday and filled our church bus with newspapers collected from the basements of many homes. With the money from sale of that scrap paper, we were able to purchase a second-hand press. However, neither one of us knew how to use our new machine. Rich was very creative and learned first and together we printed the first book and the covers and the clubbers were corralled to come each afternoon to collate them.

God was blessing Awana each summer, and Camp Awana was a vital part of our ministry. Rich was one of the key camp leaders, and it was there that God taught us so many basic principles of running a camp. I believe it was there that God gave Rich the vision and heartbeat to direct camps.

The most discouraging moment of my life came when Rich shared with me that God was calling him to leave the ministry of Awana. It was like severing my right arm, but it was obvious that God was leading him. He became youth pastor at Midwest Bible Church, and he got the Awana program going there, and before long he said that we should have interclub competitions, which developed into the Awana nationwide Olympics. With the camping heart he had, he developed the Phantom Ranch camp ministry. Then he moved on to become the pastor of the Immanuel Bible Church in Berwyn, where he developed Bible teaching materials and an audiotape ministry. Under his leadership, the amazing camp called Silver Birch became a reality.

Rich also had a heart for foreign missions, and he was selected to be the chairman of the Awana Foreign Missions program. He was also a member of the New Tribes teaching staff who taught all the missionary candidates the basic truths of the Bible and how to share the message of the gospel.

I have only begun to share the joy I had in working alongside of one of God's brilliant yet humble servants. Lance Latham, founder of the North Side Gospel Center and Camp Awana, also had an impact on mentoring Rich Wager. In turn, Rich has impacted and mentored thousands of lives, and his legacy continues today.

What an inspiration and a blessing he was to me. I thank God for sending him across my path in life. He truly was a special friend.

In Colossians 4:17, the Apostle Paul challenges every believer to "Take heed to the ministry which thou have received in the Lord, that thou fulfill it." Praise God that Rich Wager, God's servant, faithfully fulfilled the ministry that he had been ordained to do. Rich truly lived his life by 1 Corinthians 15:58: ". . . be ye steadfast, unmoveable, always abounding in the work of the Lord, forasmuch as ye know that your labour is not in vain in the Lord."

JIMMY: USED OF THE LORD

I have often said that teenagers are my special people, because they bless me so many, many times. Just to see them when they get saved and develop a real heartbeat for the Lord, how pliable and willing they are to do anything that they are asked to do in order to serve the Lord.

In that original club, at least one-third of all our club leaders were teenagers. Most of them were junior leaders in the Pals Club for the eight-, nine-, and ten-year-olds. There always came a time when we challenged them with the news that they were going to have to give their first message. I think all of us know that when you are a leader in club, it makes you very nervous when you have to speak for the first time.

One thing we always emphasize when asking people to speak is that they should do a short presentation of the gospel, letting their listeners know how Christ died for their sins and that they could be saved by putting their complete trust in Him and thus be sure of going to heaven.

The night came when it was Jimmy's turn to give his first message. He had known about this for a couple of months, but he was getting more scared as the date got closer. Every Awana Club meeting was like a prototype showcase for members of other churches to come and see just what it is that makes Awana so successful, so they could possibly start something in their own churches. On that particular night there were about a dozen potential leaders from a church up in Wisconsin coming in to observe, and they had invited a businessman who was not a Christian to come along to see what took place at these meetings.

I remember that night. They were all there watching the game period and my little friend, Jimmy, came up to me and asked, "They will all be leaving after the game period, won't they?" I told him that they were very anxious to take part in the counsel time and that they were going to hear him give his first message. Jimmy was really scared, but he had agreed to speak that evening and he wouldn't back out. When the time came for him to speak, he had his Bible in hand, and he started in. He very clearly gave the gospel of how Jesus died for all of our sins and if we would put our complete trust there, God promised to take us to heaven. Salvation is a free gift and all we have to do is to receive this free gift of His.

When we sat down I'm sure Jimmy, in his mind, said to himself, *Wow! I sure blew that one. I'll never do that again.* The old devil comes along and does those things to us. The next morning, the salesman who was unsaved made an appointment with the church and said, "Last night I was over at the Awana Club and saw what was taking place. It was amazing to see all that was happening with these kids." Then he told how he was in this meeting and a young teenager got up and showed, from the Bible, how everyone could be sure of going to heaven by putting their trust in Christ. He said, "I did that while he was speaking and according to God's Word, I am saved. Pastor, is there a place that you can use me so I can start serving the Lord?"

Well, time went on, and one day I got a phone call from this man and he asked if I would come and speak at his club. I wasn't aware of what had happened, but I found out that little Jimmy's message had really reached him, and he was now the commander of all of the clubs in that church—that church has just been a real lighthouse for God.

What does all that tell us? *It is the power of the gospel.* In Romans 1:16 it says, "For I am not ashamed of the gospel, for it is the power of God unto salvation." It does not make any difference who is giving the message. God uses His Word to reach into and take hold of the hearts of people.

I particularly want to share that message because we realize that God challenges teens to be in service for the Lord, too. Unfortunately, many churches, even ones that have a real desire to see their teens grow in things of the Lord, just teach them in Bible classes. This is very valuable, of course, but teens can do far more. Give them a real challenge to live for the Lord: give teens a ministry with kids and have them give messages. It's such a wonderful training program.

I proudly can say, "Look at the power of the gospel that was used by just a teen."

DUKE: INCORRIGIBLE CLUBBER, GOD'S SERVANT

I'm sure, if you've been an Awana leader for any amount of time, you've had some clubbers who you would consider the incorrigible type. As you look at them, you often say in your heart, *I'm not too sure I want them to be a part of our club because they would be a bad influence.* I often thought like that in those early days. But God has rebuked me many times for even having those thoughts. Let me tell you about one young teenager who came into one of those early clubs.

His name was Eddie Dubitz, but we called him "Duke." He came from a Catholic background and had developed into a cocky teenager who wanted to display his attitude to gain recognition and attention. I remember the first time I saw him. I watched his smart-aleck attitude in the game period, where he would spit on the floor and you could see the cigarettes in his pocket. It wasn't long before all the clubbers realized that he wanted to show everyone his unbridled bad attitude. Yes, I must admit, he was one that I really questioned whether I even wanted to have him come back a second time.

It wasn't very long before Duke saw his need as a sinner and trusted Christ as his Savior. It was beautiful to see how quickly he matured and grew in spiritual things. It wasn't long before he felt the need to go to Bible school, which he did for some four years. He became one of our exciting, challenging leaders who had a real burden for souls. Then came the day when he said, "God's calling me to be a missionary in Africa." Yes, Duke responded and, praise God, he served about thirty years in Africa as a missionary. Now some of his children are following in his footsteps.

I don't even know who the leader was that brought him to club, but praise God for the leadership that impacted Duke's life. To think of the hundreds and perhaps thousands of others he has touched in his life as a missionary. It's the effectiveness of the Word of God that does the work in the hearts of clubbers and leaders who allow the Holy Spirit to lead them. Yes, I could tell you many, many stories of other so-called incorrigible clubbers, but I have also learned that these clubbers, who seem to have such creative means for mischief, often turn out to be some of the most effective Awana leaders. Kids like Duke taught me never to give up on them. Just display as much patience as you can, trusting that God will see them get saved and give them a deep desire to put all that energy into serving their wonderful Lord.

BURT LONG: MISSIONARY DOCTOR

I want to take you back to the late 1920s, when I was a camper over in Michigan. It was called Camp Chic-Go-Tab, named after the Chicago Gospel Tabernacle ("Chic" was for Chicago, "Go" for Gospel, and "Tab" for Tabernacle). With my mentor, Lance Latham, as the director, it was just a pioneer-type camp with a wooden log structure almost like an army barracks divided in the middle. There was a tennis court, and because the camp was right on the shores of Lake Michigan, we went in swimming each day. When we got up in the morning, there was no running water for us to bathe in, so we all ran down the sand dunes right into the lake and that was our cleanup for the day.

While we were there, we had two hours of Bible study with Doc Latham. We all sat right in the dunes, nobody on chairs, and Doc was marvelously able to hold our attention and teach us things we had never heard before.

There were also campfires that were really precious. I can remember a young fellow standing up alongside of me and saying, "I believe God has called me to be a medical missionary doctor." He went on to say that he was going to trust the Lord to do that for him. For a fourteen-year-old boy to say that was really hard to believe. Believe it or not, he was steadfast and after he got out of high school, he went on to college, he married an Awana girl, he got a medical degree, and they headed for Niger.

There in Niger, Burt Long built a hospital and his dear wife said, "I see all of these kids here." With her Awana training, she knew the basics of how to reach kids, and she decided that she was going to set up an Awana Club there, so she started to put together some handbooks in the Hausa language. These were very primitive. The kids in Niger were illiterate, and the very first things they ever read were Scripture and portions of the new handbook that she put together for them. There they were, running this hospital, and she was running an Awana Club!

This of course was not official, but it was the first unauthorized Awana foreign club we had. For more than thirty years, Burt and his dear wife, Ruth, ministered there in Niger, and then later they went into Nigeria into another hospital where he was able to meet the people's physical needs, which were tremendous. Some people went there for eye surgery, some for cancers that had grown hanging from their arms, and on and on. There had never been anyone there before to help them. Burt did not just help them physically; to everyone who came in, he made sure they knew how to go to heaven. I had the great privilege, after about thirty years, of going down there and meeting with Burt. I took my video camera and for an entire morning I was able to video all of the operations he performed. Burt Long and I are the same age and he is doing very well. I enjoy my fellowship with him because he and his wife, Ruth, were real missionary warriors for the Lord and a wonderful inspiration to me.

THE BARKER BROTHERS: JIM AND HAROLD

I was directing the game period in the clubroom of that original North Side Gospel Center. In the midst of game period, in came a lady with two young boys by the names of Jim and Harold Barker. They had come here to visit from the hills of Tennessee. Their lifestyle was nothing like what they saw in Chicago. They stood there with their mouths and eyes wide open, watching all the activity on the game floor. It was their aunt who brought them to the church and was interested in seeing them getting involved in things for the Lord.

It wasn't long before they were regular members and participated in all the activities of those pre-Awana clubs. They were both very quiet and you often wondered if they were really absorbing what was going on. It wasn't long before we saw their keen interest in Scripture memory and fellowship with the other clubbers. Soon they were an inspiration to all the leaders and clubbers alike.

One day I saw one of the most beautiful scenes of servant leadership that I had ever seen in Awana. It was in the middle of a Pals meeting where I was leading the singing. The door to the room quietly opened and in came Jim, who was then about fifteen years of age, with a dozen Pals behind him. It was like a mother hen with her chicks following behind her. He carefully and quietly made sure they all sat down and paid attention. I was curious to know how all this came about. You see, Jimmy lived about five miles away from our club. He did not have a car to drive them there. In those days there were only streetcars for public transportation. Then I found out how all this happened.

When you first met Jimmy, you would find him to be a very quiet, unexpressive, nonathletic, and very average-looking young fellow. But God had laid a burden on his heart to become a missionary in his own neighborhood. As a devoted missionary, he walked the streets in his own neighborhood, talking to boys who were Pals age, and asking them if they would like to come to this special Pals Club. After they agreed, he asked if he could come and visit their parents, which of course they all agreed to. As he visited their homes, he persuaded the parents that he really loved their child and would appreciate it if they would let him take the boy to the Pals Club (which at that time was still not Awana). He didn't want to burden them in any way, so he took his own limited finances and offered to pay their streetcar fare.

He realized that he didn't have to go to a foreign country to be a missionary; God had called him to be one right there in Chicago. What an example he was to all of us as leaders. It wasn't long before Jimmy had his own Sunday school class.

In those beginning days of Awana, as God was challenging us to develop the program, we had to start writing some tests and putting together some books. Part of the Awana books involved crafts. Jimmy had become an expert in knot tying and many other craft areas, so he was actually the one who wrote the original craft test in those first books. Because no finances were available, we began running our paper drives to get funds to buy that first press and supplies and uniforms and awards. Jimmy was a spearhead in helping to promote the drives. What an encouragement he was!

Jimmy had a real heart to reach kids for Christ. He beautifully knew the message of salvation and had a very definite plan as to how he was going to reach these kids. He would come early to club. One piece of the equipment he used to get their attention was a small piece of rope that he kept in his pocket. As the clubbers came early, he would befriend them, and one of the first things he would ask was if they would like to learn how to be a knot specialist. Of course they would, so he told them he would be glad to show them how. It was so beautiful to see him sitting in a corner of the room teaching them how to tie knots. But it wasn't long before Jimmy had his Bible out and was leading them to Christ.

I've met perhaps a few thousand leaders in my years at Awana, but I never met a leader who in those early days won more kids to Christ than Jimmy. How beautiful it is to see God using ordinary people like us. Ordinary people are God's favorites. We know that because He made so many of us! Jimmy today is home in glory, but I will forever thank God for the impact he had on my own life to be a better personal witness.

MARTY BUCKWAL: THE CHALLENGE

Let me tell you about Marty.

Marty's mom died when he was born and he was raised by his grandparents, who were quite old at the time. I got Marty to come to club, but to get him to come to Sunday school was impossible because there wasn't anyone to get him up and get him there. So I asked his grandparents if it would be possible for them to just leave the door open and I would come into their house and if Marty was still sleeping, I would wake him up and get him dressed so that I could take him to Sunday school.

This was fine with Marty for a long time. He got saved and knew the Lord as his Savior. He was the kindest boy you could ever meet, but he had some very weird ideas as to what life was all about. He never had anyone to show him how a teenager should dress, and some of the clothes he wore were pretty shabby and not really put on very well.

Marty had a real love for my wife, Winnie, and myself. He said, "Winnie, I would like to help you when you go shopping." Winnie appreciated his willingness to help, but she thought it would be a little odd to have this fellow along with her all the time. She really did not want anybody to think that he was her son, although we did love him because he was so very kind.

Then came the time, as he got to be a teenager, that he got a job. Like most young men, his goal was to get his own car. I just could not imagine how Marty could function with a car. He had been up to Camp Awana several times and just loved it, and when we had a work day, Marty said that he would be coming up to camp to help. Soon, I just could not believe what I saw: here came Marty driving in with this old car packed with kids. It's hard to believe this, but his old car did not even have a steering wheel! He was steering the car with a big wrench that he had hooked up to the steering column. How he ever got up to camp I will never know, especially as he began bragging about how fast he was able to go. I looked at that car's tires—in those days they had tires with inner tubes—and you could actually see the inner tubes ready to pop out. I looked back and said, "Thank you, Lord!," because what a tragic accident he could have had.

Life went on and it wasn't long before Marty got married and had a son. He was so anxious for me just to hold his son in my arms while he took a picture of us. Well, time slipped by, and as it is with so many clubbers and campers, they leave and go about their lives and you don't know what happened to them. I never saw Marty again, but one thing that I am sure of is this: I will meet Marty in heaven, and I thank God for the many angels that protected Marty all those years.

OTTO MELBY: A MOTHER'S CONCERN

Back in that original club, God gave me a host of teenagers. One particular fellow there was Otto Melby. His father had died and his Norwegian mother and I had many opportunities to talk because of my Norwegian background. She would often call me, sometimes late at night, because she knew I had an interest in her son, who didn't seem to respond to the things of the Lord and was in his teenage years doing his own thing.

She would say, "Would you please help, because I do not know where my son is and he has not come home tonight?" Well, he was just a rebellious son and I would continually witness to him.

Otto Melby

Then he moved away and I lost contact with him. One day I was sitting on the platform at the church getting ready to speak and in walked Otto Melby. This was quite a few years later, and he was married and had a child. I said to the pastor, "Do you know who that is?" and he told me, "Yes, he is a fellow that is a spotlight in our church and he is so excited about getting Awana started that he has raised money for the church to buy a bus to take care of the Awana kids." He continued, "Yes, we are so thankful for him."

I told the pastor that I could hardly believe what he was telling me, but I know it is the truth. I was so excited to know that this boy grew up into a wonderful Christian young man, on fire for the Lord and doing the Lord's work in that church.

It wasn't many years later that he became a member of our Awana Board of Directors, and some time later he became our board chairman. It was hard to believe, because he was one of our incorrigible kids who was hard to understand, but behold, God had His hand on him. We constantly see that some of the most difficult kids are those whom God will raise up to be real strong Christian leaders. Otto, his wife, Donna, and their family have left a legacy down through the years that has magnified our wonderful Lord.

CHESTER SHEREN:
A DIAMOND IN THE ROUGH

I received a letter today which just reminded me of God's faithfulness in a young fellow who was really steadfast. He was one of our eight employees in our first Awana building on Belmont Avenue in Chicago. His name was Chester Sheren. He was a frail young fellow, but he had a real desire to serve the Lord and would do just about anything we asked of him in those early days, when we all wore many hats to keep Awana afloat.

Chester got married, but he had one big desire, and that was to become an Awana missionary. There was a real need for Awana missionaries back in those days, but when the board of directors evaluated Chester, they did not feel he had the qualifications to become an Awana missionary. This was a real big disappointment to Chester, as that was his big dream. I admired him because he did not allow this to divert him. He knew that God had a call for his life, and if this was not it, then God would have something else for him.

Chester left Awana, but he still wanted to be in the ministry, so he went to the East Coast and became director of a skid-row mission. He had such a love for all of these "down and outers" and he became a very successful missions director. I lost track of him until one day I got a letter from him, only to find out that he was a missionary in Honduras.

How did he arrive there? I thought. *And how did that mission board feel that he would make a good missionary?* He had such a big heart to serve the Lord that I decided to help support him, because I knew that he would use this money to glorify the Lord.

Today, as I read my letter from Chester Sheren, I cannot believe it: He has just celebrated thirty years as a faithful missionary in Honduras. I just could not comprehend that he had served there that long. How wrong I was not to realize that he was really one of God's special people, who was steadfast and faithful and didn't allow discouragement to divert him from God's leading in his life!

Yes, he is an inspiration to me and others here at Awana headquarters. We have a picture of the original eight employees in front of the Belmont Avenue Awana headquarters, and Chester Sheren is one of those in the picture.

Few people in the world have ever heard of Chester Sheren, but I am fully persuaded that in that day when the Lord hands out His awards, Chester will receive one of God's "Well Done Awards." That is what we are all striving for. Nothing in life is as important as realizing that someday we will stand before Him and He is going to evaluate how much we loved Him, how faithful we were, and, most of all, how much we obeyed Him.

Yes, Chester Sheren was a true godly example to me.

GENE GOERTZEN: A CLOSE CALL

Awana had just completed one of its thrilling missionary conferences. It's always been a joy when some of the Awana missionaries can come to headquarters for times of fellowship, instruction, and challenge to press on in the ministry to which God had called them.

I remember when a number of our missionaries had arrived at the Chicago airport to take their trip home to California. Our missionary of forty years, Gene Goertzen, was debating which plane to take, because he lived halfway between the Los Angeles airport and the San Diego airport and could take either one. One of his missionary friends was going to L.A., so Gene decided to make the trip with him. Nearby, the DC-10 that was leaving for San Diego was loading up. The plane was filled with vacationers who were going to California and some of them were going on from there to take trips to Hawaii. That plane was filled with excitement and joy.

How little did they know what was going to take place in the next few minutes. The DC-10 took off, but less than a minute later, one of the engines fell off and the plane crashed. I happened to be driving down the highway and saw this tragic accident take place. It seemed as though an atom bomb had struck. The flames from the explosion when the plane hit the ground were unbelievable to see. Of course, one of the first thoughts that came to my mind was that our missionary must be on that plane. We had just said goodbye to him, and to think that he might be in eternity was frightening.

We quickly checked with the airlines and found out that Gene had decided to take the other plane going to Los Angeles. What a thrill of joy it was to know that God had led him to go the other way. Still, we know that when God's appointments come to take us home, they are never too soon or too late, but are always exactly on time. When He says our work is done, we gladly go to Him.

Nancy and Gene Goertzen

At Awana, we constantly ask God for His protection during the millions of miles that our Awana missionaries travel either by car or plane. Yes, many of them have flown overseas, and many have been in some of the third-world countries where the condition of the planes was highly questionable. I thank God that in the sixty years of Awana, there has never been a serious injury in all the traveling that our missionaries have done.

I will forever praise God for sparing the life of Gene Goertzen, who with his wife, Nancy, has celebrated forty years of ministry with Awana. The impact they have made on perhaps millions of lives over these many years is amazing. Their love for reaching boys and girls for Christ, their camping ministry, and the many new Awana Clubs they have started have reached many, many children. So we thank God in His sovereignty, He spared the life of our precious missionary, Gene Goertzen.

STEVE CURINGTON: ADDICTION TRAGEDY TURNED MINISTRY

Steve was an exciting Awana kid who seemed to have his batteries fully charged all the time; however, he had a real desire to achieve. He got award after award after award, and he was on the winning Olympic team. He kept pursuing Awana achievements until he got his Timothy Award, which represented four years of memorizing Scripture from the club handbooks.

Steve was blessed to have Christian parents and also attended a solid, Bible-believing church. Then, when he was eighteen years old, he left home to attend college. This is an exciting time for most teens, as they get to see another world in action. It was at college that Steve saw another world that he became attracted to. It wasn't long before his new friends had persuaded him to try drugs; soon thereafter, Steve Curington was utterly addicted to drugs.

One might ask how this could happen to a young fellow who grew up at a Bible-believing church and went through the Awana program. Sometimes the devil is strong as well as wily, and he got Steve to fall down into the pit of sin. For more than ten years, Steve was engulfed in this lifestyle of sin. Remember Moses in the Old Testament? He said he chose to suffer affliction with the people of God rather than enjoy the pleasures of sin for a season. Yes, we all know there are pleasures in sin, but they are just for a season and the consequences of sin are always tragic.

While Steve was enjoying his sinful lifestyle, he drove a car while under the influence of drugs, speeding rapidly down a lonely road one night. Steve came to a real sharp curve in the road, which he did not see, and before he knew what was happening, he had hit a tree, turned his car over, and was lying there in his car bleeding profusely with ruptured ribs. While he lay there wondering if he was going to die, God seemed to bring his life before him, and he said to God, "If you will deliver me from this I will give you my life."

This accident took place in a lonely area, but God in His providence had a woman who lived nearby who heard the accident, came out and saw the tragedy, and was able to call 911 to see if they could save his life. God wonderfully spared his life and Steve said, "I know what God wants me to do. He wants me to reach the addicted people that I was fellowshipping with. I know that they are all desperate and are looking for peace and happiness, which they will never find in that lifestyle of drugs."

Steve went back to the church where he had attended Awana and talked to Pastor Kingsbury and said, "Pastor, I want to get involved again." The pastor gave him a Sunday school class because he wanted to see if Steve could attract addicted people to come to his class so that he could minister to them. It was obvious that God's hand was upon him, because before long he had a number of adults in his class. The word soon spread that there was

Steve Curington

a place in the church for addicted people, and the class began to grow. Soon
they had to have a weekly Reformers Unanimous meeting, which grew to well
over one hundred people suffering from various addictions.

These people were not only addicted to alcohol, drugs, and sex, but also
to pornography, gambling, and many other forms of vice. Steve found that it
was not just the down-and-outers who became addicted; some very wealthy
people had addictions that most people did not even know about. This was
God's sign for Steve and his pastor to make the addiction program available to other churches around the country. Before long, a school was started
where the addicted could come and live while they went through the program. This program became so successful that the mayor even named Steve
Curington "Citizen of the Year."

Today a real miracle is taking place, in that God is spreading this ministry all across the United States and into Canada. One of the most needed
ministries in all Bible-based churches today is a ministry that reaches people
with addictions. Most pastors are really groping, due to their lack of experience in this area, and so we praise God for raising up a fellow like Steve Curington, who listened to God's leading in his life and whom God is blessing
abundantly with this tremendous ministry called Reformers Unanimous.

God used the Awana ministry in Steve's life: even as he was enjoying sin, the Lord brought to his mind the Word of God that he had memorized in club. It was the Word of God that really convicted him and brought him back to a good relationship with the Lord.

I am delighted that I am personally involved in the ministry of Reformers Unanimous in these latter years of my life. I never thought that God would allow me to function in another ministry. I am fully persuaded that He has led me into this, as I continue serving the Lord until He takes me home.

HOLOCAUST SURVIVOR: GODLY EXCITEMENT

One of the most interesting visits I ever had in my office occurred some years ago, when a man came in and said to me, "I really appreciate Awana, but I think that perhaps I may appreciate Awana even more than you do." That really aroused my curiosity; why would anyone say something like that? Then he went on to give his story.

> I was born and raised in Germany under the holocaust of Hitler. My folks were devout Christians, but fear gripped them each day as they wondered if something about them would come to the surface and someone might even be suspicious about our love for the Lord. In a moment they could come in and we would be taken out and be put in a slave labor camp or even into the gas chambers. So we lived every day in fear, fear, and more fear.

Then, with a big smile on his face and great enthusiasm, he looked at me and said, "Guess what? I am an American now and I am an Awana commander. I am so excited because I look at my whole town as my mission field and I have no fears whatsoever that anyone is going to question me for what I am doing. I have no fear that someone is going to take and put me into a gas chamber or in a labor camp somewhere. I want you to know that I am so thrilled that I now have the opportunity to reach these kids for Christ and show them that there is a wonderful life ahead if they will only just believe and then give their lives to trust Him."

That was certainly a message that I thought every Awana leader should hear, to put enthusiasm into their hearts again to keep keeping on serving our wonderful Lord until He comes again.

PRESIDENT GEORGE H. W. BUSH

I received a call from our state representative, Terry Parke, that President Bush would be coming to town. He was going to be hosted at a campaign dinner to be held on behalf of Governor Edgar. Representative Parke said that whenever the president comes to town, all of the key politicians want to be invited, along with some other special people of varying degrees of accomplishment, fame, or notoriety. There are also those who will be invited if they are willing to donate anywhere from $50,000 to $100,000 to the campaign. They decided that only thirty-five people would be invited to this particular dinner. The state representative told me that he was still trying to get me one of those places, trying to persuade the key people that Awana has such a tremendous influence in the state of Illinois and could be very helpful in the election. I realized that the possibility of my getting to see the president was very remote, considering all the key people who were asking to be invited, so I had virtually given up any hope.

Then came the exciting phone call that I had been chosen to meet the president—and on its heels, the apprehension and the fear of wondering,

Meeting President George H. W. Bush

What does one say to the president of the United States? Then there were the security procedures that I had to go through: My history and character had to be thoroughly checked, and I also went through the personal security system before I could enter the banquet room. All of a sudden, I found myself in the room with all these notable guests, many of whom I had only read about or seen their pictures in the paper. Some had paid $50,000 just to have their picture taken with the president. I'm sure you realize that, as I was representing Awana Clubs International, there were no gifts forthcoming from me!

Thoughts were flooding through my mind as to how the president was going to be able to greet all these folks. Were they all going to stand in a line, so he could go down individually and talk to them? We were all given badges with our names nicely printed on them. Finally, there came the big announcement that the president was about to enter the room. We were all standing anxiously, awaiting his arrival. Suddenly, the door opened and in came the president with his Secret Service bodyguards. To my astonishment, he walked directly over to me, put out his hand, and said, "How are you doing today, Art?"

I suddenly became aware that I was shaking hands with one of the most famous men in the world. I had been praying and asking the Lord just how I should speak to the president; with all the people who wanted to see him, I knew I would have to be brief and to the point. I quickly shared with him the ministry of "Awana Around the World." I mentioned that Awana is comprised basically of volunteer leaders, many of whom have given more than twenty years of their lives to impact kids. This really impressed him. I asked him if there was any way he could help us encourage these leaders who are constantly giving of themselves, and he agreed to make a brief video for me that I could share with the leaders as an encouragement. He even gave me the contact in Washington to follow through on this. Unfortunately, some of the leadership at the Capitol changed, and the people with whom I was to work were no longer in the same positions, so we were never able to make this happen.

However, I so appreciated his friendliness, and since that day I have often thought how incidental this meeting with the president was, compared to the day when we are going to be able to meet the King of Kings, our Savior, the Lord of Lords, and we are going to be guests at the Marriage Supper of the Lamb. Just to know that we are part of royalty because we are heirs and joint-heirs with Christ. To know that in the ages to come, God is going to show the exceeding greatness of His kindness toward us in Christ Jesus. Yes, we all know the greatest person we ever met was when we came face-to-face with Jesus Christ and trusted Him to be our Savior. Even more so, to know that He is not only our Savior, but our Friend. He is the King of Kings, Everlasting Father, Prince of Peace, and what a thrill it is to have met Him and to know Him.

PRESIDENT GEORGE W. BUSH

Some years later, while I was down in Florida on vacation with my family, I received the good news that I was going to meet the younger President Bush, as he was going to be coming in from Washington to Chicago on his sixtieth birthday. A special celebration was being prepared for him.

The Speaker of the House, Dennis Hastert, was the one who made the arrangements for me to see the president. As we had years earlier, we went through the same strict procedures of being inspected and being placed in a special room at the airport, until finally we were told that we could go out to the

Meeting President George W. Bush

runway. It was very exciting to just stand there and to realize that the president's plane would soon be visible on the horizon. Perhaps the most popular man in the world was to be pulling in on that plane in just a short time, and I would get the opportunity to speak to him. All of a sudden, there were cameras all over the place waiting to take his picture as he arrived, because they were making a big celebration out of his sixtieth birthday.

Eventually, they told us to look out over the horizon so we could see his plane arriving. It got closer and closer, and then I saw it land and make its way up to the place where we were standing. The steps came dropping down and we waited for a few moments and, sure enough, out came his bodyguards and some of his key personnel. We waited a few more minutes and then out came President Bush, walking down the steps of the plane. He came up to me and I was able to greet him. I was so excited to think that I was shaking hands with the most popular man in the world! He was very friendly and accommodating and I asked him if there would be any possibility of him doing a little video for us, just thanking our Awana leaders for their services down through the years. He said that he would be glad to do that, but that it was not possible because getting through all the different gates in Washington is often very difficult.

Art and Winnie at the White House for International Year of Bible Reading, 1990

Nevertheless, we were thankful for the chance to get to meet him. I couldn't help but think, as I had the opportunity of meeting both of those presidents, that the day is coming when I am going to meet the King of Kings and the Lord of Lords. As exciting as those two events were, they are nothing compared with what we are going to see when we stand before our Lord and know that here is the Man who loves us and went to the cross on our behalf so that we would be able to spend eternity in heaven with Him. I am constantly reminded that we are to set our affections on things above and not on things on the earth. In TITUS 2:13, He says, "Look . . . for that blessed hope and glorious appearing of our great God and our Savior Jesus Christ." God really appreciates when His children look each day for His return, saying in our hearts: *Will it be today that He comes back to take us to be with Him?*

MEET MY DOG

An unforgettable visit happened when a clubber invited me to come to his home to meet his dog. That was highly unusual, as I usually went to clubbers' homes to meet their parents! His eyes were large and pleading. "Please, Mr. Rorheim. My dog is trained and he wants to meet you." Not knowing what this was all about, I reluctantly went to the boy's home to meet his dog.

As I made my way up the steps toward the door, I heard a bark and then a very deep growl. At that point I wasn't sure that I wanted to meet this dog. When I rang the bell, a very large German Shepherd came to the door with his owner close behind.

The boy instructed his dog, "You be quiet. This is Mr. Rorheim and I want you to welcome him properly. Be polite and shake his hand." What happened next I will never forget. The dog quietly approached, sat on his haunches, and lifted his paw to greet me. His little owner commanded, "Now you shake hands with Mr. Rorheim." Left without an option, I reached down and grasped the dog's paw. From deep in his throat, a low growl started and I quickly dropped his paw as soon as I felt it was polite to do so.

I often use that story as an illustration about our attitudes toward God's work. I saw a dog obeying his master's command, when in reality the dog was thinking, *I don't really want to do this. I'm just being forced to do so.* That's a lot like us Christians: Many times we don't feel like serving the Lord, and go about it while telling God the whole time, "I'm here only because I have to be." When we do that, we miss the incredible joy that we can have by being His servant doing His work.

CEMETERY DIRECTOR WITNESS

Some time ago, I went to a cemetery to see the gravesites that my mentor, Lance Latham, had given to us to ensure that Winnie and I would be buried alongside of both him and his wife, Teach. Of course, we know we will not stay in the ground, but we are all going to be raised up together when that trumpet sounds. I was interested to see just where our gravesite was located and while I was there I had a chance to talk to the director of the cemetery.

He began showing me the various types of tombstones, but I was not especially interested in that. However, as he showed them to me, I was able to share with him, and I said, "You know, I find that there is something on all the tombstones that is alike." He was a little curious as to what I was thinking about. I said there are names and everybody has a name. Then there is also on the tombstone the date they were born and the date they died—and in between those two dates there is a dash.

I was able to tell him that the most important thing on that tombstone is the dash, because that dash is actually your life. What did that dash consist of? Most of all, for the people who are deceased, where do they go? We know that their bodies go into the ground, but where do their souls go for eternity? I asked the cemetery director if he attended a church anywhere, to which he answered that he did, and then I asked him the big question: "Where are you going when you die?"

He said, "I sure hope I am going to go to heaven." Then I was able to clearly give him the gospel and to let him know that salvation is not of works, that if he would put his trust in Christ Who died on the cross for his sins, then the end of his dash would be a success.

The tragic thing about that conversation was that he said, "Nobody has ever told me like you have." I think of perhaps hundreds of Christians, pastors, and missionaries who are believers who have been to that same man to discuss all of the arrangements for a funeral, but the Lord's name was not even mentioned. We must not let the thing that our Lord has called us to do just slip away. I was happy for the opportunity to ask him whether he would trust Christ as his Savior and put his trust in Him. He indicated that he would, and I felt that here was a fellow who was now born again. I regret that I have not had any contact with him since, but I do feel that someday I will see that funeral director in heaven.

MERCEDES: OUR CAREGIVER

Mercedes is a very special lady who came into our home as a caregiver for Winnie, when Winnie was recovering from several surgeries. Mercedes and her husband came from a difficult life in Mexico and had been raised in Catholicism. Hearing the gospel for the first time in our church, they were soon led to Christ by one of our church pastors.

Godly excitement radiated from their lives, as they now knew that God had a plan for them. Each morning, Winnie and I would enjoy our devotions, using the "Awana Accountability Prayer Book" as we prayed for our missionaries and our loved ones. Another vital part of our devotion time was reviewing the chapters of Scripture we had memorized down through the years in Awana.

Our devotion time with our caregiver was a new experience for her. She had never heard Scripture recited from memory before. I asked her if she would like to memorize with us, and she got a stunned look on her face, but said that she would like to learn how to do that. For a moment I thought about what should be the first passage for Mercedes to memorize. I think we all would agree that JOHN 3:16 would be an excellent start. Mercedes was amazed at herself when she recited it perfectly. How little did she know that this was only the beginning of her Scripture-memorizing venture!

She has now memorized the following verses: JOHN 3:16; EPHESIANS 2: 8–9; REVELATION 20:15; ROMANS 3:23; ROMANS 6:23; ROMANS 5:24; JEREMIAH 33:3; PROVERBS 3:5–6; 1 CORINTHIANS 5:21; PSALM 23:1-6; PSALM 1:1-6; 1 CORINTHIANS 13:1-13; and ISAIAH 53:1–16.

What a blessing to see her proudly recite her verses. I'm sure you agree that every believer should memorize Scripture, but the big question is: How much do you really want to? How much are you willing to discipline yourself each day to make it happen? To fill the computer of your mind with the Word of God is so valuable for every Christian. Most of all, remember that it pleases God and shows Him that you really love Him.

May this life story of Mercedes challenge you today to start on a Scripture memorization venture for yourself. It will be a real challenge, but ask God to help you as you pursue this new Scripture memory challenge.

CHAPTER 6

Correspondence: Letters from Awana Clubbers

One of the most enjoyable things for me here at Awana headquarters is receiving letters from Awana clubbers. For many years, Awana would encourage letter-writing during Awana Month. Many of the clubbers were asked to write letters to me. I have received thousands of them and I appreciate so much their frankness and even cute ways of saying things. Let me share a few of them with you.

> *Dear Mr. Awana. I would suggest that you don't come to visit our club because you are too old. You wouldn't even be able to play one game. But if you would like to come and listen to our devotions, that would be OK.*
>
> *Your friend, Jim.*

This one, entitled *This is people,* was written by a six-year-old girl:

> *People are made of girls and women, also some men and boys. Men are no good until they grow up and get married. Boys are an awful bother. They seem to want everything in life except soap. My Ma is a woman and my Pa is a man. But my Pa is such a nice man I feel he must have been a little girl when he was a boy.*

> *Dear Mr. Awana, I have been an Awana clubber for some time and really enjoy it. I have often thought about what I would like to do for the*

future. Since Awana is so special to me, I am wondering if when I get old I could own an Awana Club?

Now, it's hard to understand just what went through the mind of this little clubber. Perhaps he looked at Awana as sort of a franchise. He saw the leaders collecting all the dues and maybe thought that this was a good, and profitable, business he ought to get into. That's just conjecture on my part. However, I have often said I would like to see what some of these clubbers are doing today. This young boy, I'm sure, has been successful in whatever he is doing. God has given him a good mind to think.

> *Dear Awana, I don't know if you can fully understand how much Awana means to me. Awana is like an oasis in the middle of the desert. I can't wait each week until I come to Awana. My home is very unhappy. My father is an alcoholic and fights with my mother constantly. I also believe my mother is using drugs. My older brother is also drinking and getting involved in drugs. Home is a very discouraging place. But I want you to know what a joy it is for me to come to Awana. Because there I hear the good news of God's Word and I have leaders who I know really love me. Thank you for starting this great program for me.*
>
> *With love, Betty*

One of the vital training parts of the Awana program is testimony time, to encourage the clubbers to get up and give a word of testimony on how they love the Lord, perhaps recite a Scripture verse, or say whatever God may lay on their hearts. As leaders, we often do not realize how much our testimonies are influencing the lives of these young kids. Some clubbers get the impression that a good testimony is one from a person who has had a really bad previous life and then got saved. One little eight-year-old Pal got up in the testimony meeting and said, "I thank the Lord that He saved me when I was two years old and took me away from that rough crowd I was hanging around with." He probably thought it would make his testimony more powerful.

> *Dear Mr. Awana, I like Awana very much, and I have a cool leader, he also has a cool looking daughter.*
>
> *I think Awana is the greatest club anywhere, I would much rather go to Awana than to go to Hell.*

I'm not sure if that is what he meant, but that is what came out.

I like Awana leaders because if we goof around too much they give us the right punishment and boy do they give us the punishment.

I like Awana, I like playing games, I can't run very fast, but I like it anyway.

How are you? I am fine. I want to go to Awana all my life if I can, well I can't think of anything else, but goodbye, nice talking with you.

Dear Awana headquarters, How are you? Do you guys pass sections like we do? I like Awana because I make a lot of friends and like passing sections because I like the leaders. Well, I gotta go. Bye now.

Dear brothers and sisters, I appreciate Awana a lot and I think it is the best organization in the whole world. I really like it and so do my friends. I have met new friends here too. I brung 4 to 5 new friends and they all like it. I am 11 and I have 4 dogs and a bird and I am going to get baptized pretty soon because I know I am saved and I know that is what the Lord wants me to do.

Your friend, Jimmy

Dear Awana, You'll never know how excited I am about getting my Timothy Award. I have been working on this for a long time. My next goal is to receive my Meritorious award. Even though I have been blind from birth, I know that God has exciting plans for my life.

Love, Judy

Dear Father,

I'm sorry but when you come up to camp for visiting day, I will not be able to kiss you, I hope that you will understand, but I only shake hands now man to man.

Your Son, Butch

Dear Mom and Dad,

They make you do too much here, you have to play baseball, go swimming, learn Tennis, throw a fast ball, throw football and other stuff like that. Next time I want to do nothing like the counselor.

Dear Howard,

We received your letter, could you please explain why you need 30 bandages, two splints and crutches? Mother is worried.

Love, Dad

Dear Steve,

We are all flattered that you want the family picture that is on top of the piano to put over your bed at night. We will mail it to you as soon as possible, but I am afraid you will not be able to cut your sister out of the picture.

Love, Mother

A boy came home from Sunday school one day and was asked by his father just what his Sunday school teacher had taught him. He hesitated for a minute and then described the deliverance of the Israelites from Pharaoh's army. He very descriptively told how Moses led the army to the Red Sea with Pharaoh's men close behind. Moses then quickly herded the Israelites into submarines that took them across the Red Sea. Waiting for them on the other side was a fleet of helicopters that picked them up and took them into the wilderness; the Israelites then murmured about being thirsty, so Moses took a charge of TNT and blasted the rock, and water came forth to quench their thirst. Then they became hungry and Moses gave them all automatic rifles to shoot down quail.

At this part of the story, his father interrupted and said, "Jim, is that really what she told you?" Jim hemmed and hawed for just a moment and then said, "No, not really, but you would never believe it the way she told it." It was obvious that Jim's Sunday school teacher had not really communicated what she thought she had said. The miracles of the Bible were not made "real" to Jim.

Dear Mr. Awana,

My name is Elizabeth and I go to church and Sunday school. I was saved in 1975 when I was in the second grade. I was saved in the bathroom but my older sister said that you couldn't be saved in the bathroom. I wasn't sure so in the Bible school a friend and I wanted to get saved. I wasn't as excited as the first time but after a while I felt guilty of being saved a second time because I found out it doesn't matter when or where you get saved, it's how you get saved and if you really believe that Christ died for your sins. I am really excited about trying to win my friends to the Lord. Keep Awana coming our way.

Your friend, Elizabeth

Paul Rader, an evangelist who was greatly used of God some years ago, said that one of the greatest attributes of a Christian is to be persuasive: to be able to persuade boys and girls that every portion of the Word of God is true, and to believe the precious gospel, by faith. May God teach us all, as Awana leaders, to know how to communicate these wonderful truths into the hearts of the boys and girls.

A leader's testimony: You will never know how thankful I am for Awana. My son was invited to Awana by his friends. He was [so] thrilled about going that he could hardly wait to go and he was so anxious to learn the verses in his book, so he asked me to help him. Then I started memorizing the verses with him and I saw the excitement in my son so I decided to visit this church to find out for myself. I soon found out that I needed to trust in Christ as my Savior, if I was going to Heaven. My husband and children are now Christians and today both my husband and I are both leaders in the Awana program. I thank God for Awana and how it has changed our entire family, and brought real joy to us all.

Your friend in Him, Gert

I have received thousands of letters from clubbers who have shared how much they appreciated their Awana leaders. It was because those leaders personally took an interest in them and reminded them that they were important to God and that God had something special for them. That is the ultimate secret to being a fruitful leader and instilling the lives of boys and girls with eternal values.

EXPLAIN GOD

[Written by Danny Dutton, age 8, from Chula Vista, California. This was a homework assignment given by a third-grade teacher asking the class to explain "GOD."]

One of God's main jobs is making people. He makes these to put in place of the ones that die so there will be enough people to take care of things here on earth. He doesn't make grown-ups just babies. I think because they are smaller and easier to make. That way He doesn't have to take up His valuable time teaching them to talk and walk. He can just leave that up to the mothers and fathers. I think it works out pretty good.

God's second most important job is listening to prayers. An awful lot of this goes on, as some people like preachers and things, pray other times besides bedtime. God doesn't have time to listen to the radio or TV on account of this. As He hears everything, not only prayers, there must be a terrible lot of noise into His ears, unless He has thought of a way to turn it off.

God sees everything and hears everything and is everywhere, which keeps Him pretty busy. So you shouldn't go wasting His time by going over your parents head and ask for something they said you couldn't have.

Atheists are people who don't believe in God. I don't think there are any in Chula Vista. At least there aren't any who come to our church.

Jesus is God's Son. He used to do all the hard work like walking on water and doing miracles and trying to teach people about God who didn't want to learn. They finally got tired of Him preaching to them and they crucified Him. But He was good and kind like His Father and He told His Father that they didn't know what they were doing and to forgive them and God said O.K. His Dad (God) appreciated everything He had done and all His hard work on earth, so he told Him He didn't have to go out on the road anymore. He could stay in Heaven. So He did, and now He helps His Dad out by listening to prayers and seeing which things are important for God to take care of and which ones He can take care of Himself without having to bother God with. Like a secretary only more important, of course, You can pray anytime you want and they are sure to hear you because they've got it worked out so one of them is on duty all the time.

You should always go to Sunday School because it makes God happy, and if there's anybody you want to make happy, it's God. Don't skip Sunday School to do something you think will be more fun like going to the beach. This is wrong! Besides the sun doesn't come out at the beach until noon, anyway.

If you don't believe in God, besides an Atheist, you will be very lonely, because your parents can't go everywhere with you like to camp, but God can. It's good to know He's around when you're scared, of the dark or when you can't swim very good and you get thrown in real deep water by big kids. But you shouldn't just always think of what God can do for you. I figure God put me here and He can take me back anytime He pleases.

And that's why I believe in God.

Angola Penitentiary

WARDEN BURL CAIN

One day I received a surprise phone call from Warden Burl Cain, the warden of one of the largest penitentiaries in America, Angola Penitentiary in Baton Rouge, Louisiana. I could not imagine why the warden would be calling me. He shared with me that they have a real need down there and wanted me to come down so that we could talk about this need. Burl Cain is a born-again believer.

When I went down and met with him, he shared the tragic story that the 5,000 inmates they have there are all in for life and will never have the possibility of parole. These inmates have most likely committed murder or been involved in a rape.

Warden Cain said, "I need your help." I could not imagine how I could help someone in a prison, but here is what he was asking. He said there is a flood of prisoners coming in who were the children of inmates. He asked, "What can we do to stop this flood, as the inmate children are seven times more likely to end up in prison than the average kids on the street? I believe that Awana is the only thing that I know that could have an impact in reaching these kids for Christ, so that their lives could be changed and not go the way of the world."

However, we realized that we did not have adequate Awana Clubs in the area to take care of all of these kids, so getting additional clubs was a real challenge.

He also asked me to come to a gathering where he had about 700 inmates and he wanted me to ask them the question to see if they wanted us to do something to reach their kids and grandkids for the Lord. Many of them have never even seen their children or grandchildren. But I was amazed when I asked them the question, "How many of you really would like to see your kids?" I have a very beautiful picture that shows every hand of those 700 inmates in the air, waving with enthusiasm. It was obvious that even though they had really ruined their own lives, they didn't want their children to go down the same path.

We then wondered what kind of a plan we could devise so that they could have a time with their children. We began to think that if we gave the inmates an Awana book like a clubber would have, and then an additional one to their children, perhaps there they could get some dialogue going on in which they would try and do their books together. And there has been some real progress with that program.

I also asked the warden if it would be possible to get the inmates involved in Scripture memorization, since that has been such a big part of my life. He was very excited about that and so we came up with the Scripture passage of PSALM 1:1–6 to challenge the inmates with, to see what they could do to memorize that. We offered them a reward of a T-shirt that had PSALM 1 printed on the front, with all the verses as a reminder, and told them that everyone would receive a shirt if they would recite PSALM 1. We were amazed to see their enthusiasm; at least 400 of them passed the "PSALM 1 test" and

Inmates at Angola prison

Art and Warden Burl Cain holding a list of Psalm 1 award winners

proudly received their PSALM 1 shirts. We decided to make PSALM 1 our key passage.

The next time I went down there, they had a surprise for me. One of the inmates was a very musically talented man, and he had written music to the words of PSALM 1. He taught them as a fine choir and they marched up on stage and sang the song for me. I don't know when I was ever thrilled as much as to feel the heartbeat of those inmates as they were singing PSALM 1 with their godly enthusiasm.

Since that first visit, we've been so delighted to know that more than a thousand inmates have now trusted Christ as their Savior, and to see the impact of the gospel in their lives and how it is affecting the other inmates. There is definitely a difference in them. So we thank God for this first opportunity we had to reach out and teach Scripture to the inmates at Angola.

Later Warden Cain spoke with me and said that what we'd done was a great start, but the shirts are only temporary. "Most of these inmates will probably die here, and I want them to have something permanent that will remind them all of their life just how important it is to know the Lord and to memorize His Word." Warden Cain challenged me to put together a medallion program. This medallion would be made of metal with a chain that would go around the inmate's neck. I was amazed that he would allow that in a prison—certainly there is not another prison that would allow such a thing—but he felt it was that important and God would take care of any hazards we had there. So we now have the medallion program: bronze,

Art standing with Psalm One Club flags

Children of inmates at a Returning Hearts *celebration*

silver, and gold, and then another set with red, blue, and simulated diamond stones. Each one of these represents a different portion of Scripture and we are amazed at how well they are doing after learning God's Word, and learning with great enthusiasm.

About 80 percent of the inmates never have anyone come in and visit, and of course there is nothing for them to achieve in prison where they will get individual recognition for their accomplishments. But now they are able to get involved in the medallion program; seeing them come up and receive the medallions and being able to shake their hands and see the joy on their faces really thrills my heart.

The other thrilling thing about the prison is that it has now caught the attention of other prisons all around the country, and some twenty-four other prisons are adopting the Awana program for their inmates. Most of these prisons do not have born-again wardens, and they will probably not go into the Scripture memory program for at least a while.

We are thankful for the Awana days, or, as we have titled our program, *Returning Hearts,* when the inmates' children—hundreds of them—come in for a full day to meet with their dads and enjoy being together and playing games. Our *Returning Hearts* is a very emotionally touching time. We

Angola inmate reunited with his children

Returning Hearts *celebration*

Art with a Returning Hearts *child*

have assistants from the Awana headquarters staff and volunteers from other churches who come down to Angola to help with our program of connecting the dads with their children for a day.

The children are brought to Angola by their guardians and then released to our volunteers for the day. Then they are escorted to the area where they will connect with their dads. It does your heart good just to see all of those dads sitting up in the grandstand when all of their children or grandchildren have been gathered to meet with them for the day. Some of the kids have not seen their dads for many years, and some of them have never seen their dads at all. So, as they bring the children out and call their names, just to see the inmates coming down out of the grandstands to embrace their children is an experience that once you see it, you will never be the same. To see the love that is shown between a dad and his child is very heart-rending.

During that day, they have such a good time of fellowship together with the counselor who has been assigned to them for the entire day. The sad time comes when, at the end of the day, the children must say goodbye to their dads; sometimes they don't know if they will ever see each other again. And so it is really a precious time that God has arranged for us to have the *Returning Hearts.*

Warden Burl Cain, Art, and Lyndon Azcuna; Lyndon is director of
Lifeline *and* Malachi Dads

Another vital part of the Angola program is called the *Malachi Dads,* which reaches out to both the inmates and their children with the message of the gospel. With God's guidance and wisdom, Lyndon Azcuna created and directs this program for fathers who are really interested in trying to build or rebuild a relationship with their families. Most of their relationships were completely shattered because of their lifestyle before coming to prison, but these *Malachi Dads* are born again and love the Lord. They meet on a regular basis, studying God's Word through this great program. We have a graduation service and they get certificates for their accomplishments. We are seeing wonderful results as children and their dads respond to this message.

Death Row Area

I was given the opportunity to visit the death row area. As I visited there, I found the man who was first in line to be executed, a born-again man who had already memorized PSALM 1, which really thrilled me as he recited it to me.

I will never forget, as I approached the death row area, before the gates were open, I saw a plaque on the wall with about fifteen names on it. I asked the warden just whose names were on there. He told me that these are the prisoner missionaries and that these men have trusted Christ as their Savior.

Pastor Ron Hicks, inmate at Angola, with Art

They have seen the impact of the gospel here at Angola and they want to be missionaries to the other inmates. They were willing to give up all of their rights to be able to go to other prisons to be missionaries there. I could not believe what I saw. Talk about really true missionaries who have a heartbeat to give out the gospel! I saw that so beautifully displayed there.

Contributions to Missionaries

An extra blessing to me was that I saw that some of the inmates, who were able to accumulate a little money from handicraft projects that they were able to sell, were actually contributing to the missionary fund for some of these other missionaries who had gone into other prisons. It just proves what the gospel can do when someone really gets to know the Lord and realizes that his life is not just sitting in his cell, but wants to reach out and obey whatever God lays on his heart. This truly made an impact on my life.

This is what other prisons are seeing, and they, too, cannot believe what is taking place because of the *Malachi Dads* program. These are certainly tremendous doors of opportunity. Just look at this while the doors of opportunity are open. So, let's go to them and fulfill the ministry in prisons that God has called us to.

We are so thankful for the ministry that God has given to Awana to be able to minister to the inmates at the Angola prison, which is called the *Lifeline*

Art shaking hands with one of the inmates

Ministry of Awana Angola Prison. Praise the Lord for Angola and especially for Warden Cain, as he is working with Awana to get the inmates rehabilitated and serving the Lord while they are incarcerated at Angola.

LETTER FROM AN INMATE

So, you ask me, "What's the Hype about Psalm 1, what's the meaning behind it?" First, Psalm 1 was introduced to us (Angola) as a challenge to memorize for a shirt by Mr. Art. This prison has been in a transforming stage for quite some time and the things Psalm 1 represents are good in life for both Christians and non believers. Inoder to memorize God's words you must get it in you first before you can memorize it, then you have to resight it to someone and if you don't resight it with a flow then you'll have to go back and learn it until you do. (That's how we did it in our dorm) That ensures that you know it, just like the alphabets.

Psalm 1 allows you to know how God wants his
people to live and the rewards of obeing the Lord.
Mr. Art did a beautiful thing by getting guy's
here to learn Psalms1 because it transformed alot
of people lives, in the sense that it gave them
a guideline in how to conduct themselves in line
with the word of God and also for the non believers
that were looking for a better way to live their
lives. I'm not saying that all the men who memorized Psalms 1 are christians, I'm simply saying
it effected them in one way or another. Verse one
tells you not to hang with people that are not
about what is right, because God is about the
things that are good.

Verse two explains that you should find delight
in the things that are good which are the words
of the Lord (Reading and living by the Bible) and
always think about it day and night, therefore it
will always be on your mind and you wont go astray.
Verse three enforces the fact that following the
word of God and keeping it with you day and night
you shall receive many blessings and you shall
prosper in everything that you do, God will give
the increase.

Verse four tells you that the unbelievers will
not have favor in God's sight and they will go
through many changes in life because the word of
God isn't the stabilizing factor in their lives
because God wont be guiding their steps. Verse Five
assures that the believers and the unbelievers
shall not be together. Verse Six confrims the
things in verse five, by telling us that the Lord
knows how is how and you may beable to fool the
people of this world but you can't fool God and the
unbelievers shall parish. (They shall be punished.)
The Bible terms of punished is to burn in HELL for
all eternity.

I pray that I've given you a good understanding of Psalms 1, and how it helps. Mr. Art is a good man and he's trying to help you see a better way in life, I really like Mr. Art, I can only pray that I would be that strong in the Lord and as active as he is. Make no mistakes about Bro. B, change doesn't come over night and there will be disappointments and let downs along the way, if you fail don't sweat it, get up and try again. Eventually you wont be fallin in or to those same things. No one changes over night it's a step by step process. I'm constantly fallin, but I get back up and keep going.

I'm no where near perfect and I'm shuffled out in my walk but I'm still moving forward because I know a better day is coming. Your mother told you a good thing about getting Psalms 1 tattooed on you, live it first.

Thoughts

CELL PHONES

I wonder what would happen if we treated our Bibles like we treat our cell phones.

What if we carried it around in our purses or pockets?

What if we turned back to go and get it if we forgot it?

What if we flipped through it several times a day?

What if we treated it like we couldn't live without it?

What if we gave it to the kids as a gift?

What if we used it as we travel?

What if we used it in case of emergency?

What if we upgraded it to get the latest version?

What if there were some things that made you go "Hmmmmm, where is my Bible?"

Oh, we do like our cell phones, but we don't ever have to worry about our Bibles being disconnected, as Jesus has already paid in full.

AWANA DISCIPLINES

The word *discipline* is often misinterpreted to mean punishment; really, it means education, training, and self-control as well as correction. Discipleship takes discipline. A *disciple* is one who has been taught or trained to serve our wonderful Lord. Without discipline, we are not disciples even though we profess His name and pass as followers of the Lord Jesus.

I am often reminded of the famous football coach, Vince Lombardi, who headed the championship Green Bay Packers football team. He said, "My goal as a coach is to get my players to do the things that they do not want to do, in order that they can be what they want to be." Yes! There is a price to pay if we are to be disciplined, effective witnesses for the Lord.

Apart from the Bible, which is the Word of God, discipline is perhaps the next most vital ingredient for successful Awana leaders and successful Awana Clubs. Every effective Awana Club begins with discipline. The Awana five-count has been an effective method of teaching discipline in the game period as well as other areas of Awana. Discipline is so vital because if you don't have discipline, which starts with getting the attention of Awana clubbers, you cannot teach them the Word of God.

Today we are living in an undisciplined age. Awana clubbers, coming from the most undisciplined homes, are delighted to see consistent discipline in their Awana Clubs. More clubs fail because of lack of discipline than for any other reason. Without discipline, the clubbers and also the leadership will be discouraged and before long the pastor and deacons of the church will wonder whether the club is worth having—all because discipline is not being enforced.

Discipline is imperative in our lives as Awana leaders. We need discipline in our personal prayer lives. Without a specific plan to go to the Lord each day in prayer for our personal devotion time, we soon become ineffective Awana leaders.

One of the most vital ingredients of the Awana program is Scripture memorization. In this undisciplined age, the most effective method of combating the wiles of the devil is to have Awana clubbers hide the Word of God in their minds and then, of course, in their hearts. A successful memorization plan has to be centered in discipline. Yes, on a regular basis we must take time to memorize the Word of God, review the Word of God, and embed these wonderful truths into the greatest computer that was ever invented, the mind that God gave us. The Word of God we call God's software and one blessing is that it never crashes like the computers of this world.

Discipleship requires the discipline of cross-bearing:

- Daily food for which we are to pray (MATTHEW 6:11)
- Our daily work, in which we are to be faithful (1 THESSALONIANS 4:11, 12)
- Our daily cross (2 THESSALONIANS 3:10–13).

Our Lord said, in LUKE 9:23, "If any man will come after me, let him deny himself, and take up his cross daily and follow me." LUKE 9:27 adds: "and whosoever doth not bear his cross, and come after me, cannot be my disciple."

Yes! Without discipline there is no discipleship, and without discipleship we are ineffective servants of our wonderful Lord. These are truly exciting days for us to serve our wonderful Lord. May we allow the Lord to teach us His discipline so in that day when we stand before Him, we will joyfully receive the highest award of all: "Well done, thou good and faithful servant" (MATTHEW 25:21).

THREE TYPES OF LEADERS

Some leaders are like canoes; they need to be paddled.

Some leaders are like wheelbarrows; they are no good unless pushed.

Some leaders are like footballs; you can never tell which way they will bounce.

Some leaders are like lights; they are on and off, on and off.

Some leaders are like kites; you must hold tight or they will fly away.

But the best of all are the gold-watch leaders; they are open-faced, pure gold, quietly and regularly busy fulfilling God's will for their lives.

There are also three types of leaders:

The greatest leader of all is the one who makes things happen for God.

There are those who watch things happen.

There are those who do not know what happened.

Yes, I am afraid there are leaders who fall into these categories, but oh, that we all might want to make things happen for God!

LEADERSHIP THAT LASTS

The best Awana leader has the following:

1. A mind tuned to the Lord, seeing boys and girls as the Lord sees them.
2. Ears to enjoy listening to clubbers' "small talk" as well as listening to recitation of Bible verses and sections.
3. A BT bar complete with awards, to encourage and motivate clubbers and other leaders.
4. A heart that understands kids' needs.
5. A stomach that can skip supper on club night when necessary.
6. A wristwatch, to enable him or her to arrive at club fifteen minutes early.
7. Fingers to dial a telephone, to enable him or her to stay in touch with clubbers and encourage them in their achievements.
8. A Bible and a copy of the clubbers' handbook for ready reference.
9. A customized visitation album, complete with pictures of the local club, to better explain the Awana program to parents.
10. Knees that bend as he or she prays for clubbers, parents, and fellow leaders.
11. Feet to carry him or her to club, and also on special outings and on visitation.
12. All of the above does not end in the middle of the club year.

—Author unknown

SHOULD I BE AN AWANA LEADER NEXT YEAR?

Some years ago, I received a letter from an Awana leader who so beautifully shared the spiritual battle in which she was engaged. This leader asked the big question: "Should I be an Awana leader next year?" She wrote:

> Toward the end of each club year I come to the conclusion that next year I'm not going to be an Awana leader. There is never a real peace that comes with it; only inner conflict, but nevertheless, I cling to the idea. After all, I'm tired. I'm going to take next year off; let someone else do it for a while. This often occurs after my third phone call from leaders

who won't be going to club tonight or after my third devotion that no one else wanted to give. I think, "Let someone else do it and I'll stay home because I'm tired."

Alas, these are only temporary periods of insanity when I fool myself into thinking that I am doing God a favor by serving Him. On the contrary! God is doing me a favor by letting me serve Him. Let's face it. If I don't do the job, someone else will! God's work goes on whether I do it or not: in spite of me, not because of me.

When I stand before the Lord and He says, "What, my child, did service to me cost you?" I fear I will be too ashamed to say, "Well, I gave up some time from my busy schedule—once a week" or "Sometimes it's inconvenient to be a Awana leader" or "Meals on club night are really a hassle" or "I listened to a little girl's Bible verses when I was too tired." BIG DEAL! One look at the nail-scarred hands and feet which bought me at such a cost will leave me speechless, defenseless. It's then that I realize I don't know the meaning of cost and if my service to God doesn't cost me anything, it doesn't even count. How petty is my service compared to Calvary.

Who am I to decide whether or not I'll do God a favor of serving Him next year? Who am I to pick and choose my calling? God calls— we only have to obey. That's the secret!!! You see, there is no question if I'll be an Awana leader next year—or any year. *I already am* an Awana leader. God has *already* called me. My only "choice" is whether or not to obey and follow that calling—AT ANY COST.

And then, when the right choice is made, that peace, that perfect peace that passes all understanding that only God can give, floods my heart to press on for His glory.

I trust that this letter will remind each one of us afresh that we really do not have any options in God's plan. All we have to do is to be sensitive to His leading, whatever it may be. Only eternity will reveal the fruit of the efforts we have put forth to win and train boys and girls for our wonderful Lord. "In due season we shall reap, if we faint not" (GALATIANS 6:9).

BASICS FOR A FRUITFUL AWANA CLUB

1. You must have a heart and vision to give your life to reach out to love kids and to share the lifegiving message of the gospel with them.

2. You must recognize Awana as your God-given ministry from the Lord.

3. You must treat Awana not just as an enjoyable, interesting ministry.

4. You cannot look at Awana as an interesting hobby.

5. You cannot be an Awana leader because you want to be with your friends.

6. You cannot be a leader just because you have leisure time to give.

None of these are justifiable reasons to be an Awana leader. Being a fruitful Awana leader will depend on how much you really love God. True love for God demands action. True love for God means reading God's Word daily, even when you don't feel like it. Loving God is displayed by your prayer life. Prayer will be your expression as to how much you love God. It has been said "Much Prayer, Much Power; Little Prayer, Little Power."

Your daily witnessing and giving out gospel tracts will be a normal expression of your love for God.

Your deepest desire is to see every Awana clubber that God sends across your path in life to hear the gospel and trust Him to be their Savior.

Loving God is God's commandment. Thou shalt love the Lord thy God with all thy heart, with all thy mind, and with all thy soul. He also shares the importance of love in 1 CORINTHIANS 13:1: "Though I speak with the tongues of men and of angels, and have not love, I am become *as* sounding brass, or a tinkling cymbal."

Suppose that you had to grade yourself, on a scale of 1 to 10, on how much you love God. What kind of a grade would you give yourself, based on the things we have shared already?

The greatest benefit of loving God is that the clubbers, leaders, and all persons with whom you associate will see by your life that you are obviously God's loving leader.

AWARENESS

One of the creative ideas leaders have shared with me is an "Awana Awareness Night." At the beginning of a new club season, we need to stop in the midst of our busy schedules. We must ask the Lord to give us a fresh awareness of the many facets of our ministry.

I'm reminded of the much-told story of the farmer who was selling his "trained" mule. His sales pitch was that the mule would respond to any verbal command. The man who purchased the animal found it to be the typical stubborn, unreasonable mule. Completely perplexed, the man went back to the farmer and asked him to demonstrate how the mule would obey verbal commands. The farmer immediately took a wooden 2 × 4 and swiftly hit the mule. The man who had purchased the mule replied, "Didn't you tell me that all I had to do was speak to the mule and he would respond?"

"That is correct," answered the farmer.

"Then why did you hit him?"

"Oh, I just needed to get his attention so he would hear my commands."

I'm sure we all get the moral of the story. Yes, I'm afraid at times we are like the mule. One of God's greatest concerns for you and me is to get our attention so He can give us a fresh awareness of His exciting plan for our lives.

At the beginning of a new club season, we need a God-given awareness of our goals and motives for the coming year. Let me share with you some awareness areas we need to consider:

1. Awareness that our club ministry is a calling from God.

2. Awareness of the brief time we have to reach these precious clubbers. Some we may see only once.

3. Awareness of the clarity of the gospel. God's only way of taking people to heaven is by faith in the shed blood of Christ.

4. Awareness of Satan's presence at all Awana Clubs. He's the first one to arrive at club and the last one to leave.

5. Awareness of the power of God's Word, which is our weapon against the wiles of the devil.

6. Awareness of foreign missions. God expects every Christian to have a heartbeat for the billions of people around the world who have never heard of God's way to heaven.

7. Awareness of eternal hell, without Christ, which is forever and forever and forever.

Is all the work you put forth each week in Awana leadership really worthwhile? I'm sure your answer is "Yes!"

TREASURED GEMS

- You can't lay foundations in other lives if there are only sketchy outlines in your own.

- Because of Calvary, the murky shadows of earth will one day fade in the bright glory of God's day.

- Failure to do right may be just as sinful as doing wrong.

- Many who have tons of religion have not one ounce of salvation.

- A successful marriage requires falling in love many times and always with the same person.

- To be silent about our Savior and His salvation is a serious sin of omission.

- The more you love Jesus, the more you long for heaven.

- When Satan attacks, strike back with the sword of the Spirit.

- As Christ is magnified, your ministry will be multiplied.

- The most important part of Christmas is the first six letters.

- Atheism has not convinced us that there is no God, only that there is a devil.

- It is better to look ahead and prepare than to look back and despair.

- The measure of youthfulness is largely determined by the measure of your concentration.

- You are saved by God's grace, not by our goodness; by Christ's dying, not by doing.

- The time God allows us is just enough for the work He allows us.

- Experience can be the best teacher, but only if it is the experience of obeying God's Word.

- The best way of influencing others for God is by upholding them in prayer to God.

- Buy up every opportunity; God often uses small matches to light great torches.

- True obedience neither procrastinates nor questions.

- Nothing is as contagious as enthusiasm; it is the genius of sincerity and truth that accomplishes no victory without it.

- Faith is to believe what we do not see and the reward of faith is to see what we believe.

- Self-control is to have the same ailment the other person is describing and not mention it.

- Everybody can give pleasure in some way; one person may do it by coming into a room and another by leaving.

- A college education may not hurt a man if he is willing to learn a little something after he graduates.

- It is the business of faith to overcome the world and see things that are out of sight.

- It is dangerous and presumptuous to say "tomorrow" when God says "today."

- If you are not living as close to God as you once did, you may not guess who has moved.

- God's way of salvation by grace is like a parachute; there just isn't any substitute.

- Every time you speak, your heart is on parade.

- The gospel is only for one class of people: sinners.

- A Christian's heart should be on its knees at all times.

- You must accept God's Son today if you wish to live in heaven's sunshine tomorrow.

- He who plants weeds must not expect to gather flowers.

- It is better to be in the storm with Christ than to be in the smooth waters without Him.

- Life is not a journey to the grave with the intention of arriving in a well-preserved body, but rather to skid in broadside, thoroughly used up, totally worn out, and loudly proclaiming "WOW! WHAT A RIDE!"

FAITHFUL, FRUITFUL LEADERSHIP

I minister to Awana leaders at leadership conferences, but the leaders will never know how much they minister to me! Many of them travel miles for this special day of training, fellowship, and inspiration. Just to look into their faces and see the joy of the Lord is so refreshing!

Without the devotion and faithful service of dedicated leaders, there would be no Awana today. I am keenly aware that the battle for the lives of our young people is much greater and harder now than in the early days of the Awana ministry. Just compare the results of a survey of public school teachers, taken in 2009, with the answers to the same survey in the 1950s. Teachers in the 1950 survey listed their students' most serious problems as:

1. Talking
2. Chewing gum
3. Making noise
4. Running in the halls
5. Getting out of place in line
6. Wearing improper clothing
7. Not putting paper in the wastebasket

In the more recent survey, they listed:

1. Drug abuse
2. Alcohol abuse
3. Suicide
4. Truancy
5. Pregnancy
6. Assault and battery
7. Rape
8. Arson

What a tremendous difference! Yes, there's a price to be paid by Awana leaders if we are to penetrate the strongholds of Satan in the lives of today's young people.

At each conference, I ask the leaders, "Have you considered quitting?" Almost all of them say yes. If you've been in Christian ministry for any length of time, you've discovered that there are many discouragements along the way. And discouragement is Satan's number-one tool in getting leaders to quit.

But why don't these Awana leaders throw in the towel? Because they recognize that God "has called them" to the Awana ministry. They realize they're not doing Him a favor by being leaders. All we need is a fresh look at Calvary, and our discouragements will seem so insignificant.

As Awana leaders, we must constantly be on guard that the busyness of life does not cause us to lose our sensitivity to God's leading. We must not forget that "we are called" to share the gospel of God's grace, which is the very foundation of the Awana ministry.

Remember, the awards we will receive from the Lord one day will be distributed on the basis of our faithfulness to His calling. Are you a faithful, fruitful leader?

Praise God for our leaders!

NIAGARA FALLS: WALKING BLINDLY INTO TRAGEDY

I trust that many of you have had the opportunity to visit one of the great wonders of the world: that, of course, is Niagara Falls. Just to stand there and watch God's creation, as these millions of gallons of water are pouring over the falls, you are constantly awestruck with all that is taking place.

I have often imagined this scenario. Suppose you were standing right at the edge of the falls and there you saw perhaps a hundred blind people with their canes and their walkers, and they are heading toward the edge of the falls. Somewhere along the line they received the information that they were going into a park for a beautiful band concert. So I stand there and I see them going to their deaths as they go into the falls. I stand there and have the attitude that I did not push them in, and I did not tell them where I was going, or maybe even I do not feel like talking to them today.

Now we know we have perhaps displayed that attitude many, many times when God has sent people across our path for us to witness to. Perhaps the greatest enemy we have is trying to take care of our comfort zone. Yes, we are all made that way, aren't we? We find it so easy to do the things that please us and give us comfort, but when it comes time, we realize it is not just a matter of life and death, but a matter of eternity in hell. So I trust that the Niagara Falls story might grip your heart, as it did mine. We have to be urgent witnesses for the Cross to be able to be God's witness wherever He places us.

DIRECTIONS TO OUR FATHER'S HOUSE

God's GPS:

Make a right turn onto Believers Blvd.

Keep straight and go through the Green Light (which is Jesus Christ).

There you must turn onto the Bridge of Faith, which is over Troubled Waters.

When you get off the bridge, make a right turn and keep straight,

You are on the King's Highway, heaven-bound.

Keep going for three miles: one for the Father, one for the Son, one for the Holy Ghost.

Then exit off onto Grace Blvd.,

Then make a right turn onto Gospel Lane,

Keep straight and then make another right on Prayer Road.

As you go on your way, yield not to the traffic on Temptation Avenue.

Also, avoid Sin Street because it is a dead end.

Pass up Envy Drive and Hate Avenue.

Also, pass up Hypocrisy Street, Gossiping Lane, and Backbiting Blvd.

However, you have to go down Long-Suffering Lane, Persecution Blvd., and Trials and Tribulations Ave.

But that's all right, because Victory Street is straight ahead, and that leads us to our Father's house.

And in the ages to come He will show us the amazing riches of His grace in Christ Jesus. Yes, we are ready for heaven and for God's wonderful presence as we arrive there to spend eternity with Him.

THREE SPIRITUAL LENSES

Photography has been a hobby of mine for many, many years. For about eight years I was a photographic printer, doing printing and developing thousands of pictures from people all over the United States. It was in the day when the printing of pictures was a skill that had to be "developed"; today most pictures are printed through electronic means.

I then became interested in the camera and in taking pictures. I was determined to learn as much as I could. I got a press camera, the same kind that the newspaper photographers would use. I learned how to use the camera and in the early days of Camp Awana, I shot all of the group pictures, as well as all of the activity pictures. In the beginning days of Awana, there was not enough money to hire a professional photographer, so I acted as the cameraman for all the pictures in our original handbooks.

I graduated from a photography school that taught me the basics of taking good pictures, and I was told that you basically need three good lenses for your camera. The first one is the standard lens, which is 28 millimeters; the wide-angle lens, which is 200 millimeters; and then the telephoto lens, which is a standard 55 millimeters, for most action pictures and small group shots. With the unique qualities of the wide-angle lens, I would be able to get pictures indoors. The telephoto lens is for capturing pictures in the distance, as it focuses on actions as though they were close to the camera.

Just as photography uses three lenses, Awana needs to equip leaders and clubbers with three spiritual lenses. Let's talk about the close-up portrait lens. This is the lens you look through on club night when all the action is taking place. You listen to clubbers recite verses, you hear them singing, you listen to their testimonies, and some of the clubbers you may never see again. Every night of club is vital; you can never live it over again. The Lord holds you responsible for being effective in the lives of these kids. What a privilege to share the Word of God with them each week!

Now let's take a look at Awana through the wide-angle lens. This includes the entire church ministry team. Every Awana leader must have a heartbeat for the total ministry of the church. They must realize there would not be an Awana without the church; they must have a desire to support the pastor by faithfully praying and attending the church services. Also, each Awana leader must remember that Awana, within itself, is the arm of the local church. Awana leaders should be getting clubbers into Sunday school, which is also a vital part of the church.

Then there is a telephoto lens that looks off into the distance. The Word of God says, in JOHN 15:16, "but I have chosen you, and ordained you, that ye should go and bring forth fruit, and *that* your fruit should remain." When we look into the faces of those kids each week, perhaps it should stretch our imaginations into their futures. Sometimes you cannot imagine how they could possibly turn out to be positive witnesses for the Lord. Satan will certainly do his utmost to discourage you. When the clubbers come with their batteries fully charged, too often their behavior is very discouraging, but God may have His hand of blessing on some whom you would least expect. Perhaps He is planning a special ministry for their lives, with that same telephoto lens on foreign ministry around the world.

We must remember that God loves the world and He wants us to love the world also. As we look through that telephoto lens, we see so many going into eternity every twenty-four hours. Most likely the majority go to a Christ-less grave. We must respond to what God places on our hearts, to pray and to encourage and to support missionaries financially.

These days God has challenged us to be strong in our faith, looking for every opportunity to be bold in sharing the life-giving message of the gospel. Use all of your spiritual lenses as you press on serving our wonderful Lord.

TRAGIC DEVOTION

Thy word have I hid in my heart (PSALM 199:11)

Many believers remain weak because they fail to store up in their minds help-ful passages from the Word of God. Apparently, they do not realize that in times of stress, sorrow, or temptation, the Holy Spirit can bring those portions to their remembrance to comfort, warn, and direct them.

The followers of some pagan religions are often required to saturate their minds with the sacred writings of their creed. For instance, no one can teach in a Muslim mosque until he has first memorized the entire Koran!

The Mormons have a missionary force of 26,000 volunteers. They spend 20 hours a week going door-to-door. They memorize 132 pages of material to prepare for dealing with potential converts.

One missionary told me that for twenty-one hours, she listened to a group of Buddhist priests quoting their devotional literature from memory, seldom, if ever, making a mistake.

Michael Billester once gave a Bible to a humble villager in eastern Poland. Returning a few years later, he learned that 200 people had become believers through using it. When the group gathered to hear him preach, he suggested that before he spoke, he would like each person to quote some verses of Scripture. One man rose and said, "Perhaps, Brother, we've misunderstood you. Did you mean verses or chapters?"

Billester was astonished. "Are you saying there are people here who could recite complete chapters of the Bible?" That was precisely the case. In fact, thirteen of them knew half of GENESIS and the books of MATTHEW and LUKE. Another had committed all the PSALMS to memory. Combined, the 200 people knew virtually the entire Bible.

Are you constantly hiding the Word of God in your heart? If not, begin today!

CHAPTER **9**

The Last Word

LISTENING TO SCRIPTURE: MY GREATEST JOY

What do you enjoy listening to? We all know that our minds are often captivated, perhaps by music, or TV programs . . . we could go on and on with the things that we enjoy. But more than anything else, what I enjoy is hearing people recite Scripture, recite the Word of God. At Awana, we major in Scripture memorization, and what a joy it is to hear our entire staff recite Scripture each week, because we are required to learn new verses each week and recite them as a group.

A special event occurred one day when a mother came into my office, and told me that her son would like to recite some Scripture to me. He was six years old and one of the cutest little kids you could ever meet. There he stood and recited the entire book of GALATIANS—six chapters he recited to me! And while I thought what a precious sight that was, I knew that it would never have happened if it wasn't for his mother seeing the potential that he had and persistently encouraging him to do all that memory work.

Later he learned the book of EPHESIANS, so I took him to Washington, D.C., where the president was having a reading of the Bible all through the night until it was completely read. While we were there, this little boy recited the entire book of EPHESIANS on the steps of the Capitol Building. Yes, these are precious memories.

Another precious memory is of Robert and Valerie Vaughan and their daughters, Nicole, Rachael, and Promise, who came in and said that they would

Art's office displaying Psalm One Club banner

like to recite some Scripture to me. There they all stood in my office and recited from the book of REVELATION, an entire chapter; they not only recited it, but also accompanied it with dramatic motions that made it all so very, very meaningful. I found out later that this was something they practiced in their church with all of their Awana clubbers. When the clubbers recite their verses, they do the motions right along with their leaders. So, yes, listening to them was just a delight.

But perhaps the highlight of all of my Scripture listening was when I was in Bangladesh. This is a Muslim country, and I could not believe that something like this could take place, but there were two missionaries who took on the challenge of starting Awana over there. They weren't too sure that Awana would actually work there, but they were amazed at how receptive the kids were. It wasn't long before they printed their own books, which included even more Scripture than our regular ones, and set up an award system as well.

They took me over to one of the areas where their conference was to be held and there were probably about 200 formerly Muslim boys and girls there. They asked if they could recite Scripture to me. I was just overwhelmed when I heard them recite Scripture verses, one after another, for more than

440 Memorization Club, circa 1990s

fifteen minutes. How beautiful that was, to see the fruit of putting the Word of God in their minds and, I trust, in their hearts as well. That will bear fruit in their lives in the days to come.

Then an exciting Scripture presentation was made to me while I was in Japan. The ministry there just charges my spiritual batteries! I was in the home of one of the missionaries there, and they had three children: one was three, one was five, and the other was around six. They wanted me to hear these kids recite Scripture. I thought I would maybe get John 3:16 or Ephesians 2:8–9, but I was amazed and thrilled to see them, as young as they were, recite the entire chapter of Isaiah 53, Psalm 1, and Psalm 23, all perfectly.

I went back there a year later and they said that they now had memorized Psalm 119, which has 150 verses. I just could not believe what I was hearing, but then they wanted to recite Psalm 1 to me because they knew that this chapter was very special to me. (This is the chapter of the Bible that we use in the prisons.) And so, they recited Psalm 1 to me beautifully in *three* languages: English, Japanese, and Chinese. How wonderful to hear them be able to go flawlessly from one language to another, and to think that was all the Word of God they were sharing with me there.

So I have been truly blessed to have people minister to me as I have listened to them recite the precious Word of God.

TO FULFILL GOD'S MINISTRY FOR ME

One of the main messages of this book is to demonstrate how God uses ordinary people. God is not dependent on our ability but on our availability, as we follow and obey Him and love Him. I was one of God's ordinary people with no ability to create the Awana program. He taught me from the very beginning the structure and the godly heartbeat that became Awana.

Many people have asked, "Why has God blessed the Awana worldwide ministry?" I am persuaded that there are four main reasons. From the inception, my mentor and Awana's spiritual founder, Lance Latham, said the foundation of Awana begins with:

1. A clear presentation of the good news of the gospel
2. Challenging children and leaders to memorize God's precious Scripture
3. Training godly leaders
4. Club discipline

This has been the heartbeat of Awana for more than sixty years.

For the past twelve years, Jack Eggar has served as president and CEO of Awana. Under his vision and creative leadership, Awana has expanded to 20,000 churches worldwide. Awana is now in more than 100 countries, and thousands more boys and girls have been reached with the wonderful message of the gospel through Awana and Jack's leadership during these years.

This book contains my life stories of how I have traveled to more than fifty countries. It also contains pertinent historical statistics and information on world conditions of today and of yesteryear. Furthermore, it shares the heartbeat and some of the humor from Awana clubbers.

Primarily, this book rejoices at how millions of boys and girls are now heaven-bound, because of faithful pastors and leaders who have persuaded these young lives to put their complete trust in the death and resurrection of Jesus Christ.

I am especially thankful for my dear wife, Winnie, who has had such a vital part in praying and encouraging me as we developed the Awana ministry together, under God's guidance and leading.

Jack Eggar, Awana president and CEO, and Art

Art with Jeff Schacherer, special friend and assistant, in front of the White House

Art and his assistant, Lynn Jorgensen

I want to thank God for the thousands of faithful, God-loving Awana missionaries and leaders who have crossed my path and have been such a blessing and encouragement to me over these many years.

One of the great joys of heaven will be to personally meet our worldwide Awana family. May all of us just keep on keeping on serving our wonderful Lord until He takes us home!

LIFE'S BIGGEST QUESTION

Suppose you are part of a survey team next Sunday morning. Your team's assignment is to survey every church in America: Catholic, Protestant, and all other denominations. Your responsibility is to stand outside a church in your neighborhood. As the people leave the service, you'll ask one simple question: "ARE YOU GOING TO HEAVEN?" How do you think your respondents would answer this most important question in life?

Perhaps the number-one answer would be, "I hope so." Others would say, "I think so." Tragically, few of your respondents would say, "I know I'm going to heaven because I have placed my trust in Jesus Christ, who died on the cross for me."

Some would tell you about the good works they believe will help get them into heaven. Works may satisfy someone's conscience, but even the most excellent deeds cannot merit heaven. Others would tell you they attend church and perform other religious duties. But religion represents man's efforts to reach God. Salvation is truly different. When we hear the gospel, we learn that salvation is based on what God has done for humanity, to give us a sure way to heaven.

The Awana ministry has always been about proclaiming the gospel in its simplicity and power. I believe that's one of the main reasons God has blessed this ministry. Regrettably, in many of our Bible-believing churches, the invitation for salvation is not as clear as it should be. Salvation is a 100-percent receiving proposition. If we could contribute even .0001 percent toward receiving salvation, it would not be a gift. ROMANS 4:5 says, "But to him that worketh not, but believeth on Him that justifieth the ungodly, his faith is counted for righteousness." When we, by simple faith, believe that Christ, through his death on Calvary, paid in full the penalty for all our sins, we marvelously receive eternal life. Our hope of heaven is absolutely sure.

Deby Ammons, Art's friend and encourager, with Lynn Jorgensen

I have had a great appreciation for Jim Scudder, pastor of the Quentin Road Bible Baptist Church, for the annual Grace Conference his church sponsors each year. The main purpose of the conference is to present a clear Scriptural presentation of the gospel of grace. I've heard thousands of Bible messages over the years. I've forgotten most of them, but I have never forgotten the message delivered from one little boy in just a few words. It was so profound. The world's greatest scientists have no meaningful knowledge compared to this boy's absolute assurance of going to heaven.

There are many religions and cultures around the world today, but God sees only two kinds of people: those who have accepted His gift of salvation and are on their way to heaven, and those who are lost and facing eternity in hell. When was the last time you heard a message on hell? It's not a popular subject. But if God were to allow me and you to spend just a few minutes in hell, our lives would be changed. We would apply a new, immeasurable energy to the task of taking the gospel to the world.

As an Awana leader, are you majoring in the gospel with your club? Why not end your next council time lesson with that simple, five-word question from our survey: "ARE YOU GOING TO HEAVEN?"

Winnie and Art

APPENDIX

Awana Around the World

Global Membership in Awana as of February 28, 2010

Americas	Churches	Children
Canada	404	23,000
Venezuela	297	14,681
Brazil	168	9,823
Bolivia	140	4,117
Mexico	122	4,973
Ecuador	85	4,953
Peru	83	4,727
Guatemala	61	3,871
Cuba	50	2,670
Honduras	49	3,338
Colombia	47	1,675
Argentina	36	1,664
Nicaragua	33	2,546
Costa Rica	28	1,409
Jamaica	27	880
Haiti	14	542
Dominican Republic	12	651
Puerto Rico	9	135

Americas *(Continued)*	Churches	Children
Bahamas	9	35
Aruba	8	339
El Salvador	8	254
Dominica	6	182
Paraguay	5	149
Neth. Antilles	4	257
Chile	4	146
Antigua	3	73
Trinidad	2	158
Uruguay	2	78
Suriname	1	59
Belize	1	30
Cayman Islands	1	20
U.S. Virgin Islands	1	20
	1,720	**87,455**

South Asia	Churches	Children
India	2,334	179,911
Nepal	697	18,040
Bangladesh	103	6,272
Sri Lanka	4	270
	3,138	**204,493**

Africa	Churches	Children
Kenya	476	37,084
Zambia	217	18,405
Zimbabwe	168	11,027
Uganda	135	8,987
Malawi	128	5,590
Ghana	90	5,031
Cameroon	73	2,572
Mozambique	72	7,943
Tanzania	70	3,742
Liberia	52	3,198

South Africa	48	2,593
Togo	40	1,491
Nigeria	38	3,272
Burkina Faso	32	1,354
Botswana	19	613
Chad	10	563
Benin	9	688
Senegal	5	344
Cote d'Ivoire	3	229
Mali	1	250
Swaziland	1	139
	1,687	**115,115**

Pacific Rim	Churches	Children
Philippines	139	10,185
South Korea	124	7,743
Indonesia	69	4,188
Hong Kong	51	3,605
Australia	44	1,031
Myanmar	43	2,998
Papua New Guinea	31	1,747
Japan	21	764
Fiji Islands	12	323
Taiwan	11	347
New Zealand	6	99
Malaysia	5	263
Guam	4	410
Singapore	3	177
	563	**33,880**

Europe	Churches	Children
Ukraine	225	6,419
Russia	109	3,772
Egypt	38	2,657
Moldova	26	809
U.S. Military (Europe)	23	1,529

Europe *(Continued)*	Churches	Children
Romania	17	1,050
Czech Republic	16	282
Scotland (UK)	13	275
Sudan	12	1,216
Latvia	12	233
Middle East	9	761
United Arab Emirates	7	464
Germany	5	103
Kazakhstan	4	215
Lebanon	4	155
Slovakia	4	72
France	3	68
Jordan	2	203
Spain	2	90
Palestine	2	67
Belarus	2	53
England (UK)	2	30
Hungary	2	22
Ireland-Northern (UK)	1	80
Croatia	1	45
Bulgaria	1	44
Tunisia	1	25
Morocco	1	24
Austria	1	10
	545	20,773

Totals		
Countries	104
Churches	7,653
Children	461,716

Countries with
- More than 250 churches 5
- Between 200 and 249   2
- Between 100 and 199   10
- Between 25 and 99   26
- Between 10 and 24   12
- Between 1 and 9   49

Indexes

Index to Photographs

General Index